THE BLUEPRINT FOR
STRATEGIC ADVERTISING

The Blueprint for Strategic Advertising's step-by-step approach takes a comprehensive and exclusive look into the strategic use of visual, verbal, social media, integrated, and global strategies of advertising communication. Its deconstructive process analyzes one aspect at a time, creating an invaluable research tool, which students, professors, small business owners and entrepreneurs will refer to, time and again. This useful guide will concentrate on how strategy is integrated into visual and verbal ideation.

Berman's compact, content-rich guide offers chapters detailing social media, user-centered interactive advertising and presentation strategy, closing with the creation of a "blueprint" to strategizing globally. Features include a handy reference guide to powerful strategizing, an exploration of strategies for myriad media and messaging vehicles and an examination of the strategic implementation of the visual and verbal union.

This guide will be useful to students in advertising, marketing, and business courses, as well as advertising professionals and entrepreneurs, outside the classroom.

Margo Berman is Professor of Advertising and Public Relations at Florida International University, USA.

Margo Berman's fourteenth book about advertising is some of her best work yet! The real-life examples she uses to explain different strategic approaches to solving a business challenge help the reader clearly understand the role that advertising has in the process. Her use of modern-day campaigns that don't necessarily rely on the traditional forms of advertising highlight the use of digital, experiential, and social media to create awareness of brand and communicate a message with a unique approach. It's a must-read for anyone interested in the world of advertising.

—Joe Zubizarreta, COO, Zubi Advertising

Margo Berman has written an excellent, step-by-step, how-to book for serious advertising/marketing students, as well as industry professionals. This book concentrates on the strategic thinking behind the messaging that leads to integrated, on-target and on-strategy solutions. Berman uses both her twenty years of university teaching and her creative career to produce this easy-to-understand, yet comprehensive explanation of strategic conceptualization via audience analysis, communication messaging, media selection and global application. A must-read for campaign strategists.

—Pippa Seichrist, Cofounder, Miami Ad School

In *The Blueprint for Strategic Advertising*, Margo continues to provide her trademark accessible tools that are not only relevant for those already in the communications business, but those working to break into it, as well. This latest book shares the best examples of exceptional, real-world communications to illuminate her plain-spoken, approachable analysis of advertising strategy.

—Tom Denari, President & Chief Strategy Officer, Young & Laramore

Berman shares the recipe behind the secret sauce of advertising. She not only identifies the ingredients of a winning campaign, but she also provides strategic guidance on how, when and where to combine those elements into advertising that engages with today's consumer.

—Karie Hollerbach, Ph.D., Southeast Missouri State University

Margo Berman has written a well-articulated and well-researched account of conceptual and interactive strategy. She has done it with real examples, clear writing and a comprehensive framework. Whether it's the student taking their first advertising course or the award-winning creative director polishing ideas, knowing Berman's comprehensive strategy techniques are crucial in today's digital world.

—Craig Davis, Ohio University

Berman provides the perfect formula for developing advertising strategies that work. Her step-by-step approach makes strategic and creative thinking one seamless effort. Each advertising strategy presented is supported with real world campaign examples and easy-to-follow how to's. Berman's entertaining writing style and clarity of purpose make *The Blueprint for Strategic Advertising* the perfect choice for academics and professionals alike.

—Patricia Mark, Ph.D., University of South Alabama

THE BLUEPRINT FOR STRATEGIC ADVERTISING

How Critical Thinking Builds Successful Campaigns

Margo Berman

Routledge
Taylor & Francis Group

NEW YORK AND LONDON

First published 2017
by Routledge
711 Third Avenue, New York, NY 10017

and by Routledge
2 Park Square, Milton Park, Abingdon, Oxon OX14 4RN

Routledge is an imprint of the Taylor & Francis Group, an informa business

© 2017 Margo Berman
Illustrations by David Leonard

Library of Congress Cataloging in Publication Data
Names: Berman, Margo, 1947– author.
Title: The blueprint for strategic advertising : how critical thinking builds successful campaigns /
    Margo Berman.
Description: 1 Edition. | New York : Routledge, 2016.
Identifiers: LCCN 2016015412 | ISBN 9780765646576 (hbk) | ISBN 9780765646583 (pbk) |
    ISBN 9781315618661 (ebk)
Subjects: LCSH: Advertising. | Critical thinking. | Strategic planning.
Classification: LCC HF5823 .B4537 2016 | DDC 659.1/11—dc23
LC record available at https://lccn.loc.gov/2016015412

ISBN: 978-0-7656-4657-6 (hbk)
ISBN: 978-0-7656-4658-3 (pbk)
ISBN: 978-1-3156-1866-1 (ebk)

Typeset in Goudy
by Florence Production Ltd, Stoodleigh, Devon, UK

To Brian Friedman, Debbie Emmons and Jennifer Minnich.
—Margo Berman

CONTENTS

FIGURES

BOXES

INTRODUCTION

The Blueprint for Strategic Advertising—
How Critical Thinking Builds Successful Campaigns

The goal of this book is to demonstrate how strategic thinking drives visual, verbal, digital, interactive and global campaign messaging. It describes how to fine-tune critical thinking skills to create well-integrated, on-target and strategy-focused multimedia, multiplatform campaigns. Each of the chapters will examine a specific type of campaign strategy built on analytical consideration. The evaluation process starts with strategy development in Chapter 1. Then, systematically moves through a detailed examination of specific strategies, from audience, creative, conceptual, verbal and visual communication to media, interactive, campaign and global.

You will find the following recurring themes woven throughout the book. They indicate the importance of each to the creation of a strategically sound campaign.

1. Storytelling to express these and other messages. They include the way the campaign delivers the:

    a. Brand's story
    b. Consumer's benefit story
    c. Educational story
    d. Emotional story
    e. Engagement story between brand and consumer
    f. Love story of families and relationships
    g. Social change story
    h. Testimonial story about the brand

2. Interactivity to strengthen the brand and consumer relationship
3. Engagement to entertain, inform, play with and excite the audience
4. Universal truths to make a point that is easily understood and accepted
5. Relevance to make message relate to the consumer and the brand
6. Resonance to deliver an authentic message

You will discover that it's not enough to be well-versed and skillful in writing, visual, media-selection, interactive and global marketing techniques. That is just the beginning. These competencies need to correlate with and support the Creative Strategy Statement. That ensures every specific strategy will relate back to the key campaign strategy like a spider web, with each component weaving into another from the center. Another way to think of strategies is to picture the structural, webbing systems of suspension bridges. These show a well-engineered design to support weight-varying, moving vehicles, much like the interdependent, weight-bearing elements of a solid campaign strategy.

The Creative Strategy Statement will be fully explored in Chapter 3: Creative Strategy. It will tie back to the Creative Brief, showing the pair's inter-reliant relationship. This is where a campaign's *Structural Components* are first examined.

Chapter 2 moves on to the investigation and identification of the audience: Audience Strategy. This section scrutinizes different lenses through which to categorize target markets. It begins with VALS (values and lifestyles). Does the audience include Emulators (Wannabes), Achievers, I-Am-Me-ers, Experientials, Makers and so on? Is the target comprised of people with like interests (bikers, gardeners, musicians) or similar values (political, religious, cause-related)? Are they connected by age-group attitude (Baby Boomers who are forever young) or simply by age group (demographics)? It also discusses how else current or prospective audiences could be grouped. This is demonstrated as the *Architectural Perspective*.

In Chapter 3, the Creative Strategy Statement is dissected and explained. Strictly structured and formulaic in nature, it is a single sentence that includes these four components:

1. The verb
2. The audience (in a few words)
3. The consumer benefit
4. The brand support statement (answers "why buy?")

This condensed version of key brand information, deep in content, is terse in expression. Clear and concise, it encapsulates the overall creative direction and acts as the backbone to all campaign decisions.

Then, all of the answers to the questions in the Creative Brief, which will be discussed in Chapter 1, will relate back to and will be checked against the content in this one, summarized statement. This is why it is critical to understand how to develop an accurate Creative Strategy Statement: All solutions lead back to the vortex.

This is the heart of strategic thinking: One facet reflects and connects another. Not one aspect is determined without calculating its impact on the whole. In short, it is the *Structural Support Webbing,* discussed in Chapter 3, that connects the components to the audience, preparing for the next chapter.

Chapter 4 delves into the basics and practice of Conceptual Strategy, demonstrating how the earlier chapters, which covered Strategic Thinking, Audience Strategy and the Creative Strategy Statement, influence each other and are reflected in a *Presentation Drawing* to guide the next steps.

Chapters 5 and 6 discuss Verbal and Visual Communication Strategies. They emphasize and illustrate how well-chosen words and compelling graphics deliver the message directly to the target audience in a voice that clearly represents the brand. Verbal messaging is the *Architectural Rendering* of the campaign, balanced by visual communication presented as the *Design Drawing*.

This is followed by the discussion of Media Strategy in Chapter 7. Here, the choice of media-specific messaging and media intersection leads to powerful, consumer touchpoints. *The Multi-Tier Application Development* assists in the media choices. Critical thinking about consumer insights helps guide solutions to reach the targeted audience where they are. Whether they're on their mobile devices, online or in transit, interrupting them in the middle of their everyday routines helps messages fly in under the radar, before the anti-advertising shields go up.

Next, Chapter 8 examines Interactive Strategy and how engagement that is extended in a target-focused medium strengthens consumers' emotional bond with the brand. Here, audience insight, conceptual thinking and interactivity merge to create a dynamic dialogue between the target and the product. Just introducing interactivity may not be the solution. However, applicable interactivity with a vested consumer can result in an authentic relationship through *User-Centered Design*.

Chapter 9 brings all of the strategies together to explain the thinking behind an on-course Campaign Strategy. One by one, each strategy from the previous eight chapters is applied to develop an all-encompassing, relevant, on-target and consistent message, which serves as the *Architectural Model*.

The final chapter (10) demonstrates how well-engineered campaigns become the *Architectural Blueprint* behind global advertising. The foundation is set with a systematic analysis of the audience. This insight integrates creative and conceptual strategizing, which is executed through Visual and Verbal Communication Strategies. It is then distributed through media-specific messaging, including interactivity, when appropriate. The result is a Global Strategy-based campaign that can spin out in multiple platforms and can be re-engineered into myriad markets around the world.

For easy reference, the chapters' organization is summarized below:

Chapter 1. Development of Strategy: *Structural Components*
Chapter 2. Audience Strategy: *Architectural Perspective*
Chapter 3. Creative Strategy: *Structural Support Webbing*
Chapter 4. Conceptual Strategy: *Presentation Drawing*
Chapter 5. Verbal Communication Strategy: *Architectural Rendering*
Chapter 6. Visual Communication Strategy: *Design Drawing*
Chapter 7. Media Strategy: *Multi-Tier Application Development*
Chapter 8. Interactive Strategy: *User-Centered Design*
Chapter 9. Campaign Strategy: *Architectural Model*
Chapter 10. Global Strategy: *Architectural Blueprint*

While using this book, plan enough time to fully apply the information in each chapter. Carefully explore and contemplate the following:

1. Embrace the specific strategy.
2. See how it relates to that aspect of advertising.
3. Consider how each strategy relates to another.
4. Review the overall creative direction to see how to keep the campaign on strategy.
5. Examine the charts and diagrams.
6. Complete all or some of the exercises.
7. Become a deconstructionist. Analyze messages in all media.
8. Challenge your strategic thinking every day.
9. Be open to criticism and apply the suggestions before rejecting them.
10. Become a strategic engineer for current and future campaigns.

What I created is a blueprint to develop strategic floor plans for messages that target audiences across all platforms and in all media. Utilize influential language and commanding graphics to express your message clearly to your target. Get out your proverbial drafting pen and design well-engineered advertising campaigns.

1

DEVELOPMENT OF STRATEGY
Structural Components

Strategic development is a systematic evaluation process. It begins with the end. The final result is what drives the original thinking. To have an understanding of the process you start with thorough analysis. Research of the brand and its competitors, paired with consumer insight, guides the strategy of the brand. To develop the campaign's overall direction, you must be able to create or at least critique a Creative Brief. Think of it as the CPS: Creative Positioning System from which other creative solutions will be established.

Basically, the brief is a series of key questions. The answers enlighten the agency teams, including account planning, creative, digital/traditional and interactive media. These answers serve as the floor plan to the campaign's architectural structure. Where are you headed? What is the purpose of the communication? What are you trying to say? How are you going to say it? Who's speaking? Who's listening? How can you reach them? Who else is targeting them? What makes your brand unique? What's your main message? Where will you deliver it?

To fully explore the possible answers, first you must have an understanding of the brand, the competitors, the audience(s) and the media through methodical research. This would include primary research, which incorporates new information gathered by researcher-compiled methods, such as one-on-one interviews.

Primary research, gathered to gain consumer insight, involves asking people questions. This can be collected in the following and other manners:

1. *Focus groups* (meeting consumers in small groups).
2. *Mall interceptions* (approaching them while shopping).
3. *Copy testing* (showing them ads for their reactions to the message before releasing them).
4. *Pre-testing* (discovering their aided and unaided awareness of the brand and its ads, plus brand name familiarity, opinion, use and loyalty).
5. *Surveys* (conducting them on-site, one-on-one or through off-site correspondence).
6. *Observational or ethnographic research* (visiting them at home and noting their lifestyles).
7. *Media consumption preference or multiplatform research* (finding out their favorite way to access content: TV, online, mobile, etc.).
8. *Digital consumer activity or digital anthropology* (tracking their preferred websites, podcasts, videos, virtual communities and how long they stay engaged).
9. *Post-testing* (measuring a campaign's impact through recall, comprehension, response, purchase, etc.).

Unlike primary research, which speaks directly to targeted audiences, secondary research gathers and applies data previously gathered by other researchers publicly available through published articles, reports, the Internet, books, libraries, surveys and other sources.

For brand information, account teams usually turn to secondary research, which includes statistical findings, a review of current literature (a "lit review"), case studies, market research, brand performance, sales and more.

For media effectiveness and online activity, measurement tools are used to track and report consumer behavior. Some methods include primary research, such as reporting usage via daily diaries and surveys. Other methods use secondary research tracking devices to observe and gather consumer behavior, such as online-buying cycles, consumer-created content, repeat visits, length of visits, trial purchases, retweets, followers, blog posts, online comments and engagement.

The Creative Brief

The point is, all strategic thinking begins with research that answers specific questions. This compilation of data serves as the foundation for the completed Creative Brief: the cornerstone of all advertising campaigns. So, let's take a close look at the brief and its core questions. (For ease of reference the words "brand," "product" and "service" will be used interchangeably.)

Although there are shorter briefs, the 14-question form is more detailed and offers a more in-depth strategic guide. (Box 1.1) The author added two questions that consider these campaign questions:

1. What is the point of view (#11)?
2. Why would the tactics create buzz (#14)?

Just remember to answer the questions in phrases, not in sentences. That keeps the brief . . . brief!

Box 1.1 The Creative Brief

1. Why does the brand (product or service) *want to advertise*? What is the goal?

    CREATIVE STRATEGY STATEMENT TEMPLATE:

    To _____ _____ that with _____, they will _____ because
        (verb)   (audience)   (brand)   (benefit)

    of its _____.
        (support statement/reason why)

    EXAMPLE:

    To <u>persuade</u> <u>trendy teens</u> that with <u>Diesel Jeans</u> they will <u>get a cool, sexy fit</u> because
        (verb)   (audience)   (brand)   (benefit)

    of its <u>edgy, body-contouring designs</u>.
        (support statement/reason why)

---

2. Who is the *audience*?

   a. *Demographics*—Explains age, income, education, gender, occupation (job position)
   b. *Psychographics*—Portrays particular lifestyles, personal values, interests, types of behavior (such as personal brand preferences) and VALS (described later)
   c. *Geographics*—States where they live (urban, suburban, rural)

3. Who are the *brand's competitors*? (Just list them without any commentary.)

4. What do they (consumers) *currently think* (about product, service or brand)?

5. What do you *want them to think* (about product, service or brand)? (This should match and rephrase the "benefit" described in the Creative Strategy Statement.) *It answers W-I-I-F-M, "What's in it for me?"*

6. *Why should they buy* this product, service or brand? (This should paraphrase the "support statement" made in the Creative Strategy Statement.).

7. What is the *big message* you are telling them? (*State it in a tagline*, also known as a slogan.)

8. What is the *brand's* (product's or service's) *positioning*? *What do you want consumers to say about it?* It's portable, innovative, durable, safe, versatile, etc.

9. What is the *brand's USP* (unique selling proposition or point)? *What differentiates it* from others (competitors) in the market?

10. What is the *brand's character* or personality? To define it, answer these questions:

    a. What are the *brand's traits*? (What would it *be like if it had an actual personality*?)
    b. If the brand *were a celebrity* (movie star, athlete, comedian, etc.) who would that be?
    c. *What role* would this person play in your life? (cool friend, fun uncle, caring teacher, kooky neighbor, outgoing sister, etc.)
    d. How would that person (friend, brother, boss) *speak to you* (the consumer)? How would a best friend *speak to you*? Look for a descriptive adjective. A coach would be authoritative, encouraging, concerned, etc. This is the brand's *tone of voice*.

    (Rephrase it in #11 below.)

11. What is the *tone of voice*? (The way you speak to the consumer: friendly, humorous, cool, seductive, authoritative, etc. It's an adjective. See #10d, above.)

12. *Who's speaking*?

    a. *The Brand* = Self-Serving (for example: "We're number one in customer safety.")
    b. *The Consumer* = Testimonial (for instance: "I lost ten pounds eating my favorite foods!"

c. *The Conscience* = Emotional Blackmail (What could happen if you don't use the product?)

d. *The Brand Icon* = Brand Stand (like Snuggles the Bear for the fabric softener)

13. What *kind of tactics* (which media) would you use to execute the strategy? Would you choose interactivity, social media, ambient, transit, out-of-home, print, broadcast, mobile, or other platforms? Don't just list them; specifically explain how you'd use them. (For example: a Facebook campaign that invites "likes" or "tags." The first consumers who do so win the product.)

14. How would the above-mentioned tactics *create buzz and garner press coverage?*

Questions and Answers: The Creative Brief

Before we proceed, we'll examine each question of the brief one at a time to see how each impacts the creative direction. Answering the questions is only part one. Part two occurs when you evaluate the ultimate significance of the answer. You will determine if these are basic beams in the framework or key support beams that are crucial to the campaign's structural integrity.

The first question addressed the need to understand the *objective of the advertising campaign.* If you are unclear what the purpose of the communication is, your message will fail to have focus. The Creative Strategy Statement condenses and summarizes the campaign's core idea. It succinctly describes the audience in a few words, without full detail as in question #2: "*Who is the audience?*" After identifying the targeted consumer, such as "young, time-pressed executives," it explains the promised Benefit. Then it explains how the brand will deliver it (the Benefit) through key features expressed as the Support Statement. (The Creative Strategy Statement will be further explored in Chapter 3.)

Question One

Why does the brand (product or service) *want to advertise?* What is the goal?

CREATIVE STRATEGY STATEMENT TEMPLATE:

To _____ _____ that with _____ they will _____ because of its

    (*verb*) (*audience*)   (*brand*)   (*benefit*)

_____.

   (*support statement reason why*)

Question Two

The second question—*Who is the audience?*—looks more deeply into the targeted audience with these descriptive identifiers:

a. *Demographics*—Explains age, income, education, gender, occupation (job position)
b. *Psychographics*—Portrays particular lifestyles and attitudes (called VALS), personal values, interests, types of behavior (like personal brand preferences)
c. *Geographics*—States where they live (urban, suburban, rural)

By studying each of these three facets of the audience, we will be able to gain deeper insight into whom we're targeting. In Demographics (part 2a), we're looking at how old our target is. What do they do for a living? What is their family household income (HHI)? What is their education level? The responses draw a profile of consumers' age group, education level, financial position and employment status.

Although these facts alone don't give a definitive description, they can hint at a certain lifestyle, which is explored in part 2b: Psychographics. This part of the audience definition categorizes the audience into different groups. Each group enables creative talents to more clearly visualize their target. In that way, they can more effectively create relevant messages specifically impacting those particular consumers. For instance, if you are speaking to highly motivated Achievers, who are outer-directed, these are people who have reached a relatively high level of accomplishment, yet they relish approval from others. If the consumers see themselves as unique individuals who are not affected by others' opinions, these are I-Am-Me-ers who are mainly inner-directed.

Labels, which include "Achievers" and "I-Am-Me-ers." are called VALS (Values Attitudes and Lifestyles). They define specific common characteristics, attitudes and behaviors that group people together. As wine or movie lovers share the same interests. Likewise, people who have common values, such as environmentalists or animal rights activists, are bonded by what they protect, defend or condone. Political party members would be one such group, who share common values: the depth of their political beliefs.

Arnold Mitchell, a social scientist, created VALS in 1978. Although there are three main VALS groupings, there are visible similarities. For example, the "Survivors" in one VALS is "Strivers" in another. By comparing the labels, it's easier to examine the groups. In Chapter 2, we'll take an in-depth look at 1) some of the ways the same groups have different labels and what they represent; 2) how they relate to product use, preference and loyalty; and 3) how they specifically fit into campaign strategies.

Now back to the Creative Brief. Part 2c identifies where the audience lives. Although, it's only necessary to state urban, suburban or rural, each word draws to mind a specific way of life. The fast rhythm of city life. The comfortable, more relaxed life in the suburbs. And, the laid-back pace of the pastoral setting with sprawling farms and acres of open land. As you can see, location can strongly influence consumers' perspective. It's a significant contributor to behavior, attitudes, interests and values.

Question Three

The third question *addresses the competitors*. They have to be direct, not just industry competitors. That means that a hotel like the Four Seasons would be in competition for the guests at W Hotels, but not guests of Motel 6 or Days Inn. Likewise, Saks Fifth Avenue would compete for the same audience as Lord & Taylor, not the Kmart or Wal-Mart shopper. In the brief, you only need to list the competitors, not offer any descriptions. The list is for reference when you want to review campaign tactics (use of media).

Question Four

The fourth question, *"What do they (consumers) currently think?"* is the key to under - standing how consumers presently view the brand. This is from their perspective, not from the brand's marketing team. Often, the audience's opinion may be difficult to accept. Restaurants can't claim they're the best seafood in Maryland when the audience says the crabs are chewy. This is why the next question is so critical.

Question Five

Question five, *"What do you want them to think?"* can only be answered after you determine what they think now about the brand. Are they fans, critics, unaware of it? Knowing this will help you create a campaign message that either reinforces, changes or shapes their opinions. This part of the brief must directly refer back to the consumer's benefit (What's In It for Me?) stated in the Creative Strategy Statement. If you said that applesauce is a nutritious, natural snack in the CSS, you can't say you want your audience to think it's a time saving treat. That's an off-strategy benefit.

Question Six

Likewise, the sixth question, which asks, *"Why should they buy this product, service or brand?"* must relate back to the CSS's support statement. This discusses brand features that show how they can deliver the above-stated benefits to the consumer.

Question Seven

Next, question seven poses, *"What is the big message you are telling them?"* Think slogan. Think succinct. Think persuasive. Think brand promise. Does it fit the targeted audience and reflect the brand's personality? What can you say that would express a single message that could be used in all communications? From traditional and nontraditional to digital and interactive. The creative talents will develop the slogan; however, the brief needs to provide direction.

Question Eight

Question eight addresses this: *"What is the brand's positioning?"* "What does the audience think about the brand?" If you say Rolls-Royce, most people would say "expensive" or "luxury." This is the brand's position. It could be about performance like BMW or family fun like theme parks. It's what first comes to mind when the brand name is mentioned.

Question Nine

Question nine challenges you to *determine the brand's USP. What's unique about it?* How does it set itself apart from the brands? What is different? Consider the elasticity of Silly Putty, the Slinky springs that enable it to walk down stairs, the reusability of Etch A Sketch and the versatility of Lego. When you hear this tagline, it's a perfect example of USP (unique selling point): "See it jiggle. Watch it wiggle. Jell-O." No other food claimed this unique trait. So once Jell-O said it, it owned it. Yes, puddings move, but many are Jell-O products.

Question Ten

In question ten, you are asked to *define the brand's character or personality*.

To determine it, take your time to answer these questions:

a. What are the *brand's traits*? Is it playful like Lego's? Serious like a hospital? Entertaining like Nikon?
b. What *celebrity* would depict the brand's traits? "Out there" like Jim Carrey? Funny like Whoopi Goldberg? Sexy like Angelina Jolie?
c. If you knew this celebrity *how would you know him or her*? Maybe a prankster-loving friend, a tough coach or a kind brother?
d. How would that friend, coach or brother *speak to you*? Choose a few clear adjectives. For instance, a mischievous friend might be daring. Your description is the brand's *tone of voice*. You would then restate or reuse it in the next question (#11).

Question Eleven

Question eleven addresses this question: *"What is the tone of voice?"* (The way you speak to the consumer: friendly, humorous, cool, seductive, authoritative, etc. It's an adjective. Refer to #10d, above.) For example, if you're advertising a weight-loss program, you might choose an encouraging tone of voice.

Question Twelve

In question twelve, you must answer this: *"Who's speaking?"* Who's delivering the message?[1] Is it the brand, the consumer, someone's conscience, or a brand mascot or spokesperson, like the M&M'S characters or Dennis Haysbert (with his rich, distinctive voice) for Allstate Insurance?

a. *The Brand*—Self-Serving lets the brand present itself. It can boast about its awards for these and other achievements: customer service, sleek design or innovative technology.
b. *The Consumer*—Testimonial gives the consumer free voice to explain how the product solves a problem, such as how Proactiv helped Adam Levine conquer teenage acne.
c. *The Conscience*—Emotional Blackmail enables the conscience to warn consumers about the consequences of not using the brand. The iconic Mac versus PC instantly comes to mind. Some comparisons showed how Macs seldom get viruses compared to the frequently assaulted PCs.
d. *The Brand Icon*—Brand Stand passes the message to a recognizable representative like Halle Berry for Revlon.

Question Thirteen

In question thirteen, we finally get to the execution of the strategy with, *"What kind of tactics will be the vehicles for the campaign?"* This is where understanding the consumers' behaviors is crucial for media selection. For a young, digitally devoted audience, mobile, online, social media (Facebook, Twitter, Instagram, Foursquare, Google+, Friendster, Flickr, Pinterest) easily reach this group. You want to select appropriate media platforms for

Figure 1.1 Creative Problem-Solving Process

specific audiences. Be careful here. The wrong touchpoint or media intersection (place where the media and audience meet) will miss the mark.

Question Fourteen

At the end, in question fourteen, we reassess our choices and answer: "*How would the above-mentioned tactics create buzz and garner press coverage?*" This is where you double-check that the tactics you choose are strong enough to attract attention from consumers and the press. You can see how the creative problem-solving process works in Figure 1.1.

By answering the above-listed questions, readers will be able to create strategically accurate, well-targeted campaigns. Now let's see how to use the answers, while addressing other questions.

Creative Process and SWOT Analysis

Once you've thought through the brand, its competitors, its personality, voice and point of view, you developed the tactics and checked that they were both on-strategy and on-target. That means they align with the Creative Strategy Statement and the details in the brief.

If in the CSS, you said the benefit was whiter clothes for a detergent and the main message discussed savings, the message is off-strategy with strategy development. These are the structural components that support the campaign's architectural design. Just as bridges have webbing systems, these connective strategies fortify the underlying communication's core.

Without a clear understanding of the core objective, chances are you won't find a cogent solution. For example, the compiling of data cannot provide answers in and of themselves. The results must be analyzed and interpreted. In order to develop a campaign strategy, many details must be considered. These include fully comprehending all the pertinent points of the research: the brand, the competitors, the audience, the tactics and the campaign's effectiveness.

Basically, each advertising blueprint solves a particular challenge. This is why the art of designing a foundation moves through a methodical process much like the five steps of problem solving. Notice how similar the thinking is. (Box 1.2)

In engineering, any concrete or abstract plan, you must know where to start. There are four levels or cycles in a brand's growth. The first is its birth or product launch. This *brand-introduction* phase is where its identity is presented. Its features and benefits are showcased. (We will discuss features and benefits in Chapter 3.) The second is its *brand-maintenance* period when it has established its presence in the product skyline. This is when you want to keep current customers and cultivate new ones by carefully monitoring new trends, technologies and threats (see next paragraph). The third is its *brand-reposition* stage when you modify the product and/or the message. Think about how Lexus repositioned itself to attract a wider audience by creating minivans. Any new model added to an existing product line is called a brand extension. Just as candy bars, which are now available in bite-size portions, reach a calorie-conscious, not just chocolate-loving audience. The fourth is its *brand-decline* stage. This is the last step in the life cycle. Either it will be reconstructed or it will implode and vanish from the marketplace. Many dying companies have rallied back like Hush Puppies (a line of comfortable shoes).

Box 1.2 Five-Step Creative Problem Solving

1. *Insight*—The first step is to have a clear understanding of exactly what the problem is that you're trying to solve. You cannot begin without a full understanding.

2. *Preparation*—This is where the research fits in. Both primary and secondary research provide data that will fuel the problem-solving process. Gathering of research that adds insight into consumer behavior, attitude and lifestyles; competitor performance; brand *SWOT* analysis (discussed later on) and media evaluation open the path to a conceptual breakthrough.

3. *Incubation*—Put the problem aside. The less you think about it, the sooner you'll solve it. After a little bit of time, "mental marination" leads to the sudden second of discovery.

4. *Eureka*—This is when the lightning bolt hits with a quick strike and suddenly you have the answer. It's the "Aha! moment." It's the second when all the information comes together in a harmonious whole.

5. *Verification*—Here's the time when you validate that the answer you came up with solves the original problem. Sometimes, you'll develop a brilliant solution, but it's:

   Off-strategy—Doesn't answer the objective
   Off-target—Is missing the target audience via an:
   - Inappropriate medium
   - Irrelevant message

To postpone and hopefully prevent the brand's demise, it's crucial to constantly check the supporting structure and brace it to weather the assault of negative marketplace elements.

Now we will examine what a SWOT analysis means, as mentioned in *Preparation* (#2 in Box 1.2). It's an acronym. Each letter represents a word. In this case, they are Strengths, Weaknesses, Opportunities and Threats. When looking to develop internal retrospection you must scrutinize the internal and external influences impacting the brand. The internal aspects are Strengths and Opportunities. The external components are Weaknesses and Threats. You might ask why would Weaknesses be external? They should be internal. Right? Although that's true, it's always better to address the weaknesses as outsiders see them. These are the ones you, as the brand's directors, might need to discover. Therefore, weaknesses can and should be reviewed from both points of view: internal and external.

Let's see how these words work to help build a brand that can withstand the pounding elements in an ever-changing marketplace environment.

SWOT Analysis: Strengths

Strengths are the traits that the brand already has. It's reliable, durable, versatile, easy to use, delicious and so on. They're intrinsically part of the brand's identity. Ultimately, they contribute to the brand equity. This key asset is the brand name's power, how well known it is. It commands respect and loyalty because people perceive that it is superior to unknown brands.

SWOT Analysis: Weaknesses

Weaknesses are primarily characteristics that the target audience believes need improvement. They can be slow service, poor customer service, unreliable performance, or any other perceived problem. Secondarily, they are also issues that brand employees know need to be corrected. Both sets of observations need to be considered when revising the brand.

SWOT Analysis: Opportunities

Opportunities are prospective partnerships, marketing connections, media vehicles, promotional venues, alternative audiences and other brand-building possibilities that the internal brand team should explore. Sometimes, the most obvious connections have been overlooked.

SWOT Analysis: Threats

Threats challenge the brand from outside, such as present or emerging competitors, new technologies, changing on-site and online traffic patterns and so on. What is threatening the brand? Think about the movie *You've Got Mail*. The owner of a little bookstore had to close because a giant bookstore chain moved in across the street.

Brand analysis, like self-introspection, may be painful to look at, but necessary for growth. It reveals what is working and what needs to be fixed. By looking from insiders' and outsiders' perspectives, you get a clearer view of what needs repair or reinforcement. You can use your SWOT analysis in a new way to design your communication (Figure 1.2).

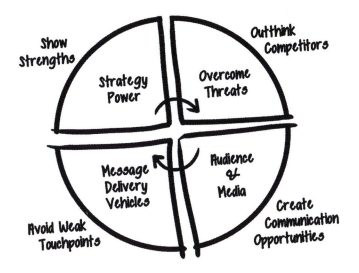

Figure 1.2 SWOT

Now let's look at the process of campaign development.

Stages of Campaign Construction

There are multiple phases before any campaign is launched. No construction can begin without the above-discussed, preliminary steps. First, the brand's team must determine the objective and go through the self-evaluation process. Second, it needs to identify what makes the brand unique (USP). And third, it has to create an appropriate brand personality with a matching tone of voice. These are just three parts to the 14-question Creative Brief. No communication can start before it is completed.

Ultimately, the agency will guide the campaign through this eight-step process before it is released into the media.

1. *Develop the Creative Brief* from the information gathered from the client and account team.
2. *Draft the creative strategy* directly based on the details in the brief.
3. *Design the creative solution* for on-strategy and on-target messaging.
4. *Present the concept* to the creative director (CD) to demonstrate how it supports the assigned strategic direction.
5. *Incorporate suggested revisions* based on CD feedback.
6. *Gain approval of the creative idea* first from the agency creative director, then the client (brand).
7. *Execute the campaign* by producing it with a digital design, out-of-home or other production company for the specified multiplatform media. This could mean to design a billboard, construct a website, create a TV spot, develop a mobile message or establish a social media campaign.

8. *Schedule the message* to run (on air, in print, online, etc.) in the appropriate media. Determine when and where the advertising should appear. For example, on highway billboards or main city streets, on sports or lifetime channels, on websites or social media sites.

After the campaign runs, the agency must analyze its effectiveness through post-testing, media analytics and other measurement tools. From then on, monitor and tweak the communication as needed.

Brand—Building Communication

Although we'll go into this in deeper detail in Chapter 2, it would be beneficial to set the groundwork for audience communication. It wasn't that long ago when advertising was a one-way communication. The brand or product delivered a message through different media. These included TV, radio, print, out-of-home, direct mail and so on. The audience only absorbed or ignored the information. That is no longer the case. Today, the product wants to engage the audience and create a two-way dialogue or community conversation.

Audience interaction can only occur when brands know where, when and how to reach their target. Are they commuting in their cars? Catching buses, taxis and trains? Are they sitting online? Are they involved in blogging, Facebook, LinkedIn, Foursquare Twitter, Instagram or other social media?

When you know the way consumers access and digest information, you can create touchpoints. These are places where the message interrupts the target. Media-specific messages reach precisely concentrated audiences in those select vehicles. Wise marketers target male-oriented programs for a primarily male-dominated audience. Likewise promoters looking to reach particular political loyalists would look to news media that slants in that direction.

As you can see, there are multiple ways to talk to a selective audience: media-specific communication, like-interest media, myriad touchpoints (out-of-home, transport, TV, magazines, social media, online) and so on. In Chapter 4, we'll consider different creative strategies to communicate with numerous consumers via multiple platforms.

Creating a corporate identity is another way to depict the brand, speak directly to an audience and solidify a relationship with a target. Common ways to do this are listed below (Figure 1.3—Figure 1.10).

1. *Logo*—This is a visual depiction of the brand. Instantly differentiating it from other competitors in the field. Visual strategies—discussed later in Chapter 6—can be represented in graphic and/or typographic manner.

Figure 1.3 Logo

2. *Slogan*—Here a phrase or word portrays the brand. The purpose of a slogan is to encapsulate the benefit or the identifiable USP (unique selling point or proposition). We will look deeper into verbal communication in Chapter 5.

Figure 1.4 Slogan

3. *Jingle*—Although these musical logos are less common than they have been in the past, they are still used. Some of them are still full-length jingles that run throughout the commercial. Here are some unforgettable jingles and musical "logos."

Figure 1.5 Jingle

    a.   "Snap, Crackle, Pop"—Rice Krispies
    b.   "I am Stuck on Band-Aid and Band-Aid's Stuck on Me"—Johnson & Johnson Band-Aid
    c.   "Like a Good Neighbor, State Farm is There"—State Farm Insurance

Others have been shortened to just a few notes, such as the:

    d.   Three-note phrase for NBC (music only, without jingle lyrics)
    e.   Five-note close ("Open Happiness") for Coke
    f.   Five-note close ("Da-dah-da-da-dah") before four notes with lyrics ("I'm Lovin' It") for McDonald's
    g.   "Bong" for Taco Bell

4. *Color*—A specific color is instantly attributed to the brand. When you think of colas, red immediately brings Coke to mind, whereas blue conjures up Pepsi. For detergents, orange signifies Tide and green represents Gain.

Figure 1.6 Color

5. *Recognizable word*—Some brands own a word. These include "believe" for Macy's and "pleasure" for Publix Supermarket.

Figure 1.7 Word

6. *Icon*—A visual depiction of the brand can be:

    a. An *animated mascot* like the Pillsbury Dough Boy, M&M'S or the Michelin Man
    b. A *brand character* like Ronald McDonald
    c. A *famous cartoon character* like Snoopy for MetLife or Garfield for Embassy Suites
    d. An *illustrated image* like the Monopoly Man

Figure 1.8 Icon

7. *Celebrity*—When a celebrity is strongly aligned with a brand, such as Michael Jordan and Nike, they are inextricably connected and can be thought of concurrently.

Figure 1.9 Celebrity

8. *Benefit*—A specified consumer W-I-I-F-M is stated. Some familiar ones are durability for Timex, coolness for Apple and gas saving for hybrids like Toyota Prius.

w-i-i-f-m

Figure 1.10 Benefit

Strategy Teams: Agency and Brand

One team doesn't develop the campaign's strategy. Several teams do. The development process begins with the account team. This group maps the client's goals and directives; supervises and analyzes primary and secondary research on the brand, audience, competitors, trends; and diagrams the results to present to the other teams. Together these and other teams, such as creative, digital, media and production, work to construct the foundation for the campaigns.

In reviewing the chart below (Figure 1.11), you can see how the collaborative efforts work. With the groundwork set on the brand and audience set, the teams can use the insights gathered from the research to design the preliminary architectural details. An effective and symbiotic relationship allows for a free dialogue, leading to creative solutions.

Notice how the teams' cooperative pursuits are interconnected with the collective research objectives. Each relies on the other. The teams must understand the audience's perceptions and behaviors as much as they have to be intimately familiar with the brand's footprint and imprint in the market. Pay attention to the word lists in each part of the circle. They will help in building the brand's strategic communication. Review the words below the Agency Teams and learn what they represent. Next, look at the Brand and Audience words and explanations.

1. Account Team: Supervision of Research and Summary

   Preparation—Reviewing the client's (brand's) goals and understanding the critical issues.
   Evaluation—Analyzing the primary and secondary brand audience research.
   Comprehension—Recognizing the brand's and audience's current and intended relationship.
   Calculation—Computing the possible communication platforms and touchpoints to depict the brand and reach the audience.
   Application –Combining research, platforms, touchpoints with client objectives to design the basic strategy.
   Validation—Checking that the creative direction is on-strategy and on-target.

2. Audience: Explanation of Insight and Values

   Information—Gathering demographics, psychographics and geographics.

Observation—Watching the audience through ethnographic (observational) research.
Investigation—Studying audience behavior, attitudes, values, needs and desires.
Identification—Categorizing the brand, using VALS, Maslow's Hierarchy of Needs, common values and interests, etc.
Reaction—Researching audience's response to messaging and brand performance.
Participation—Pinpointing brand loyalty and relationship status.
Interaction—Evaluating audience's engagement with brand (consumer-created content, contests, blog posts, Twitter and other social media).

3. Brand: Identification of Equity and Core Values

Investigation—Exploring the brand's positioning.
Evaluation—Analyzing the brand's goals.
Examination—Reviewing the brand's core values.
Exploration—Searching for common core values between brand and audience.
Compilation—Assimilating the brand's past performance, strategies and tactics.
Explanation—Describing who the brand is to the audience.

4. Creative, Digital, Media Teams: Development of Message and Delivery

Collaboration—Working together to develop conceptual ideas.
Concentration—Focusing on audience insights.
Interpretation—Translating audience needs into message strategy.
Consideration—Examining which touchpoints would best reach the target.
Summarization—Consolidating research and creative/media direction.
Communication—Developing key messages for headlines and slogans.
Recommendation—Suggesting final strategic concepts and media tactics.

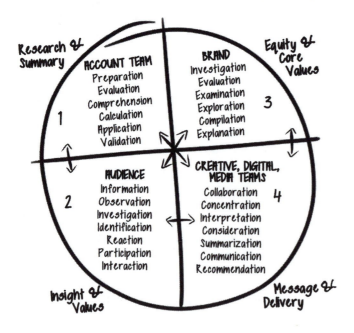

Figure 1.11 Organizational Chart

Take into consideration the entire strategy-building process for every campaign before brainstorming. This methodical approach ensures that the teams have explored a thorough analysis of the brand and the audience before proceeding to developing any strategic messages and tactical media solutions.

Step-by–Step Strategy Summary

To review, we'll look at each of the analytical steps that lead to developing a strategic campaign. The five-step creative process serves as a blueprint. *Step one*: Understand the problem. What are you trying to solve? *Step two*: Compile information to prepare you to find solutions. *Step three*: Let the problem simmer. Put it on the "back burner" of your mind. Let it "mentally marinate." *Step four*: Welcome the instant answer when it shows up unexpectedly. Eagerly embrace the "Eureka moment." *Step five*: Confirm that the answer you discovered addresses the original problem.

Much like the creative process, you need to dissect the advertising challenge and clearly understand the campaign goals or objectives. Next, you must gather research on the brand's history and its 1) audience, 2) current positioning in the marketplace, 3) positioning in the consumer's mind, 4) competitors, 5) key message, 6) unique selling point and 7) prior tactics. Then evaluate the research and see how to use it to guide the brief. This can be primary (surveys, focus groups, observational, etc.) or secondary (articles, books, websites, etc.) research. Finally, you need to apply critical thinking so you can assimilate the data and draft a fully designed, on-strategy and on-target model: the Creative Brief.

As we've already read, the first question in the brief asks why you're advertising at all. Your answer, the Creative Strategy Statement, drafts the overall direction. It describes the target (audience), states what they get out of the product (consumer's benefit) and explains why they should believe it (brand's support statement). Every part of the CSS relates to another question in the brief. That means the benefit must be rephrased in question five: "What do you want the audience to think about the brand?" How does it help them? Likewise, the answer to question six, "Why should they buy the brand," should reflect the support statement stated in the CSS.

In fact, the verb you choose at the start of CSS (to inform, convince, persuade, educate, warn, assure and so on) indicates the way to tell the audience about the brand. For example, if the product is a medication, you might use a cautionary voice.

Astute thinking aids in diagramming a cogent campaign plan. Take your time. Create concise responses. Use the most descriptive words in your answers. Write compact phrases packed with content. For example, state the benefit clearly. Instead of saying the car will give you "a fast ride," say "an exhilarating experience." Yes, these are longer words, but they boost the benefit. When you describe the support statement, point out what specific features the brand offers to fortify the benefit. So, instead of saying the car has a "powerful engine," say it is a "super-charged, turbo." It's a more precise promise and more compelling reason to buy.

Remember that question five, *"What do you want the audience to think?"* reinforces the CSS benefit and question six, *"Why should they believe it?"* is the reason why or support beam for the CSS support statement (Box. 1.3).

Box 1.3 CSS Connection to Benefit
and Support Statement

To persuade trendy teens that Diesel Jeans **will give them a cool, sexy fit**
  (verb)   (audience)   (brand)   (benefit)

because of its **edgy, body-contouring designs**.
  (support statement/reason why)

Creative Strategy Statement *benefit* connects to #5 in the brief:

  Question five: "What do you want the audience to think?" **(tight, head-turning fit)**

Creative Strategy Statement *support* statement is restated in #6 in the brief.

  Question six: "Why buy?" **(snug, fashion-forward styles)**

Consider what the main message is (question seven). Ask, "What am I trying to say?" If you can't articulate it out loud, you're still not clear on the message.

For question eight, can you identify the brand's positioning in the mind of the consumer?

The ninth question asks you to present the *brand's USP* and stress what differentiates it.

In question ten, you present the brand's personality by ascribing human traits and a distinct manner of speaking to the brand.

Question eleven states the above-assigned tone of voice as an adjective.

The next question, twelve, identifies the point of view by asking, "*Who's speaking?*" These are the four possibilities with their labels. (Box 1.4)

Box 1.4 Point of View

Who's Speaking	Label
a. *The Brand*	Self-Serving
b. *The Consumer*	Testimonial
c. *The Conscience*	Emotional Blackmail
d. *The Brand Icon*	Brand Stand

In question thirteen, you determine, state and explain the audience-specific tactics to be used in the campaign. Look for touchpoints that accurately reach your target segment.

Finally, question fourteen forces you to review your choices to confirm that this campaign would attract press and create buzz.

In summary, the construction of the Creative Brief leads to an on-target and on-strategy answer through all the following three steps:

1. The creative solution, presentation and concept approval from the agency and client.
2. The campaign execution for each specified medium.
3. The scheduling and running of messages in the assigned media.

However, before the campaign goes into production, there are brief-related considerations. First, there's the SWOT analysis, which studies the internal and external influences on the brand: Strengths, Weaknesses, Opportunities and Threats. Other ways to apply this classic analysis to campaign messaging are shown earlier in Figure 1.2.

In order to finalize the creative direction, there are other brief-related considerations. These include structuring a corporate identity that quickly portrays the brand image in myriad ways: 1) *Logo*, 2) *Slogan*, 3) *Jingle*, 4) *Color*, 5) *Word*, 6) *Icon*, 7) *Celebrity* and 8) *Benefit*.

In strategic thinking it's most important to contemplate (Figure 1.12—Figure 1.18):

1. What you're saying (State the *main message*.)

Figure 1.12 Message

2. How you're saying it (Decide the *tone of voice*.)

Figure 1.13 Tone of Voice

3. Who's speaking (Show the *point of view*.)

Figure 1.14 Point of View

4. Who's listening (Target the *audience*.)

Figure 1.15 Audience

5. Where they're finding it (Identify the consumer *touchpoints*.)

Figure 1.16 Touchpoints

6. How and when they're receiving it (Select the specific *media*: online, mobile, TV, etc.)

Figure 1.17 Media

7. How they're being engaged (Create *interactivity* between the brand and consumer.)

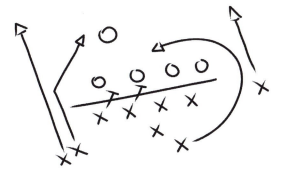

Figure 1.18 Interactivity

Combined, these steps fortify your strategic thinking so you can make well-engineered multi-platform communication. Applying all of this chapter's methods and the other strategy-based techniques in the subsequent chapters will lead you to campaigns built on solid architectural design.

Strategy Development Exercises

Exercise 1: Identify several strategies for a building-block toy designed for three- to five-year-old children. What kind of parents would this toy maker target?

a. List VALS categories.
b. Describe a group of parents with common values.
c. Pinpoint a target with common interests.

Exercise 2: What media would you use to reach these audiences? For example:

a.   Which social media (Instagram, Twitter, Facebook, Foursquare, Pinterest, etc.)?
b.   What kind of out-of-home messaging (transit, billboards, signs in parks)?
c.   Which magazines (*Parents, Highlights* for the kids, etc.)?

Exercise 3: If you wanted to target the grandparents, which media would you choose? For example: would you choose any of the above listed in Exercise 2? If so, which ones?

Exercise 4: What *big message* would persuade both audiences (parents/grandparents) to make a purchase? Try to think of a slogan, such as "Under construction."

Exercise 5: What is the *brand's personality?* Review *Question 10* in the brief. To help remind you, here's a quick summary. To determine the brand's personality, answer these questions:

a.   What are the *brand's traits?* Is it exciting like a theme park?
b.   What *celebrity* portrays the brand's traits? Warm and humorous like Matthew Broderick?
c.   *What role* would this celebrity have in your life? A lovable uncle?
d.   How would that person *speak to you?* Think adjective. Loving, caring or maybe encouraging? The adjective is the brand's *tone of voice.*

Note

1.   Margo Berman, *The Copywriter's Toolkit: The Complete Guide to Strategic Advertising Copy* (London: Wiley-Blackwell, 2012), 34–35.

2

AUDIENCE STRATEGY
Architectural Perspective

Before we examine the various ways to structure targeted messages, we need to discuss how to categorize diverse audiences. In addition to examining three main categories most often referred to in the Creative Brief, we will also explore how these categories affect brand and consumer communication. Let's first review the three categories.

1. *Demographic*—Age, income, gender, education, ethnicity
2. *Psychographic*—Lifestyle, age-related perspectives, interests, viewpoints, purchase-motivations, purchase-deciders and influencers
3. *Geographic*—Where they live: urban, suburban or rural areas

Within each category, there are subcategories with distinctive differences among the audiences. For example, under Demographics, the wide disparities in age, income and education are clearly evident. You could immediately see how speaking to a teen would greatly differ from a senior. Products that target the wealthy would avoid the disadvantaged. A fundraising event for a museum would target a sophisticated, educated audience.

Psychographics and Geographics also point out easy-to-spot differences. People interested in poetry most likely would not be interested in tractor racing. Farmers in rural areas would probably be more interested in sturdy, rather than designer jeans. The important point is not just to learn the categories, but instead, to see how they redirect your message construction.

Oftentimes, creative talents focus more on the lifestyle or psychographic profile. They want to picture the audience in their daily lives: where they shop, what their hobbies are, what causes they support and so on. However, there are many campaigns where demo - graphics are the directional starting point. Other times, products and brands target residents exactly where they live or wish to relocate. We will explain these differences as we move along. We'll begin with groupings based on Demographics.

1. Demographics

Group One—Age Groups

The first way to target certain market segments, is focus in on age-group categories. In this way, you can match age-specific products with their respective consumers. For example, advertise arthritis medication to a 50-plus market or a Lego walkie-talkie that spans one-and-a-half miles to kids over six or the latest smartphone to young adults. Age alone is not necessarily the right way to go for all products or services. However, when it is, it's an easy fit. Likewise when the message or product is off-target, it just as easily fails.

Although some researches have specific-year differences for each category, let's use the following as our age-grouping guide (Box 2.1).

Box 2.1 Audience by Age Grouping

1. *Baby Boomers*: 1946–1964

2. *Generation X* (Gen X): 1965–1976

3. *Gen Y* (Millennials, Gen Next): 1977–1994

4. *Gen Z* (Net Generation, Digital Natives, Verge Generation): 1994–2004

As you think about strategically targeting a certain age group, analyze what these people's lives were like as they were growing up. What were the economic, social and political climates? What were the common beliefs people held? What were their everyday concerns? What were their methods of communication? What were their common courtesies? What were their unifying values? Consider the times they were living in. What was it like then as opposed to now?

You can't write to an audience whose lifestyle you can't imagine in a three-dimensional, animated image. When you immerse yourself in consumer insights, you can understand their point of view and frame of reference. After you can picture yourself having a one-on-one conversation, you're better prepared to develop an on-target messaging strategy. Be sure you can pinpoint their sweet spot, their media consumption and their decision-buying influences.

In your mind, see their reactions to possible touchpoints, product-driven solutions and diverse message styles. Would they be more comfortable seeing a billboard, a try-before-you-buy offer or a direct response mechanism, such as a toll-free number? Would they appreciate a BOGO deal or a mobile coupon? What would trigger their interest and ultimately, a purchase?

When thinking about your target, you already know more than you think. For instance, you won't use radio spots or newspaper ads as key touchpoints for Digital Natives. Why? Because those are not content-delivery vehicles for them.

Besides appropriate media choices, equally important is the correct match of products to respective ages. With that in mind, you wouldn't pitch skateboards to Baby Boomers or anti-aging creams to Millennials. But, strategic audience targeting isn't just about products and their corresponding age groups. It's also about seeing which products they're familiar with and which ones they use.

Take a moment and consider this: Baby Boomers lived before digital technology blossomed. That means they didn't have personal computers, DVRs, movies on demand, GPS devices, TV-online connectivity or even the Internet. They didn't have e-mail, Facebook, Twitter or Instagram. They saw the introduction of car air conditioners and color televisions. Cable channels and satellite TV did not exist. There were only the four or five major networks, not hundreds of channels. And no, there weren't any plasma TVs or smartphones.

Just take a moment, and compare that digital-free period with today's technology-dependent times. This kind of insight helps hone your consumer-analysis, critical and comparative skills.

Although age alone can pinpoint a specific audience, it's not the only targeting method.

Every consumer-lifestyle factor should be evaluated for its relevance and significance when working through any strategic plan. Later, under Psychographics, we will consider the common viewpoints of each group, one-by-one.

Some of the Demographic and Psychographic groups overlap. For example, under the soon-to-be-discussed VALS categories, household incomes are brought together under labels, such as *Survivors* (lowest income) to *Integrateds* or *Fulfilleds* (highest income). Let us first focus on the importance of income levels when considering campaign messaging.

Group Two—Income-Level Groups

It is clear that luxury items are targeting those in the highest-income bracket. However, some luxury brands and retailers reach out to a middle-income bracket because members of this audience want to emulate the ultra rich. Those in the lowest-income group, who struggle to feed their families, may not be interested in high-priced, designer brands. But, if they were, they could buy similar items in thrift stores, wait for sales or buy at discount chains. These audience groups are not assigned specific incomes because high, middle and low income-level categories vary. Perhaps it would be easier to say the top 10 percent, the bottom 10 percent and all the other earners in between.

Group Three—Gender

This group has gained more attention over the years, with a higher acceptance level of those who don't fit into just the male and female categories. Marketers today are reaching beyond and speaking to groups with diverse sexual orientation, including same-sex couples, transgender, bisexual and other individuals. Rather than condemning behaviors, marketers are embracing those differences by creating promotional campaigns that target them. For example, the ANZ bank, Australia and New Zealand Banking Group, created GAYTMs draped in colorful patterns, studded with rhinestones in leather, denim and other unexpected fabrics to honor the Sydney Gay and Lesbian Pride Parade. Hand-designed by talented artists, the ATMs printed out receipts with rainbows in the background.[1]

Many campaigns specifically target men or women, just as they can target kids or seniors. Some brands have created protein snack packs for men. Others solve a specific problem for women, such as Degree Ultra Clear, which prevents white stain marks on clothes.

Group Four—Education

Education is another audience delineator: those who are more educated and those who are less. With education comes an appreciation of the arts, an understanding of a wide range of knowledge and an awareness of various points of view from philosophy and literature to evolution and technological advances. Many people who like to learn, like to read. Book clubs would attract that audience. These members fit into a similar interest category, mentioned below under Psychographics (#8).

When talking to a sophisticated audience, messages can be written using more complex language and product descriptions.

Group Five—Ethnicity

Grouping consumers by their ethnicity can be an effective way to reach a specific ethnic group. For example, Goya, the Spanish Food Company, La Tienda, Despaña and other Spanish-product manufacturers and distributors target Hispanics as their primary target. A secondary, non-Hispanic audience has also become fans.

Other companies, including resorts, such as Holiday Inn, have also sought to single out consumers by ethnicity. When hotel-chain marketers learned that African Americans enjoyed family reunions, they created special group rates for these consumers. As more resorts discovered other ethnic groups were having location-destination reunions, they joined in and offered family-rate plans. Cruise lines and other travel-industry businesses have also offered discount packages.

2. Psychographics

Creative talents often examine psychographic categories to connect with different consumers. These include 1) VALS (Values, Attitudes and Lifestyles), 2) age groups, 3) age-related perspectives, 4) similar interests, 5) similar views, 6) purchase-motivator categories and 7) primary and secondary consumer audiences. The reason why it's important to understand these diverse groups is because it helps you single out and speak to particular target markets, using appropriate strategies.

The entire creative direction hinges on the architecture perspective developed here. Think of a miniature, model home where all the details are in place. Putting the audience first is like focusing on the future resident. What kinds of amenities would best serve their needs? These amenities are strategies that offer consumers the following benefits: 1) resolve problems, 2) address basic needs and 3) fulfill desires. When you think strategically, you're developing the archetypal consumer dialogue.

Group Six—VALS: Values, Attitudes and Lifestyles

Understanding the various VALS categories helps you view the audience as three-dimensional people with families, hobbies, interests and opinions, not as statistical data. The more vividly you picture the audience, the easier it will be to address them as individuals in related groups. For example, people who are struggling financially (Survivors or Sustainers) can only buy what they absolutely need. Therefore, you would not sell them luxury items. Likewise, for people who like adventure and thrills (Experiencers/Experientials), you would not feature ordinary vacations. They would want to climb the Himalayas, trek through the Amazon Rainforest or hike through the Australian outback.

Imagine the actual consumers within each category. Get a sharp picture and hold it. Next, consider how your campaign message would strategically single them out. How they live their lives (psychographics) is as important as where they live (geographics) and what their income-, age-, education-based information reveals (demographics). Their specific preferences, passions, affiliations and personal pursuits give you an accurate impression of who they are.

VALS 1

As we learned in Chapter 1, Arnold Mitchell developed the original VALS categories in 1978. Within the three main VALS groupings, there were visible similarities. For example, the "Survivors" in one VALS was "Strivers" in another. By comparing the labels, it's easier to examine the groups. Normally, they're arranged from the lowest income to the highest (original VALS), and levels of motivation and skillsets (VALS 2 and 3). So, be sure to review the generalized first VALS list below.

Mitchell's original categories included these nine, sound-like-what-they-are groups:

1. *Survivors*—Struggle to get by financially.
2. *Sustainers*—Are just able to meet their families' basic needs.
3. *Belongers*—Enjoy joining groups, like reading clubs, religious groups and gardening groups.
4. *Emulators*—Imitate those who succeed, while working to move up.
5. *Achievers*—Set professional and personal goals, then reach them.
6. *I-Am-Me-ers*—Are self-guided and individualistic (Figure 2.1).

Figure 2.1 I-Am-Me-ers

7. *Experientials*—Try new activities, like skydiving, parasailing, bungee jumping (Figure 2.2).

Figure 2.2 Experientials

27

8. *Societally Conscious*—Care about preserving the environment and forms of life.
9. *Integrateds*—Sit at the pinnacle of accomplishment, at the summit of success and are now concerned about philanthropy.

VALS 2

In 1989 and again later, VALS was revised (VALS 2 and VALS 3) to focus more on beliefs (attitudes) and what was important to them (values) rather than personal endeavors (activities) and hobbies (interests). It examined people by: 1) how they saw themselves (self-orientation), 2) which goals they set and 3) what actions they took to strengthen, maintain or revise how others saw them. To develop these distinct categories, researchers used myriad methods (resources), such as education, finances, influence, self-assurance, enthusiasm, wit and so on.

VALS 2 includes the following eight key categories. The ones in italic closely match the original VALS labels.

1. *Survivors*—Struggle to get by financially.
2. *Makers*—Enjoy building, baking, gardening, repairing (Figure 2.3).

Figure 2.3 Makers

3. *Experiencers* (was Experientials #7 in VALS 1)—Try new activities, like skydiving, parasailing, bungee jumping.
4. *Strivers* (was Emulators #4 in VALS 1)—Imitate those who succeed, while working to move up.
5. *Achievers*—Set professional and personal goals, then reach them.
6. *Believers*—Are comfortable with established societal morals, religious organizations, familiar products.
7. *Thinkers*—Care about preserving the environment and forms of life.
8. *Innovators* (was Integrateds #9 in VALS 1)—Sit at the pinnacle of accomplishment, at the summit of success, now concerned about philanthropy.

VALS 3

As mentioned above, there was another modification, creating VALS 3. It includes the eight consumer types listed below. Most of the names are the same as VALS 2. Only the order was changed. The asterisks indicate the labels and positions that did not change: *Survivors* (#1) and *Innovators* (#8).

1. *Survivors*—Struggle to get by financially.
2. *Believers* (was #6 in VALS 2)—Are comfortable with established societal morals, religious organizations, familiar products.
3. *Thinkers* (was #7 in VALS 2)—Care about preserving the environment and forms of life.
4. *Achievers* (was #8 in VALS 2)—Set professional and personal goals, then reach them.
5. *Strivers* (was Emulators #4 in VALS 1 and #3 in VALS 2)—Imitate those who succeed, while working to move up.
6. *Experiencers* (was #3 in VALS 2 and Experientials #7 in VALS 1)—Try new activities, like skydiving, parasailing, bungee jumping.
7. *Makers* (was #2 in VALS 2)—Enjoy building, baking, gardening, repairing.
8. *Innovators* (was Integrateds #9 in VALS 1)—Sit at the pinnacle of accomplishment, at the summit of success, now concerned about philanthropy.

In addition, there is another group of people who don't fit into any of these categories. According to different VALS groups, they're labeled *Actualizers* and *Fulfilleds*. They have reached all of their personal and financial goals. They are often involved in philanthropy. As you can see, strategies to reach each of these audiences would differ. You could also use the VALS categories to predict the target's brand choice, usage and loyalty.

Group Seven—Age-Related Perspectives

Box 2.2 Audience by Age-Group Viewpoints

1. *Baby Boomers* = Never get old

2. *Gen X* (Generation X) = Independent

3. *Gen Y* (Millennials, Gen Next) = Team players

4. *Gen Z* (Digital Natives, iGen, Gen Wii) = Tech savvy

The above-mentioned groups (Box 2.2), comprised of unique individuals, have commonly held ideas and similar outlooks. These similarities invited succinct, yet descriptive tag names. These pithy labels enabled marketers to better grasp their collective viewpoints. As demonstrated by the high activity levels and attention to maintaining a youthful appearance, the Baby Boomers (Figure 2.4) are referred to as the "never-get-old" group. Unlike the grandparents of the past, the Baby Boomers are not sedentary, let-the-world-pass-me-by, rocking-chair seniors. Many keep up with fashion trends, societal changes and new technologies.

Others retire and still stay active. To reflect this audience, Prudential Financial created a campaign, which featured seniors on their first day of retirement. Instead of shuffleboard

Figure 2.4 Baby Boomers

or bingo, these retirees were starting second careers as filmmakers, boxing coaches and teachers. Engaged and involved, they were shown as they began the second chapter of their lives.[2]

The *Generation X* (Figure 2.5) group is viewed as "independent" types. Highly educated, they don't just accept the news; they develop their own opinions. They take charge of their careers, have confidence in their life choices, are family-focused and establish a balance between work and family. They're eager to right the wrongs they see, including corruption, human rights and repressed freedom. Accepting of diversity, they don't prejudge people according to ethnicity, nationality, sexual orientation or culture.

The *Gen Y* (Figure 2.6) members, also called Millennials and Gen Next, are "team players." Civic-minded, hyper-connected with friends and social media, these optimistic young adults often carry the not-necessarily-true stigma of being narcissistic and entitled. Yes, it's true; they share endless details of their personal lives and love selfies.

However, having witnessed their parents' layoffs, a depressed economy and a weak job market, they face a new kind of uncertainty. Burdened with high student debt, they anticipate the prospect of unemployment and job insecurity.

Figure 2.5 Gen X

Figure 2.6 Gen Y

Unlike their parents and grandparents, they have less company loyalty, expecting to stay at a job two years and then move on. On the job, they want to be valued and appreciated, recognized for their abilities and rewarded for their contributions. That's why they'd accept a lower salary at a job they enjoy, rather than more money at one they detest. Understanding how quickly wealth can be lost, they choose to buy less. When making purchasing choices, they skip over luxury and brand names in favor of more organic items, which support environmental causes, local farmers and ethical growers.

With that being said, many still think everything will work out in the end. Idealistic, they want to reduce global warming, social inequity, governmental controls and ecological imbalance. As a group, when they rally behind a cause shared through social networking, they raise funds to help those in need, startup companies or ecological issues. They socialize in groups, work well in teams and create interactive communities. "Grown-ups" today are fascinated with this group as is evidenced by the more than 122 mentions in *The New York Times* articles alone, just in the first eight months of 2014.[3]

The last group, *Gen Z* (Figure 2.7) is "tech savvy." They are referred to by these and other monikers: Digital Natives, iGen and Gen Wii. Unlike the earlier generations of technological immigrants, digital natives easily adapt to new advances, showing an innate fluency using the latest devices.

Exposed to multiple sources for news, information and social connectivity, they fluidly move from one platform to another, often barely noticing which devices they're on. They

Figure 2.7 Gen Z

mastered the virtual and physical realms. They can't imagine being "stuck" watching live TV without the freedom to skip ahead. Or life without smartphones, GPS navigation, text messaging or social networking.

Socially diverse, they embrace all cultures and ethnicities. Inclusive, rather than exclusive, they would avoid restrictive country clubs or other discriminatory associations. Having been raised during social upheaval, terrorism, suicide bombers and war, they are drawn together by an increased exposure to 1) political agendas; 2) global power struggles; and 3) multinational/multicultural interactions.

A 2013 study by DDB, referred to in an *Adweek* article[4] revealed an insightful comparison between Baby Boomers and Millennials (omitting Gen Xs). Listed below are some of the findings. You might not expect that Millennials would think men are naturally better leaders. However, you might presume that they'd be okay having camera crews in their personal lives to get TV exposure. You might be surprised to discover that they're optimistic about the future. To test how well you know Millennials, take a look at this list of their opinions compared to those of Baby Boomers. The first number indicates the opinions of Millennials. The second one reflects those of Baby Boomers.

1. Favor same-sex marriage (56% vs. 45%)
2. Favor outside-your-race marriage (84% vs. 79%)
3. Believe men are naturally better leaders than women (32% vs. 25%)
4. Would let cameras follow them around 24/7 just to be on TV (22% vs. 9%)
5. Expect the quality of life to improve this year (56% vs. 29%).

Some of the higher Baby Boomers opinions in these areas might surprise you and some might not. They support legalized abortion, capitalism, gun ownership, stay-at-home dads, religious pursuits, the death penalty, less governmental intrusion and politics. (Again, the first numbers state Millennials' opinions and the second ones show Baby Boomers' beliefs.)

1. Favor legalized abortion (48% vs. 57%)
2. Are interested in politics (40% vs. 51%)
3. Believe there's too much government interference in life (43% vs. 57%)
4. Think owning a handgun is a right (68% vs. 75%)
5. Favor death penalty (58% vs. 69%)
6. Think religion is an important part of life (47% vs. 58%)
7. Think capitalism is what makes America great (41% vs. 56%)

With all the gunshot victims portrayed in the news, it's no surprise that Millennials would be less inclined to think everyone should have the right to buy a gun. Also, all the controversy around abortion influenced their opinion. The inclusion of TV programs and films with actors portraying characters of different sexual orientations and multiracial couples has helped the general public become more tolerant of cultural differences. Therefore, it would be expected that Millennials, who grew up with these references in storylines, would support same-gender and interracial marriages.

When examining how these different audiences are grouped together, marketers must always realize they are speaking to individual consumers, each with similar, yet unique views, wants and desires. Picturing one singular person always helps creative talents sharpen their consumer-targeting precision.

Group Eight—Similar Interests

Another way to group audiences is to consider their hobbies and interests (Figure 2.8). Often people, with like interests, cross age, gender and cultural boundaries. Photographers, word puzzle enthusiasts, gourmands, art aficionados, book-club members, museumgoers, music lovers, wine connoisseurs, artists and writers could be any age, any gender and nationality.

Although some groups might fit better in a narrower age category like young adults for gamers and techies, members could still span a couple of generations. What unifies them is a common interest, appreciation or passion.

Figure 2.8 Guitar Lovers

Therefore, when you're advertising products, such as motorcycles (Figure 2.9), which appeal to people with a love of two-wheelers, your message should talk about the thrill and freedom of the open road. Capture the feeling. Illustrate the exhilaration. Emphasize the experience. In other words, depict the joy of riding from their point of view. Share their fervor.

Figure 2.9 Motorcycle Enthusiasts

When you can hit the audience's sweet spot, the place where all ad resistance melts, you can engage a deep interest. Why? Because you're talking about something they love. And you're showing how your product can fulfill their desires and/or needs.

Group Nine—Similar Views

Audiences with similar views is yet another method to categorize audiences. People can relate to each other based on political views, environmental issues, social causes, charitable funding, religious affiliations or other shared concerns. These views surpass any other group-defining labels.

Sometimes people with a common interest may also be drawn together by a similar cause. For example, across cities in America, motorcycle groups band together by the hundreds to deliver toys to underprivileged children. These toy-delivery motorcades go by many names, including the Annual Toy Ride, Bikers' Toy Run and their Toys for Tots Caravan. Events like these demonstrate how shared passions and common causes unify one or more groups: 1) those who like biking, 2) those who are concerned citizens and 3) those who belong to both. Although all kinds of motorcycles are part of the processional, Harley-Davidson has been a dedicated sponsor for decades.

Consider the power of other closely tied relationships. The Shriners Hospitals develop campaigns to help sick children. The Lions Clubs raise funds to provide guide dogs for the blind and eyeglasses, eye surgery and more for the visually impaired.

The Tap Project campaign funded one long-term goal of Unicef: to provide clean drinking water to those without it. Originating in New York, the Tap Project was an extremely effective, yet simple promotion. Here's how it worked. Restaurant servers simply asked diners if they would be willing to add one dollar to their bills to support clean water around the world. Millions of everyday New Yorkers instantly said "yes." Most New Yorkers eat out every day and servers got behind a global cause.

This connection shows the strength of fundraising through grassroots efforts generated from people also grouped together by jobs and lifestyles.

Just as church congregants create prayer chains to help those with failing health, groups of doctors donate their time performing free, reconstructive cleft lip and palate surgeries. One famous organization's team of doctors, the Smile Train, travels the world to correct facial deformities for children in impoverished communities. So far they have passed the millionth-smile mark.

People concerned about abused and abandoned animals create dog, cat, horse and other rescue groups. They band together to offer entertaining, fundraising fairs where people can learn about adoption, make a donation or purchase some pet-related item in support of the vendors and exhibitors. The drive behind these associations is a simple love of their furry friends. Some groups promote diversity and fight sexual-orientation intolerance. Others work together to aid battered women, assist exploited and abandoned children, abolish human trafficking and eradicate other unconscionable atrocities.

By forming alliances to help others, these concerned and devoted citizens make a positive change in their communities. These can include religious, political, environmental, ecological and many other like-minded affiliations. When companies present campaigns that embrace a particular charity or cause, they are also connecting to advocates of those issues. Shoppers today, especially Millennials, select brands that exhibit civic-mindedness and social consciousness.

Group Ten—Purchase-Motivator Categories

These categories group people into three key consumer or market-segment motivators. Based on the earlier described VALS identifiers, these labels point out the underlying drive behind a purchase. Below are explanations for the need-driven, outer-directed and inner-directed consumer groups.

1. *Need-driven*—They can only financially afford to buy what they absolutely need, not what they might want. This group cares about ideals and has three divisions. 1) *Survivors*. Financially challenged, they would shop in thrift stores, such as Goodwill. 2) *Strugglers* and *Believers*. They are also in a low-income bracket and shop at stores like Wal-Mart and Costco. 3) *Sustainers*. They can be found making purchases at deep discount and outlet stores.
2. *Outer-directed*—They make purchases to impress others, such as items that are considered high-status symbols. Achievement is their motivation and they enjoy attaining and showcasing their accomplishments. Although they have a higher household income, they still work towards increasing their annual earnings.
3. *Inner-directed*—They buy what interests them and are not influenced by the opinion of others. Driven by *self-expression*, they like to experience life, create things by hand and support environmental causes. They could be found mountain climbing, engaging in do-it-yourself home improvements and helping to save endangered species.

When you understand what drives people to buy, you can hit their sweet spot. When you're speaking to those who are need-driven, your message must convey how this particular product or service will solve a problem and address a need. For the outer-directed audiences, you need to emphasize how the product will elevate their status, especially in their core circles. Then, for those inner-directed consumers, you must demonstrate how they will have a unique experience that fulfills a personal dream, ambition or goal.

Each group can be addressed based on the consumers' key motivating force. Remember to whom your campaign is directed and why they buy. This will help you develop on-target communication.

Group Eleven—Primary and Secondary Consumers

In addition to the six, above-mentioned audience labels, you need to also consider both primary (main) and secondary (subordinate) consumers. Understanding who does what in the buying process helps you distinguish precisely to whom you're speaking. There may be times you're targeting the *Initiator*. For example, if you were creating a campaign for an exciting new digital game, you might speak to children. They, in turn, would introduce the idea to make a purchase. Then, they might even become strong *Influencers*, persuading parents to buy (*Purchasers*). But, ultimately, they would be the *End-Users*. As you can see, one person might serve several roles during the decision-making process.

Obviously, your communication in words, (verbally), images (visually) and media (touchpoints) would depend heavily on the recipient. You might develop a more enthusiastic message for kids and a more descriptive one to parents. When promoting educational games, for example, kids would want to hear about the fun factor and parents about the mental-fitness benefits. Games that are teaching tools, which require quick thinking and strategic decisions, can enhance learning.

Look over the following list and contemplate how your communication language, imaging and media vehicles would differ from each of these targets (Box 2.3).

Box 2.3 Five Targets in the Buying Process

1. *Initiator:* Person who recommends purchasing the product or service

2. *Influencer:* Individual who persuades or discourages the buyer

3. *Decider:* Consumer who is the final decision maker

4. *Purchaser:* Person who purchases the product or service

5. *User:* Customer who is the actual product user

Although these groups seem obvious, if you asked yourself who were the five people involved in making a purchase, you might not think of all five. You might only think of the primary target: the buyer. So let's examine them one at a time. Be sure you're thinking about the message for each one as you read on. First, there's the *Initiator* (Figure 2.10) who says, "It's time we get this," "We need to buy this," or "This is on sale and we should buy it now." This is someone who puts the buying process in motion.

Figure 2.10 Initiator

Second, there's the *Influencer* (Figure 2.11). This individual guides the group toward or away from the purchase with comments like "Let's wait," "I saw something even better," or "We really don't need this at all."

Figure 2.11 Influencer

Third, there's the *Decider* (Figure 2.12). This is the person who makes the final decision, "Yes, we'll get it" or "No we won't."

Figure 2.12 Decider

Fourth, there's the *Purchaser* (Figure 2.13). Taking all opinions into consideration, this is the customer who places the order online or on-site and pays for the product or service.

Figure 2.13 Purchaser

Fifth, there's the *User* (Figure 2.14), also called the End-User. This is the audience member who actually uses the product. This could be the student who received the computer or the child who went to get eyeglasses or the person who registered for a language, computer or scriptwriting class.

Figure 2.14 End-User

Sometimes the buying process includes just one person who handles the entire purchasing process. Other times, two people play multiple roles, for instance, as the Initiator, Influencer and Decider. Either way, your messages would vary for each of the five consumer roles. For the Initiator, you might be driving home the point that it's about time to take action.

Mattress campaigns that suggest replacements every eight years would remind Initiators to think about buying a new mattress. For the Influencer, you'd focus on the why this product is better than another. For the Decider, you'd highlight the unique selling point (USP). For the Buyer, you'd stress the reason to act now. Finally, for the User, you'd highlight the consumer benefits. Campaigns that span the key reasons to take action reach several types of buying groups.

One example is the Amazon Fire Phone TV campaign that has children casually talking about its features while using the phone in front of young adults. Their digital fluency makes the Millennials look like technological dinosaurs. One funny closing line in the "Hipster Kids" spot includes the young boy's comment that he's never, in all of his nine years on earth, seen anything like it. In this case, he would be the Influencer, even though in one of the spots, "Investment," he's buying an investment property from all the cash he stashed from the sale of his startup. The humor in these spots is exceptionally well crafted. The creative team also brilliantly cast two gifted child actors to deliver the messages.

3. Geographics

There may be times when targeting a certain region would best suit a brand, product or service. A feed store with grains, harnesses, animal pens and so on would obviously look to talk to ranchers and farmers. Veterinarians specializing in livestock would be looking to care for farm animals, not only house pets.

Retailers in strip malls most likely would be in the suburbs. Their campaigns seek to reach local residents. Luxury stores and fashionable boutiques in metropolitan cities like New York and Chicago would be targeting world travelers as much as local, wealthy buyers.

Relevant geographic information can be paired with demographic and psychographic profiles for more structurally sound messaging.

Group Twelve—Urban Consumers

Urban consumers' needs most likely would vary from rural-region residents. The fast-paced city life with its trendy, posh lifestyle and designer boutiques caters to specific audience members. Of course, not all city dwellers can afford a wealthy lifestyle; however images of upscale "city-ites" are prevalent. Other shops, such as chain-store-laden shopping centers reach out to other inhabitants.

In most urban areas there are cultural centers, museums, art galleries, theaters and other venues that support arts-centric activities. Although everyone can buy tickets and attend public events, people who are financially funding them are usually high-income patrons. For them, special patron-only galas and premiere performances, back-stage parties and first-day exhibits are open just to them.

Many urbanites eat out regularly, so restaurants cater to regulars throughout the month. Local residents shop several times a week at mini food markets or gourmet shops, buying just what they need, keeping bundles manageable. With the efficiency of public transportation, cars are not necessary. Locals use buses, subways and taxis. The ultra rich would have their own drivers.

In general, brands that target urban occupants can more easily deliver messages at a faster pace that reflect the residents' quick patter.

Group Thirteen—Suburban Consumers

You can picture it. The slightly slower pace of the suburbs with its green lawns, larger homes and tree-lined streets. Residents here may work in the city and retire to the suburbs at day's end. These locals often frequent area strip malls and expansive shopping centers. With cars a necessity, they can buy in bulk, unlike those who live in the city. They can shop in groups and have the luxury of taking leisurely drives to parks, mountains or beaches, depending on the location.

Brands targeting them could offer entire-mall discounts, frequent shopping cards and specific-day offers to encourage repeat visits or purchases.

Group Fourteen—Rural Consumers

Farmers, ranchers and country dwellers have a more leisurely pace. In many small cities across America, everyone knows everyone. In close-knit communities like these, people chat on neighbors' porches, in family-owned shops and in country fairs. Kids help with farm chores and get old-fashioned fresh air. Many lemonades, quilts and pies are still homemade. It almost seems as if decades pass more slowly and quality of life surpasses all. Less consumed with Internet activity, many people actually enjoy weekends and down time.

Brands that celebrate and showcase the joys of country living would speak personally to this audience's pleasurable pastimes.

The Audiences in Summary

In reviewing all fourteen categories, remembering them is equally important to knowing what they represent. Ultimately, you want to use these to identify key characteristics of your target audiences. You want to be sure you know how they think, what they value and how they see the world. Knowing what's important to them gives you an advertising advantage. Consumer insight leads you to develop campaign messages that address their points of view, reflect their societal concerns and ignite their passions. What compels them to support a cause? What drives them to make a purchase? What special interests do they pursue in their free time? In short, who are they and what do they care about?

As we have learned, there are seven general ways to categorize audiences. In review, these are shown below (Box 2.4).

There are many kinds of indicators and identifiers. When they belong to a book club, they immediately fit into two groups: 1) VALS *Belongers* (VALS 1, #3) and 2) passionate readers. Fitness enthusiasts belong to at least three groups: 1) *VALS Experiencers/Experientials*, 2) *I-Am-Me-ers* and 3) health-conscious consumers. Don't just reach for a category off the "shelf." Be judicious in your group selection. Be studious in your consumer research. And be disciplined in your message making.

Box 2.4 Audience Checklist

1. *Demographics:*

    a. Age group
    b. Matching income brackets
    c. Comparable education levels
    d. Parallel ethnic backgrounds

2. *Psychographics:*

    a. VALS
    b. Age-related perspectives
    c. Same interests
    d. Similar viewpoints (causes, cultures, etc.)
    e. Purchase motivations (need-driven, outer-directed, inner-directed)
    f. Primary and secondary groups (purchase-decision members from Initiators to End-Users)

3. *Geographics:* Common locations: urban, suburban and rural areas

---

Just because people are in the same age group may not be enough to target them. But, if you can also pinpoint their viewpoints, causes and hobbies, you can more precisely hit their sweet spot. Always remember to see the audience as multidimensional individuals and like-minded consortiums, not just numbers of nondescript clusters.

Audience Strategy Exercises

Exercise 1: Identify one product that would target both Makers and Belongers listed in the VALS categories.

a. Name what activity or interest would tie these two groups together.
b. Pinpoint one common interest.

Exercise 2: What two media vehicles would reach these audiences? For example:

a. Would they use social media, such as Instagram, Twitter, Facebook or Pinterest?
b. Would they be out and about so they could view out-of-home signage?
c. Would they shop at a certain type of store?

Exercise 3: Now, select another product or service that would speak to an age-related perspective. For example, wrinkle cream for a 45+ market.

Exercise 4: What could you show or say to convince this audience of the benefits? How would you portray a fewer-visible-signs-of-aging message?

Exercise 5: Pick one type of purchase-motivator (need-driven, outer-directed or inner-directed). What product would target them more than the other two groups?

Exercise 6: Pick three members from the purchase-buying process (Initiator, Influencer, Decider, Buyer, User).

a. Select one product that they would all be interested in buying or using. For instance, ice cream.
b. Decide one key point in a message that would target each of them. For instance, what would you say to get the Initiator interested? Who would be the Influencers? For instance, how could you make kids beg their parents to buy it? What would help the Buyer go to the store today? Would you offer a coupon?

Notes

1. "Bank Transforms ATM into GAYTM," www.goweirdfacts.com/bank-transforms-atm-into-gaytm. html (accessed August 20, 2014).
2. Ken Wheaton, "Prudential Inspires with Second Acts: 'Chapter Two' Effort Features Retirees who Aren't Ready for Mahjong and Early Dinners," *Advertising Age*, May 5, 2014: 77.
3. Sam Tanenhaus, "Generation Nice: The Millennials are Emerging as a Dominant Demographic Force. What Does That Mean for the Rest of Us?" *The New York Times*, August 17, 2014: ST 1, 7.
4. Lucia Moses, "Data Points: Generation Gap: Study Shows Millennials Could Learn a Thing or Two from their Parents about Manners," *Adweek*, January 23, 2013, www.adweek.com/news/ advertising-branding/data-points-generation-gap-146654 (accessed August 14, 2014).

3

CREATIVE STRATEGY
Structural Support Webbing

Creative ideas that are instantly understood become the net under all other campaign components from media to execution. It often starts with storytelling that is disruptive, unexpected and entertaining. A story that portrays a universal truth and highlights consumer benefits enhances the brand's image.

There are many ways that the creative strategy can serve as the impetus behind all messaging. The ten techniques listed above (Box 3.1) present specific methods to add brand memorability and increase viewers' attention because of their impact. As you review each approach, think about other campaigns you've seen that would fit into these categories. In later chapters, we'll discuss sight, touch, execution and delivery in more detail.

Box 3.1 Ten Creative Strategies

1. *Storytelling*

2. *Talent*

3. *Sound*

4. *Scent*

5. *Taste*

6. *Voice*

7. *Sight*

8. *Touch*

9. *Execution*

10. *Delivery*

---

1. Storytelling—Presenting the Brand in an Unforgettable Way

Figure 3.1 How Stories Depict Brand's Character

What makes good storytelling? Riveting plots? Surprise endings? Fascinating characters from underdogs to heroes? Emotional-appeal storylines from comedy and satire to pathos?

Storytelling, when featuring an underlying universal truth, will resonate with the viewer (Figure 3.1). Universal truths, expressions that cross cultural, age and gender differences with common acceptance, can be found in some of the most memorable campaigns. These expressions are listed along side each example below. See if you can think of other truths that would also work equally well.

a.   "The Force"—Volkswagen 2012 Super Bowl

In this spot, a little boy, dressed up as Darth Vader, stretches his arms out to use his imaginary powers on different objects around the house, as well as his doggie. After failing time and again, he goes outside and tries his powers on his dad's VW Passat. When his dad, watching from the living room, sees him, he remotely starts the car. The boy is shocked, surprised and delighted that his powers worked.

Universal truth: This demonstrates how the dad wants to encourage his son's imagination: "Anything you can imagine, you can achieve."

b.   "Pick Them Back Up"—P&G (Procter & Gamble) 2014 Winter Olympics

This campaign featured athletes whose moms encouraged them when they repeatedly fell during practice as they honed their skills.

Universal truth: The support shown by the moms demonstrated "there's nothing like a mother's love."

c.   "Wheelchair Basketball"—Guinness 2014 spot

The grit, which a basketball team of wheelchair athletes exhibited, showed admirable qualities: dedication, camaraderie and tenacity.

Universal truth: These athletes exemplify a "never-give-up" spirit.

d. "Jr. Driver"—Subaru Legacy 2014

Dad asks five-year-old son if he's ready to drive the car. The child imagines what it would be like, as he pictures impatient drivers, parking tickets and other everyday frustrations.

Universal truth: These images, from the child's perspective, drive home this point: "Enjoy your childhood. There's plenty of time to be an adult."

e. "The Car is Broken"—Subaru Legacy 2014 campaign

Son's remote-control car is broken and he asks his dad if he can fix it. Dad drives his car, pretending to be guided by the remote control. When the boy says he has to break more toys, his sister helps out by tossing her stuffed horse to the ground, hoping dad can fix it in the same way.

Universal truth: This clever spot, which portrays dad as the hero, characterizes "there's always a solution" message.

f. "Puppy Love"—Budweiser 2014 Super Bowl

Puppy falls in love with a Clydesdale and keeps returning to the stalls to visit.

Universal truth: The loyalty the puppy shows depicts the "love knows no bounds" concept.

g. "Love Them Back"—Cesar dog food 2013 campaign

Different commercials portray the bond between owners and their dogs. In one spot, the puppy is chewing on everything he shouldn't. He's changing channels with the TV remote, setting off the car alarm and so on. The spot explains how puppies should chew on something healthy: Cesar dog food.

Universal truth: These adorable scenes reinforce the idea that "man's best friend deserves the best."

h. "Anti-Bark Dog Collar"—This consumer-created spot for Doritos aired in the 2013 Super Bowl. It won $650,000 and was created by Josh Svoboda with cast Rosie, the Golden Retriever puppy, for associates Wes Phillips and Nick Dimondi from 5 Point Production in Raleigh, NC. It cost $400 to create, including dog treats. The $650,000 Doritos award came from two contests: 1) $600,000 from *USA Today* Ad Meter and 2) $50,000 from Frito-Lay "National Ad" competition.

Universal truth: When the dog outsmarts the man, it verifies the familiar saying: "Never underestimate your opponent."

i. "Keep Love Strong"—Iams dog food 2014 campaign—In one spot, a female soldier's pet Rocky, an Irish Wolfhound, anxiously whines as he looks through the window, waiting for her to return home. When she finally arrives, he enthusiastically jumps up, nuzzles, kisses her and finally lies on top of her. In another spot, a little girl named Gwen is playing dress up with Duke, her Great Dane doggie. She even paints his toenails pink. It closes with the announcer conveying this idea: For a love this strong, she'd only feed him Iams.

Universal truth: The message, "when only the best will do," is easily understood. Among other universal truths that would work is the one mentioned above in "g": "Man's best friend deserves the best." (See Cesar dog food.)

j. "Time Machine"—The 2014, $1 million-winner of "Crash the Super Bowl" Doritos contest[1] was Raj Suri. His consumer-created commercial cost only $200 to produce. He worked with Ryan Thomas Andersen, the director, and shot it at Andersen's parents' Arizona home.

Universal truth: Here the spot portrays an "anything is possible" idea.

Storytelling is the webbing behind the brand strategy. People respond to stories and can relate to them in an emotional way. Look at some of the most popular Super Bowl commercials. There's often a vignette (mini movie) with a message that speaks to you.

2. Talent—Casting Believable and Relatable Actors

Figure 3.2 How Talent Delivers the Message

Famous actors, celebrities, athletes, musicians and other talents can pique the viewers'/ listeners' attention, especially if the audience members are fans. Some beloved comedic actresses, such as Betty White, add instant recognition and immediate entertainment (Figure 3.2). Look at the list below and see which celebrities would make you pay attention.

a. Female Celebrities

1. Actress Betty White—"Hungry" Snickers 2010 Super Bowl commercial—In this spot, Betty White portrays a football player who is not showing his athletic prowess. Accused of playing like Betty White, he eats a Snickers and turns back into himself, proving the brand's slogan: "You're not you when you're hungry."

Universal truth: "You can't concentrate when you're hungry." When you're hungry, you underperform because you're distracted.

2. NASCAR driver Danica Patrick—"Body Builder" GoDaddy 2014 Super Bowl commercial—The spot shifted from the sexy Danica to the buff Danica. Wearing a body suit, she runs besides male body builders, racing to the tanning salon. The message is: With a GoDaddy website, your small business will gain online traction and on-site customers.

   Universal truth: "Business is booming." This happens when you create online presence with a GoDaddy website.

3. Model Kate Upton—"You Missed a Spot" slow-motion car wash Mercedes-Benz CLA 2013 Super Bowl commercial—Several guys are washing the CLA Mercedes and are distracted by Kate who's walking toward the car. She stops and says, "You missed a spot."

   Universal truth: "Nobody's perfect." It's easy to lose focus when a beautiful girl catches your attention.

4. Comedic actress Julia Louis-Dreyfus—She replaced Amy Poehler in Old Navy campaigns.—Portraying a self-absorbed woman, Julia stops in the middle of one of her monologues to dart off to Old Navy. Both she and Tina Fey, mentioned below, are relatable characters, who can be pictured as a friend or next-door neighbor.

   Universal truth: "Don't let your ego get the best of you." This spot depicts how even egomaniacs can be in love with something other than themselves.

5. Comedic actress Tina Fey—"Everyday Moments" 2014 American Express campaign —The TV spots featured glimpses of simple, everyday experiences. In one scene, "Yogurt Facial," her young daughter gave her a facial. The next scene showed Tina buying more yogurt at the store with some of it still in her hair. When the cashier commented, she just said, "It happens," and casually licked it off, as if that were a common occurrence.

   Universal truth: "Don't sweat the small stuff." What's a little yogurt in your hair when your daughter gives you a facial?

6. Actress Salma Hayek—"Out of Milk" 2012 Got Milk? campaign—One spot shows Salma as a mom who suddenly discovers she's out of milk. Frantically rushing from one store to another as one is out of milk and another is closed, she tries catching a cow in the field. Finally, in a disheveled state, she desperately flags down a milk-truck delivery drive. He gives her a gallon and she looks as if she's received a gift from the heavens.

   Universal truth: "You'll stop at nothing to get what you want." Through rain, disappointment and travails, Salma won't quit until she gets a gallon of milk.

7. Sofia Vergara—"Mom Knows Best" Head & Shoulders 2014—The commercial demonstrates how Sofia's entire family has flake-free hair by using the shampoo.

   Universal truth: "Always look your best." Most people care about how they present themselves. Head & Shoulders gives them one less thing to worry about: dandruff.

b. *Male Celebrities*

1. Actor Clint Eastwood—"Imported from Detroit" Chrysler 2012 Super Bowl commercial—It shows the grit and tenacity that's the heart of Detroit. It's taken a beating, but it hasn't accepted defeat.

    Universal truth: "Never accept defeat." Even the toughest challenges can be faced with bravery, as Detroit residents have demonstrated.

2. Rob Lowe—"Worse Rob Lowe" 2014 DirecTV campaign—It features worse versions of the actor, such as "crazy hairy," "less attractive," "painfully awkward" and "scrawny arms" Rob Lowe. The spots compare the lifestyles of each. Naturally, the original Rob always has DirecTV.

    Universal truth: "Be cool." Having DirecTV makes you more appealing.

3. NFL athlete Isaiah Mustafa—"The Man Your Man Could Smell Like" Old Spice 2010 Super Bowl Commercial—This spot depicts how this product can make your man transform into a sexy hunk, just by using the product.

    Universal truth: "One small thing can change your life." Naturally, this spot is an exaggeration of this truth, but it presents the possibility that it could make a difference.

4. George Clooney—"George Not Included" Fiat 2013 spot—This one showed George admiring a Fiat, climbing inside and relaxing. The sexy owner looks in and seeing him so comfortable, just smiles. The humorous superimposed text read, "George not included."

    Universal truth: "Dream on." The Fiat has everything you could want . . . almost.

5. Gary Sinise—"Anthem Army Strong" U.S. Army 2014—This commercial showcases the leadership and fearlessness of soldiers who serve to protect and guard around the world.

    Universal truth: "Be your best." Army training will strengthen your leadership skills, teach you bravery and develop your strength of character.

6. Actor Dennis Dexter Haysbert—Allstate Insurance campaign—All the spots use this actor's rich tone as the voice of the company. Confident, compassionate and warm, it reflects the brand's message.

    Universal truth: "Someone you can trust." When problems strike, you can count on Allstate to be there.

7. Actor Dean Winters—"Mayhem" character in Allstate Insurance 2013 Super Bowl commercial—This demonstrates the chaos we all go through when disaster strikes. This clever and memorable concept reminds everyone that it's good to have Allstate in your corner.

    Universal truth: "Murphy's Law." In life, you can expect mayhem to show up. Now you have a solution: Allstate.

8. Musicians Ozzy Osbourne and Justin Bieber—Best Buy "Buy Back Program" 2011 Super Bowl commercial—In this one, Ozzy uncomfortably starts the spot promoting

4G network, then the 5G. Acting confused, he asks, "How many bloody 'g's' are there?" Then, Justin steps in and confidently holds up a 6G smartphone. Best Buy offers a buy-back program allowing shoppers to keep up with technology.

Universal truth: "Keep up or be left behind." Not knowing new technological advances makes you out-of-touch and passé.

The right talent can be the support straps in the woven pattern in the strategy, giving strength and personality to the brand's voice.

3. Sound—Creating Attention–Grabbing Jingles

Figure 3.3 How Music Creates Memorability

There's no question that a well-constructed jingle can make a brand's name instantly recognizable (Figure 3.3). The frequently asked question—What makes a jingle unforgettable?—is answered by Linda Kaplan Thaler, CEO and chief creative officer of the Kaplan Thaler Group, in a *Forbes* article:[2]

> *First of all, it has to have huge sticking power. A jingle is not successful if you listen to it once and like it. You have to listen to it and want to sing it. Essentially you become the advertiser for the brand.*

A 2014 *Ad Age* article[3] quotes Roger Bensinger, executive vice president of Prolitec, an ambient-scenting technology company, whose AirQ service is used by brands, such as Abercrombie & Fitch, Hard Rock Hotel & Casino and Giorgio Armani. His following comments reflect how the importance of scent advertising has grown:

> *As brands continue to search for innovative ways to distinguish themselves, scent marketing is becoming another tool in their arsenals. We're where music was 15 years ago.*

Here's a short list of well-known jingles. Some may have been overused and possibly have become grating. You can make your own decision. You'll usually find that musical signatures with just a few notes are easily identified. Here are some examples.

Famous Jingles without Lyrics

1. Coke: five-note musical tag for "Open Happiness" (2009—E-C-D-E-C)
2. NBC: three-note chime sequence (1929—G-E-C)
3. Taco Bell: one-sound bell "Bong" (c. 2001)
4. Intel: five-note musical sound mark, called "Intel Bong" (1994—D flat, D flat, G, D flat, A flat)

Other jingles are remembered because the lyrics are easy to recall. Some jingles use some of the 16 slogan techniques,[4] such as 1) *product name*, 2) *rhyme*, 3) *alliteration*, 4) *play on words*, 5) *parallel construction*, 6) *statement of use or purpose*, 7) *testimonial*, 8) *simile*, 9) *onomatopoeia*, 10) *emotional blackmail*, 11) *imperative*, 12) *interrogative statement*, 13) *vernacular*, 14) *reason why*, 15) *challenge* and 16) *combination*.

Memorable Jingles with Lyrics

1. Nationwide Insurance: easy-to-remember "Nationwide is on your side." (1966)

   Techniques: product name, rhyme and statement of promise

2. Oscar Mayer: "Oh, I wish I were an Oscar Mayer wiener . . ." (1963). These were the original lyrics: "Oh, I'd love to be an Oscar Mayer wiener"

   Techniques: product name and testimonial

   "My bologna has a first name. It's O-S-C-A-R . . ." (1973)

   Techniques: product name and testimonial

3. Doublemint Gum: "Double your pleasure. Double your fun. Doublemint. Doublemint. Doublemint Gum." (1960—uses rhyme, alliteration, parallel construction, product name). These were the original lyrics: "Double your pleasure. Double your fun. With double-good, double-good, Doublemint gum."

4. Campbell's Soup: "Mmm mmm good." (1950)

   Techniques: alliteration and statement of purpose

5. Kit Kat: "Gimme a break. A Kit Kat break." (1986)

   Techniques: imperative, vernacular and product name

6. Band-Aid: "I am stuck on Band-Aid 'cause Band-Aid's stuck on me." (1970s by Barry Manilow)

   Techniques: product name, play on words, statement of purpose and reason why

7. State Farm Insurance: "Like a good neighbor, State Farm is there." (1971 by Barry Manilow)

   Techniques: product name and simile and statement of promise

8. Folgers Coffee: "The best part of wakin' up is Folgers in your cup."

   Techniques: product name, rhyme and statement of promise

9. Alka Seltzer: "Plop. Plop. Fizz. Fizz. Oh, what a relief it is." (1971)

   Techniques: rhyme, parallel construction, statement of purpose, onomatopoeia and reason why

10. Toys "R" Us: "I don't wanna grow up." (1982 by agency owner, Linda Kaplan Thaler, founder of the Thaler Group)

    Techniques: testimonial and vernacular

11. Dr. Pepper: "I'm a Pepper. He's a Pepper. She's a Pepper. We're a Pepper. Wouldn't you like to be a Pepper, too?" (1977 by Randy Newman)

    Techniques: product name, parallel construction, testimonial and interrogative statement

12. G.E.: "We bring good things to life." (1977 by Randy Newman)

    Techniques: product name, play on words and statement of purpose

13. Nestlé: "N-E-S-T-L-E-S Nestlé's makes the very best chocolate." (1955)

    Techniques: product name, statement of purpose and reason why

14. Sara-Lee: "Everybody doesn't like something, but nobody doesn't like Sara-Lee." (1958 by Mitch Lee, creator of Broadway musical, *Man of La Mancha*)

    Techniques: product name, parallel construction and challenge

15. Rice Krispies: "Snap, Crackle, Pop. Rice Krispies!" (1932)

    Techniques: product name, parallel construction and onomatopoeia

16. Empire Carpet: "800–588–2300 Empire" (1996 by copywriter Lynn Hauldren[5])

    Techniques: product name

17. J.G. Wentworth: "877-Cash-Now" (2008) Used in humorous commercials including the opera version, the jingle begins with the famous line: "I have a structured settlement and I need cash now."

    Techniques: product name and statement of purpose

18. Meow Mix: "Meow. Meow. Meow . . ." (1970 by composer/producer Shelly Palmer)

    Techniques: product name, alliteration and reason why

In a 2014 article, Professors Henard and Rossetti examined the influence that consumers of chart-topping hits had on advertising commercials. They examined a thousand number-one hits over a fifty-year span: January 1960 to December 2009. They pinpointed 12 main themes and specific words that occurred most frequently: loss, desire, aspiration, breakup, pain, inspiration, nostalgia, rebellion, jaded, desperation, escapism and confusion."[6] Henard and Rossetti explained that these themes proved to be emotional rather than cognitive in nature. They also revealed the impact these themes have on the audience:

> *The communication themes identified here are those that resonate with a diverse and large population of consumers and extend beyond the field of music. These themes are universal*

in the sense that most individuals have experienced them at some point and can relate to the message presented.[7]

Ultimately, the authors conveyed their belief that communication themes from hit songs offer advertisers a solid idea about "which themes best resonate with a mass audience at a particular point in time."[8]

Sound effects

It is impossible to ignore the power of sound effects in various advertising vehicles, including online videos, radio and television spots. The sound of cars crashing amplifies the danger of everyday car travel. The snap of a can opening, followed by the pouring of liquid into a glass is a reminder of a refreshingly cold beer, soda or sparkling water. The cries from a baby monitor can immediately alert parents.

Well-chosen sounds can instantly connect to a targeted audience, just as key words, phrases or lyrics can. Hearing a witch's cackle to advertise the Broadway musical *Wicked* conjures up images to the listener. The purring of a cat projects contentedness, a reward to pet owners. Listening to a dog's running and panting with praise from someone confirms that healthy dogs are happy ones.

Whenever you see a video or TV spot, or listen to a commercial, pay full attention to the sound effects. Notice how they place you in a particular setting and draw an emotional response from you. Sounds can stimulate a need for a service, create a desire for a product and influence the buying decision for a particular brand. Never underestimate the psychological pull of sound.

Figure 3.4 How Feelings Fuel Audience Reactions

4. Scent—Engaging Emotions and Memories

Besides musical identifiers, scent can also be used for brand differentiation. In fact, it's being used more and more in advertising (Figure 3.4). Pedigree dog food used scent in a novel way. It created scented, floor stickers with a three-dimensional image of a full food bowl. Doggies, drawn to the scent, vigorously licked the stickers demonstrating how aromatic the food was. Although pet owners were surprised, they weren't disappointed like their unsatisfied pets.

Today, the global scent-marketing industry generates $300 million. Roger Bensinger, executive vice-president of AirQ by Prolitec, steers the creation of customized, scented environments, like "olfactory logos," for international brands such as Abercrombie & Fitch, Hard Rock Hotel & Casino and Giorgio Armani.[9] Mitzi Gaskins, vice president and global brand leader for JW Marriott, believes that scent, in addition to overall décor and color scheme, has the same impact on the consumer as music, lighting, and flowers.[10]

Other businesses, such as Ocean Mark and Ford Motor Company (Lincoln brand), have created exclusive scents that distinguish the brand. The Ocean Bank scent is called Ocean Blue and may be added to pens and checkbook covers.

Ford Motor Company, seeking to emit a comfortable, posh environment has used a blend of jasmine and tonka fragrances in its showrooms. To develop this, Ford worked with SensoryMax and expert perfume creator, Rene Morgenthaler, who stated that the scent reflected "luxury and warmth."[11]

At unexpected places in several UK cities, including London, Manchester and Glasgow, McCain Ready Baked Jackets recreated the scent of its oven-baked jacket potatoes. These ambient messages occurred at ten smelly bus stops and in supermarkets' chilly frozen-food sections.

The bus stops invited travelers to push an oversized potato to release the scent. The invitation surprised and entertained commuters. It also masked some of the noxious odors, built brand awareness and reminded consumers that these five-minute potatoes smell yummy.[12]

In the frozen aisles, Blue Chip Marketing, the agency for McCain Ready Baked Jacket, was the first to introduce technology that offered fragrance in frozen-food areas. The results were higher sales in more than 600 Tesco and Asda stores.[13]

So why is scent so powerful? Every time you smell anything, your smell receptors send messages to the olfactory bulb, which sits inside your brain's limbic system. That message triggers an immediate response, subconsciously stimulating memories and emotions. The fact is that no other sense instantly reaches the limbic area of the brain, causing this kind of visceral reaction. Other senses are directed to the cognitive region.[14]

Consider how delicious food product scents draw you in at shopping malls, such as fresh-baked cookies, Cinnabon rolls, pizza, baked goods, fudge and pretzels. Just the smell not only makes you hungry, but also brings up memories of special times and places. The next time you notice a yummy smell from a bakery, you might remember how you felt when you ate your favorite pie or a birthday cake you enjoyed as a child.

5. Taste—Creating a Specific Brand "Flavor"

One exceptionally innovative campaign was created in Dubai. It allowed migrant laborers, mostly from India and Pakistan, to use Coke bottle caps in place of coins in a Coca-Cola-created phone booth. This served as both a brand-building campaign, as well as one that answered the needs of workers who wanted, but couldn't afford to call home frequently.

People lined up with their caps and could make a three-minute call anywhere in the world. What an ingenious way to extend the "Open Happiness" campaign. The brand demonstrated compassion and caring, while highlighting the core strategy of sharing a Coke. Now, every Coke purchase enabled these homesick, indigent laborers to share a few moments with loved ones.[15]

Figure 3.5 How Taste Drives Consumer Interest

These unique campaigns makes product sampling, through the mail and at stores, seem so ordinary, even though they still work. Notice the next time you try a sample at a supermarket or other store, did you consider buying it? Perhaps you tried a new hors d'oeuvre or dessert. Maybe you tasted a new wine or alcoholic beverage. These tastings awaken and expand your product awareness without a purchase (Figure 3.5). Companies know how the try-before-you-buy promotions work for both consumers and brands. You might find a new favorite food or beverage and they might gain another consumer in just a few seconds.

6. Voice—Using Talent with Unique Voices

Figure 3.6 How Talent Delivers the Message

When casting talent for commercials, agency producers often look for highly distinctive voices that will be intrusive and pique the listeners' and/or viewers' interest (Figure 3.6). You don't necessarily have to hire a celebrity; however you should look to hire a talent with a unique sound. Notice how when the names Heidi Klum and Mario Lopez are mentioned, you can hear their voices.

Sometimes it's the timbre or tone of the talent's voice. For example, it could be that it's rich and deep (James Earl Jones). Or it could be the way actors speak: their delivery, pace and inflection (Melissa McCarthy and Jack Nicholson). For example, it has a breathy (Marilyn Monroe) or nasal sound (Fran Drescher). It could be the particular accent (Rosie Perez or Woody Allen) or a certain way they enunciate words (Denzel Washington).

These identifiable voices pull you in, not just because they belong to famous stars, but because of their specific characteristics that set them apart. Their voices and delivery are instantly distinguishable. See how many more actors, musicians, athletes you can add to the list.

Female actors

Diane Keaton
Whoopi Goldberg
Kyra Sedgwick
Rosie Perez
Kim Basinger
Melissa McCarthy
Scarlett Johansson
Kirsten Dunst
Jennifer Tilly
Mila Kunis
Fran Drescher
Viola Davis
Meryl Streep
Queen Latifah
Jodie Foster
Betty White
Katherine Heigl
Rosanne Barr
Winona Ryder
Salma Hayek
Kate Winslet
Cate Blanchett
Tina Fey
Susan Sarandon
Beyoncé Knowles
Charlize Theron
Cameron Diaz
Sandra Bullock
Natalie Portman
Sigourney Weaver
Téa Leoni
Helen Hunt
Anna Faris
Christina Ricci
Drew Barrymore
Marilyn Monroe

Male actors

Denzel Washington
Anthony Hopkins
Sylvester Stallone
Arnold Schwarzenegger
David Duchovny
Al Pacino
Robert De Niro
Harrison Ford
Liam Neesen
Geoffrey Rush
Alec Baldwin
Sean Connery
Gary Sinise
Woody Allen
The Rock
Kevin Costner
Vin Diesel
Jack Nicholson
Eddie Murphy
Christopher Walken

Other types of voices include catchphrases that become memes, meaning they're repeated, spread and integrated into popular culture, whether from campaigns, such as the Budweiser word, "Whassup?"; the California Milk Processor Board phrase, "Got milk?"; the Las Vegas Convention Board famous line, "What happens here stays here"; and the Life Alert catchphrase, "I've fallen and I can't get up." In film, there are many ones to recall, such as "I'll be back" and "Hasta la vista, baby!" from *Terminator*, as well as "You had me at hello" or "Show me the money" from *Jerry Maguire*.

In Chapter 5, we'll examine another type of "voice," namely the language of communication and its delivery techniques. This includes 1) tone of voice (how the brand speaks, such as authoritatively, casually, etc.), 2) point of view (who's delivering the message, such as the brand, the consumer or the conscience), 3) message (what's being said) and so on.

7. Sight—Raising Brand Awareness with Images

Many successful campaigns use specific visual cues to portray the brand (Figure 3.7). As mentioned in Chapter 1, it could be an icon (such as animated mascots, famous cartoon characters, brand characters and animals), a spokesperson, a consumer, a company executive or founder who can personify or portray the brand's personality and core values (what the brand stands for). Brands can also use packaging to present a specific idea, such as holiday themes in the designs or integrating beauty shots (photos of the product) to draw in a worldwide audience.

One Cadbury Valentine's Day campaign in India featured heartfelt messages to loved ones. As a reflection of gift giving, Cadbury had implemented holiday-inspired blended with quirky campaigns. In honor of the Hindu festival, Raksha Bandhan, which honors sibling relationships, Cadbury created an opportunity to show love to your sister(s). It invited

Figure 3.7 How Visuals Strengthen Recognition

consumers to express their affection with messages using social media: Facebook, Twitter and YouTube. Popular musicians from India composed beautiful songs from forty-six selected, personalized greetings.[16] This campaign's emotional appeal stirred talk value and generated buzz. Here are some ways to connect to your audience.

Brand Icons

a. Animated mascots

1. Geico—Pig and Gecko
2. Cap 'n Crunch cereal—Cap'n Crunch
3. M&M'S—M&M'S characters
4. Planters—Mr. Peanut
5. Trix—Trix Rabbit
6. Lucky Charms—Leprechaun
7. Aflac—Duck
8. National Crime Prevention Council—McGruff the Crime Dog

b. Brand characters (actual people, with or without costumes)

1. McDonald's—Ronald McDonald
2. Geico—Caveman
3. Charmin bathroom tissue—Mr. Whipple
4. Chef Boyardee canned pastas—Chef Boyardee
5. National Federation of Coffee Growers (Colombia)—Juan Valdez

c. Famous cartoon characters

1. Disney—Mickey Mouse
2. MetLife Insurance—Snoopy

3. Alpo cat food—Garfield
4. Fruity Pebbles—Fred Flinstone
5. Honda—Strawberry Shortcake

d. Animals (live, not animated)

1. Budweiser—Clydesdales and Dalmatians
2. Busch Baked Beans—Duke the Dog
3. Taco Bell—Taco Bell Dog
4. 9 Lives cat food—Morris the Cat
5. Target—Bullseye (formerly Spot) Bull Terrier
6. Bud Light—Spuds MacKenzie (1980s)

e. Celebrities

1. Snickers—Betty White
2. Nike—Michael Jordan
3. Verizon—James Earl Jones
4. Priceline.com—William Shatner
5. CoverGirl—Rihanna
6. Revlon—Halle Berry
7. H&M—David Beckham
8. Chanel No. 5—Brad Pitt
9. Dior—Charlize Theron
10. Pepsi—One Direction (top-charting boy band)

f. Recognizable spokespersons

1. Progressive insurance—Stephanie Courtney (Flo)
2. Trivago –Tim Williams
3. Allstate Insurance—Dean Winters and Dennis Haysbert (deep, rich voice)
4. Old Spice—Isaiah Mustafa
5. PC guy (from Apple commercials)—John Hodgman

g. Consumers, company founders and executives who became spokespersons

1. Jenny Craig—Monica Lewinsky (infamous consumer)
2. South Beach Diet—Dr. Arthur Agatston (founder and cardiologist)
3. Atkins Diet—Dr. Robert Atkins (founder and cardiologist)
4. Chrysler—Lee Iacocca (chairman)
5. Virgin Group—Richard Branson (founder)
6. Men's Wearhouse—George Zimmer (founder)
7. Hair Club for Men—Sy Sperling (founder and president)

We will discuss more visual techniques in Chapter 6, such as the use of infographics, illustrations, photographs, colors and so on.

8. Touch—Creating Fun, Audience Engagement

Figure 3.8 How Involving Consumers Creates Loyalty

With so many digital touchpoints and social media connectivity, brands are utilizing them in interactive campaigns. Although we'll go more into depth in Chapter 8, audience engagement heightens the consumer–brand relationship. The purpose of brand interactivity, which we'll also discuss in more detail in Chapter 8, is to increase customer loyalty and strengthen the emotional bond (Figure 3.8).

TD Canada bank created an innovative "Thank You" campaign that rewarded consumers in fun, unexpected ways. The unanticipated interactions make the campaign go viral with people sharing how they were thanked and appreciated for their loyalty.

The bank's staff members reached out to twenty customers, inviting them to test its new ATM-Thanking machines, placed in specific branches. Unsuspecting participants were greeted by name by a voice that first welcomed and then, thanked them for being loyal customers. The ATM voice said, "I'm an Automated Thanking Machine." When a side window opened, they received gift-wrapped presents, tickets, flowers. But, the bank didn't stop there. It created even more personalized thanks for select customers. These included:

1. A sports fan received the official Blue Jays cap and team shirt, glove and tickets. Next, he caught a ball from his favorite player. Then finally, he got to throw the first pitch at a game!
2. A young mom who received two piggy banks with $1,000.00 checks for a mom's kids to open their accounts, along with all-expense paid trip to Disney for the family.
3. An elderly mom whose daughter in Trinidad was having cancer surgery received plane tickets to visit her.

Of course a compassionate campaign went viral. People couldn't believe the thank-you gifts, especially the personalized ones.[17]

Campaigns that include the sense of touch can be as simple as test-drive-a-car, kiosks in malls, textured greeting cards and other hands-on tactics.

Brands have discovered, after much research that when more than one sense is mentioned in ad copy, it heightens consumers' positive sense-related responses. Therefore, when advertisers can actually integrate, not just mention one or more senses, the effectiveness increases.[18]

9. Execution—Articulating the Story Details

Figure 3.9 How Orchestrating the Parts Enhances the Campaign

After building the creative ideas, you must consider how you will use the senses to best express the storytelling. Targeted senses that connect the blueprint need to be blended together in an architecturally sound manner. This means the execution needs to bring the structural forces together so they support one another for greatest impact. Just using sight, sound, touch, etc. isn't enough. Each sense needs to speak directly to the audience in a relevant way to reinforce the message (Figure 3.9).

Will you use celebrities, spokespeople, consumers, executives or company founders? How will they present the spot? Emphatically? Gently? Intimately? Authoritatively? Later, in Chapter 5, we'll discuss, in more detail, the brand's tone of voice. Here, we're looking at not just how the brand speaks to the audience, but also how exactly that voice will be presented. How much emphasis? What kind of articulation? How slowly? How quickly? And so on. The delivery is created in the studio and reflected, as much as possible, in other media.

The same goes with music. Will it be original or existing? What style will you choose? Where will you place it to accentuate the most important points? Sound effects also need to be created or selected. You must carefully decide where to strategically place them for maximum effect.

When using scent, you have to be judicious in your choices. Placing the smell of fresh-baked cookies at a bus stop with a "Got Milk?" message, as was done in San Francisco, created a backlash. The controversy was driven by the question of how painful it is to commuters to smell the cookies and have no way to get them. It just created hunger and a sense of deprivation. On the other hand, when Avon used higher-priced scent strips in magazines that emitted the fragrance only when consumers scratched them, they showed compassion for allergy sufferers.

Next review how you will use taste through product samples as:

- In-store handouts
- Innovative equipment, such as the Coke Freestyle Machine, with more than 104 flavors
- Unique campaigns as the above-mentioned, cap-for-coin Coke concept in India

For the actual talent's voice, do you want a distinctive one, such as Helen Hunt or Matthew McConaughey? Notice how Eddie Murphy brought the Donkey character to the foreground with his delivery in *Shrek*. Just as in advertising, animated films cast talent with an individual and identifiable sound.

When establishing a singular, notable image, consider how that particular mascot, character, cartoon, celebrity or animal projects the brand character. Look how the Aflac Duck brought instant recognition and became the face of a successful, yet unknown insurance company.

Finally, how will you create a physical interaction with the audience? What interactive mechanism will you use to get the consumer to interact with the brand? Games, contests and comments, consumer-created content and other methods allow people to play with the brand. The more the sense of touch, the more tactile and real is the relationship.

Using one or more senses will stir a response in consumers, making them feel closer to the brand.

10. Delivery—Implementing Ideas for Innovative Media Usage

Figure 3.10 How Appropriate Vehicles Create Impact

Although the media delivery systems were determined before the creative process, you need to check how these sensory techniques will work in the planned vehicles. Although we'll look into this more in Chapter 7, let's take a quick look at how the ideas need to match the specific medium. Consider the best use of talent, sound, scent, taste, voice, visual and touch to make the campaign's "story" come alive (Figure 3.10).

What if you could create such an exciting interaction that everyone shares the fun? Remember what TD Canada bank did with its ATMs (Automated Thanking Machines) with personalized gifts. Or how ANZ bank designed colorful "GAY-TM" machines to participate in the Gay and Lesbian Pride Parade in Sydney, Australia, as discussed earlier in Chapter 2.

Prior to every Super Bowl, Doritos challenges consumers to create a TV commercial for its Crash the Super Bowl contest. Creators of the first-place spot by popular vote on Facebook and/or *USA Today* Ad Meter win a cool $1 million. Here are a few past winners: "Free Doritos" (2008) by Joe Herbert of Bates, Indiana; "Pug Attack" (2010) by J.R. Burningham of Burbank, California; "Sling Baby" (2011, Facebook) by Kevin T. Willson of Los Angeles, California; "Man's Best Friend" (2011, *USA Today*) by Jonathan Friedman of Virginia Beach, Virginia; "Goat 4 Sale" (2013) and "Time Machine" (2014).

Even though "Underdog: Anti-Bark Collar" (2009) came in second, creator William Kyle Gerardi of Cary, North Carolina still won $650,000. Another contestant, Tynesha Williams of Santa Monica, California won $400,000 with her "House Sitting" spot.

As you think about how to interact with the consumer, ask yourself what campaigns created buzz and enhanced the brand image? How could you use interactivity to stimulate participation, connect better with your audience and create talk value? Stretch your imagination and challenge yourself so you can create an audience-relevant, brand-centric concept that engages and entertains. This will make the campaign unforgettable.

Creative Strategy Exercises

Exercise 1: Identify one powerful storytelling campaign? Dissect why it worked.

a. List the senses it targeted.
b. What media was used?

Exercise 2: Name one campaign that used a famous talent. Answer these questions:
a. Did that talent make the campaign more memorable?
b. Would you have used a different talent? Which one?
c. Would you use two talents together? Which ones?

Exercise 3: Name one jingle that you immediately recall. Can you identify the advertiser?

Exercise 4: Which campaign used scent to reach its audience? Where was it used?

Exercise 5: Have you experienced a taste sample? Did it make you buy the product? Where else would you have let the public taste the product?

Exercise 6: Choose a campaign that used a talent with a specific voice.

a. Did it fit the brand?
b. Did it speak to the audience?
c. Did it sell the product/brand?

Exercise 7: Select a campaign that used a memorable visual to represent the brand.

a.   Was it a mascot, brand character, consumer, etc.?
b.   Did it stay as the representative for more than ten years?
c.   What made it so distinctive, entertaining and/or appealing?

Exercise 8: When did you interact with a brand or product using touch? Was it through:

a.   Social media? If so, which one?
b.   A contest or game? Why did you enjoy it?
c.   A product test, a try-before-you-buy campaign or a trial offer?

Notes

1. Jim Edwards, "Doritos' 'Time Machine' Super Bowl Ad Cost Just $200 to Make," February 2, 2014, www.businessinsider.com/doritos-time-machine-super-bowl-ad-2014-2#ixzz3PIEv83IQ (accessed January 19, 2014).
2. Ken Bruno, "Best-Ever Advertising Jingles," *Forbes*, June 30, 2010, www.forbes.com/2010/06/30/advertising-jingles-coca-cola-cmo-network-jingles.html (accessed January 23, 2014).
3. Minda Smiley, "Dollars & Scents: From Clothes to Cars to Banks, Brands Seek Distinction through Fragrance," December 9, 2014, *Advertising Age*, http://adage.com/article/cmo-strategy/smell-money-marketers-sell-scent/296084/ (accessed January 16, 2015).
4. Margo Berman, *The Copywriter's Toolkit: The Complete Guide to Strategic Advertising Copy* (London: Wiley-Blackwell, 2012), 50–54.
5. Empire Carpet Man, Lynn Hauldren, www.empirecarpetman.com/the-empire-today-jingle (accessed January 16, 2015).
6. Matt Shipman, "Analysis of 50 Years of Hit Songs Yields Tips for Advertisers," March 18, 2014, https://news.ncsu.edu/2014/03/wms-henard-hits2014/ (accessed January 19, 2014).
7. David H. Henard and Christian L. Rossetti, "All You Need is Love? Communication Insights from Pop Music's Number-One Hits," *Journal of Advertising Research*, June 2014: 62.
8. Henard and Rosetti, "All You Need": 63.
9. Smiley, "Dollars."
10. Smiley, "Dollars."
11. Smiley, "Dollars."
12. John Metcalfe, "Inside Smellvertising, the Scented Advertising Tactic Coming Soon to a City Near You," February 9, 2012, www.citylab.com/design/2012/02/inside-smellvertising-scented-advertising-tactic-coming-bus-stop-near-you/1181/ (accessed January 16, 2015).
13. Blue Chip, http://wearebluechip.co.uk/ (accessed January 15, 2015).
14. Scent Marketing, "Why and How Scent Marketing Works," www.scentmarketingusa.com/scent-marketing-works.html (accessed January 16, 2015).
15. WhackyIdeas, "Top 3 Most Touching Marketing Campaigns," December 11, 2014, http://whacky ideas.net/2014/12/top-3-touching-innovative-marketing-campaigns/ (accessed January 16, 2014).
16. WhackyIdeas, "Top 3 Most Touching Marketing Campaigns."
17. WhackyIdeas, "Top 3 Most Touching Marketing Campaigns."
18. Ryan S. Elder and Aradhna Krishna, "The Effects of Advertising Copy on Sensory Thoughts and Perceived Taste," *Journal of Consumer Research*, February 2010 (published online June 25, 2009) (accessed January 28, 2015), 750.

4

CONCEPTUAL STRATEGY
Presentation Drawing

Concept is everything. It drives the creative direction, talks to the audience, matches the medium and embodies the brand. The goal is to develop an idea that works equally well in all vehicles, while delivering a message in a unique, relevant and entertaining fashion. Campaigns that are novel are instantly recognizable. They're the ones that draw a picture of the brand and cleverly present that portrayal to the audience. Let's look at some of those with a unique approach, one at a time.

In 2013, Kleenex turned to Google Flu Trends, a flu-tracking device with 90 percent accuracy, to forecast cold-and-flu-outbreak regions three weeks in advance. The idea was to persuade consumers to load up on Kleenex before they got sick. The MyAchoo.com campaign targeted highest at-risk cities where germs would most likely hit next. Using exaggeration and humor strategies, TV spots exaggerated what people would do when they didn't have a Kleenex on hand. After sneezing, some wiped their hands on their family dogs. Others used party streamers. The campaign also used digital ads in singled-out geographic areas.[1]

For the 2015 Super Bowl, McDonald's celebrated Valentine's Day and honored its patrons with a February "Pay with Love" spot. For a short time before the holiday, select customers didn't have to use cash for their orders. Instead, they followed cashiers' directions and displayed love with hugs and kisses to family and friends.

These are the kinds of concepts that create talk value, which in its very nature extends the campaign long past its scheduled media. They connect to the consumer in myriad ways. They could 1) interact with them, 2) make them laugh, 3) make them feel an emotion, 4) thank them, 5) cast talent that resembles them, 6) share their opinions, 7) make them sympathetic, 8) show them the core brand essence, 9) remind them of the brand position itself, 10) cause them to change their beliefs, 11) portray the brand's social conscience and commitment and 12) have fun with the audience (Figure 4.1). Of course, there are even more ways messages can inspire the consumer.

In this chapter, we'll examine these concept strategies, one-by-one. Some campaigns blend concepts by engaging the audience while sharing humor. Or reflecting the brand's audience along with epitomizing consumer opinions. As we discuss each of them, think about other campaigns that utilize these strategies. Pay attention to commercials, campaigns and promotions and analyze the concepts and their messages as you view or hear them. This will strengthen your evaluative and critical-thinking skills.

Now, let's move forward and consider each conceptual strategy technique.

Box 4.1 Twelve Conceptual Strategies

1. *Engaging the Audience*

2. *Sharing Humor*

3. *Sparking an Emotion*

4. *Rewarding the Audience*

5. *Reflecting the Audience*

6. *Epitomizing Consumer Opinion*

7. *Showing Compassion*

8. *Portraying a Brand's Core Values*

9. *Reinforcing Brand Position*

10. *Changing Audience Perception*

11. *Supporting a Cause*

12. *Playing with the Audience*

1. Engaging the Audience

Figure 4.1 How Brands Interact with Consumers

Many brands target audiences during specific holidays and events. If the promotion is particularly relevant to consumers, it will succeed and get attention (Figure 4.1).

For example, to announce its new relationship with 1-800-FLOWERS and recognize Valentine's Day, Visa Checkout created a "Footballentine's Day" cross-promotion. The promotion, which started in September 2014, used multimedia including national TV spots, retail promotions, digital and social media, including Facebook, with this easy-to-remember hashtag: #FootballentinesDay.[2]

There were several related Visa campaigns with ordering deadlines and promo codes. To get ready for the game, one September 2014 campaign offered $18 double-the-flower bouquets. Another one gave away 30,000 free bunches of 18 multicolored roses until supplies ran out on a specified date. Participants only paid $14.99 for shipping and handling.

All campaigns targeted loyal football fans. They, in turn, could honor loved ones who supported their football passion with flowers. NFL stars and supermodels like Brooklyn Decker were engaged for pitching and handing out flowers. ESPN hosts Mike and Mike even discussed it.

A.1. Steak Sauce reached its fans in an entertaining campaign, shared via social media. Known for its 185-year popular pairing with steak, the brand created a Facebook profile as if it were a real person, not a brand. Soon, "he" invited others to friend him. Soon A.1. Steak Sauce was "friends" with Salmon, Pork, Fish Tacos, Meatballs, Corn on the Cob and so on creating other new relationships. Announcements appeared in humorous comments, such as "Me and Potato hittin' the town!" Another funny online dialogue was created when Steak asked, "Hey, want to go to the steakhouse this weekend?" To which, A.1. Steak Sauce replied, "Can't. I already have plans with Lobster." Soon, as in real life, the friendship was fraught with problems and they drew apart. To cheer "himself" up, A.1. Steak Sauce created a Potluck event where all his new friends appear in various dishes. What an inventive approach. Now creating friendships with other ingredients, A.1. Steak Sauce shows fans other delicious combinations they might not have considered. (It's worth seeing on YouTube: www.youtube.com/watch?v=I2XFglTo6bg.)

By tying the promotion to the consumers' passions, these kinds of campaigns reignite the emotional response to the brand. And make them feel appreciated.

2. Sharing Humor

Figure 4.2 How Amusing the Audience Works

In 2014, the owner of Foley's NY Pub & Restaurant, Shaun Clancy, introduced an Irish Baseball Hall of Fame for his patrons. Showing his sense of humor, Shaun sold $1 million in sports collectibles, including Manhattan's reputed-to-be oldest urinals and an actual can of insect spray used by umpires in the bug-biting 2007 Yankee's playoff game (Figure 4.2). To keep the entire month of March in 2008 upbeat, he barred the singing of the depressing song "Danny Boy," especially on St. Patrick's Day.[3]

One hilariously funny, favorite commercial featured a father and child in the supermarket. When the boy was denied the candy he wanted, he kept yelling, "I want the big bag." That quickly escalated into his screaming, running through the aisles, knocking items off the shelf and finally having a full tantrum on the floor. The only words are the boy's bellowing. The spot closes on a close-up of the desperate dad's face with this line below it: "Use condoms." If you can stop laughing long enough, you'll see the advertiser was Zazoo condoms. Pay special attention to the talent. They couldn't have been more perfectly cast. The little boy was credibly irritating with an ear-splitting scream. The dad looked resigned to his fate. Part of creating a powerful message is to carefully choose the talent who's delivering it. Here's one of many YouTube links to see it: www.youtube.com/watch?v=oEd1m16Lls0.

In 2015, Bud Light released an entertaining spot that asked a Budweiser fan at a bar if he'd agree to do something unexpected in exchange for a bottle of his favorite beer. He reads the bottle, which invites him to some "old-school fun." He and two friends leave the bar and find a giant coin on the sidewalk with a huge coin slot on the building. Caught by surprise, they find themselves greeted by a group of celebrating partygoers. The patron, who accepted the challenge, is led into in a life-size Pac-Man game. He is told he is Pac-Man character and is pushed into the giant maze. Suddenly, he's fending off attacking Pac-dots. Accompanied by music and sound effects, which emulate the game sounds, he runs through as the crowd cheers him on. This fast-paced, energy-packed commercial instantly engages the audience's attention. They are intrigued to continue watching to see what happens. When he wins, he gets another Bud Light, and stunned with this experience, asks, "What is going on?" It's a fun-to-watch spot that successfully captures Super Bowl excitement and anticipation.

3. Sparking an Emotion

Figure 4.3 How Feelings Help Consumers Bond with the Brand

Unforgettable campaigns generate an emotional response from the audience. They may awaken consumers' senses so they feel concerned, sympathetic, considerate, compassionate, impassioned, joyful, amazed, stimulated, moved and so on (Figure 4.3).

In a *Forbes* article, Susan Credle, chief creative officer at Leo Burnett, commented on the emotional effect of successful campaigns:

The most memorable spots don't just make us laugh or cry, they change a conversation.[4]

One way for consumers to display their feelings was to turn their tweets into songs. To promote Sony Mobile, agency MRY teamed up with two programs to execute its plan: #TweetSinger. First, it used Oddcast to turn type into speech. Then, it implemented Songify to convert the speech into music. Now, tweets could express emotions through the chosen genre of music. The result? In the first thirty days, consumers across the world shared TweetSongs in 176 countries. Within three months, 1) TweetSongs rose to more than 70,000, 2) replays reached 300,000, 3) Sony Xperia's exposure grew and 4) www. SonyMobile.com site visits stretched to an impressive seven minutes.[5]

Tata Safari, the SUV, made-in-India manufacturer, also integrated music to bond with consumers in its "My Day My Way" campaign. Targeting Experientials, the campaign spoke directly to the off-road warriors who love behind-the-wheel adventures, from dune bashing and mudding to cross-country endurance events. They were invited to share videos and photos of their Tata Safari escapades and post them to #SafariTrails. Next, these consumer-created visuals were set to lyrics and became part of the Tata #SafariTrails "My Day My Way" song, composed by Vasuda Sharma, Gaurav Dagaonkar and Sidd Coutto.[6]

An Australian anti-smoking commercial, "Boy Loses Mum for a Minute," shows a little boy holding his mother's hand at a busy terminal. Suddenly, he's alone without his mom. He looks around desperately, but doesn't see her. In a few moments, he's crying. The announcer asks a poignant, introspective question, like this: If your child feels this bad when you're gone for a minute, imagine how he'd feel if you're gone for a lifetime?

This stirring commercial evokes a sense of abandonment and loss. The goal is to make smokers realize the ultimate pain their death would cause to family members, especially their children.

4. Rewarding the Audience

Figure 4.4 How Consumers React to Being Appreciated

In 2014, WestJet surprised Xmas passengers with an event that was voted the best viral student video with 37.9 million views and 2.2 million social shares. Behind the "Christmas Miracle" music video, the narrator delivered a modified version of the famous poem, "Twas the Night Before Xmas," accompanied by Tchaikovsky's "The Dance of the Sugar Plum Fairy" from the beloved *The Nutcracker* ballet. In preparation of the surprise, crewmembers asked unsuspecting, pre-boarding passengers what they wanted for Xmas.

The Canadian airline engaged 150 employees scrambled to complete the following tasks before the plane landed: shop, gift-wrap, label the gifts and get them through security.

After arriving, passengers discovered that their wishes were granted. As they waited for their luggage, gift-wrapped presents labeled with their names, came down the luggage carousel. The shocked and delighted passengers, screamed, cried with joy and then gratefully hugged a jolly, blue-suited WestJet Santa (Figure 4.4).

No wonder this stunt received so much attention. One thrilled, disbelieving family even received a large, flat-screen TV! How many consumers wouldn't be thrilled to receive their dearest wish?[7]

In 2012, Coca-Cola rewarded point-saving Coke drinkers with free, official NASCAR gear. One commercial, "Thank You Race," showed animated characters representing the world's fastest race car drivers, dashing across the country to deliver the collectible items from this high-speed sport. Car hoods, steering wheels, driving helmets and more are tossed to eager fans. It was a fun way to thank their loyal fans.

Another more basic campaign that rewarded consumers was the hassle-free Bank of America Cash Rewards Card. It awarded one percent back on every purchase. Without money-back limits, annoying restrictions or complicated rules. This made it easy to get an actual, legitimate bonus from its clear-cut, no-nonsense promise.

Although this campaign for www.ThankYouWater.org also fits under the Supporting a Cause concept strategy, it focuses more on thanking those who have bought water as a way to donate to the mission. As a result of the purchases, fresh drinking water was provided in water-deprived regions. One commercial featured heartfelt images of gleeful children catching water from newly installed outdoor faucets. The message thanked all of those who chose to buy specifically marked bottles with the www.ThankYouWater.org logo. The spot showed consumers how they personally impacted the lives of those less fortunate. This feel-good commercial ended with a call to action asking viewers to visit the organization's website.

5. Reflecting the Audience

Smart marketers are brave. They'll risk consumer backlash to promote consumers' attitudes. For example, in 2014, they showed a bi-racial couple and daughter in a commercial: "Gracie" (www.youtube.com/watch?v=LKuQrKeGe6g). With more and more mixed-race families, Cheerios wanted to acknowledge one of its many consumer groups. Although some viewers were appalled, others were pleased to see the growing number of interracial couples reflected.

CNN reported that one in ten heterosexual couples are biracial. The 2010 U.S. Decennial Census (conducted every 10 years) survey showed that of the unmarried couples, 18 percent of the opposite-sex and 21 percent same-sex couples were interracial.[8]

NPR also discussed the same 2010 U.S. Census that stated a 28 percent increase in interracial couples between 2000 and 2014. In fact, more than 5.3 million couples are comprised of different races and ethnicities[9] (Figure 4.5).

Figure 4.5 How Featuring Shoppers Connects Them to the Brand

Not only did the spot create backlash and buzz, it inadvertently fueled a consumer Facebook page: www.facebook.com/mixedandhappy. Smiling, mixed-race families holding boxes of Cheerios shared their photos and comments. As part of the Family Breakfast Project, launched by Cheerios, the Murphy-West couple realized they were among 15 percent of all newly married couples that were biracial. Inspired by the controversial TV commercial, Michael and Alyson developed the WeAreThe15Percent.com website, in celebration of all the other couples like them.[10] The site attracted hundreds of mixed families to post pictures and perspectives. Another consumer posted a video that celebrated family diversity on YouTube.[11]

The Febreze "Noseblind" campaign included a series of commercials that depicted pet owners in an unexpected and honest manner. Many don't realize their homes and cars reek from animal odors. Through a hilariously exaggerated campaign, images show pet lovers in different situations. In one, "Driving Dog Odors," the Old English Sheepdog has its head out the car window, enjoying the breeze. The announcer mentions that your car smells fine to you, but it really smells like this: The entire car converts into a giant Sheepdog, with the same dog hanging out the window. It's so funny because it's so unexpected. Another spot, "Cat Couch Odors," shows a woman on her sofa surrounded by cats. The announcer makes the same comment and the couch becomes a gigantic cat with the other housecats lounging on it, as they did before the transformation. The campaign, in a delicate way, tells pet "parents" that they've become "noseblind" to pet odors. The answer? Febreze room and fabric deodorizers can neutralize even the strongest, yet undetectable-to-them odors.

6. Epitomizing Consumer Opinions

When Moen marketing executives learned that its customers looked at their bathroom fixtures as jewelry, not hardware, they wanted to depict that opinion in their ads (Figure 4.6). What did they do? They asked jewelry designers to create necklaces, using fashionable Moen faucets as their muses. The result was enchanting and attractive wearable works of art.

Next, they applied stylized photographs that highlighted the jewelry as it graced a model's neck. This graceful pairing dramatized the faucet's beauty, reflecting the consumers' point of view. The campaign acknowledged fashion-conscious buyers' opinion that Moen

Figure 4.6 How Mirroring Perception Increases Communication

enhanced their bathrooms and kitchens, turning them into showplaces that visibly displayed their personal aesthetics.[12]

Angie's List campaigns focus on the power of consumer reviews. Instead of hiring repair, construction and other laborers sight unseen, consumers can rely on the opinions of others. Now they can have work done and feel confident in the companies they employ. The subscription-paid fee promises authenticated reviews, a consumer-complaint resolution team and data certification. Ad messages drive home these points and give consumers a sense of protection when they allow strangers into their homes.

Even in its early years, Amazon knew the importance of consumer opinion. It asked for customer reviews, which encouraged others to make purchases. For books, for example, customers purchased two to three books before the introduction of reviews. After that, buyers increased their orders to about five books. Once established as a persuasive and trusted peer-to-peer assessment, purchaser reviews expanded to its other products. Shown to be an effective sales-generating method, other companies also adopted it.

Many brand marketers today that target Millennials, such as Gap, Aeropostale, Urban Outfitters, H&M and finally, Abercrombie & Fitch realized this audience prides itself on individual style. Not wishing to be a billboard for any brand, these young people prefer to mix and match brands to create their own unique look. The idea is not to look like the crowd, but rather to create a distinctive image. Gap taglines reflect these consumers with messages, such as "Simple clothes for you to complicate."[13]

7. Showing Compassion

Aiming to epitomize true friendship, Guinness released a commercial, "Friendship," created by BBDO New York. Viewers saw a high-energy, super-competitive game of basketball. What drew the audience in was to see all the athletes racing around in wheelchairs. When the game ended, everyone got up except for one player. He was the only one of the group who was actually physically challenged. The rest were friends showing their support and making him still feel like one of the gang. What a touching way to depict friends who care (Figure 4.7). The spot closed with the announcer saying this poignant line: "The choices we make reveal the true nature of our character."

Figure 4.7 How Empathy Shows Caring

Advertising can also portray pain consumers feel. Many heartbreaking commercials created for organizations, such as Mothers Against Drunk Drivers (M.A.D.D.), made viewers empathize with moms who lost their children to inebriated motorists. Public sympathy was so intense that the association drew instant support for its cause and made drunk drivers punishable by law. They changed the public's perception from acceptable to indefensible behavior and influenced legislative rulings that made these types of accidents a criminal offense.

One Thai commercial, "Unsung Hero," features an ordinary young man kindly helping people who are struggling with small gestures every day. For example, he helps a street vendor lift her cart. He gives money to a mother and a child begging in the street to raise money for the little girl's education. He even feeds a homeless dog some of his food. He leaves a bunch of bananas on a senior neighbor's door. He repositions a dying plant so it can get some water. Skeptics who witness him every day shake their heads, disapprovingly. You can only imagine them thinking, "What a fool," as they look on.

Day after day, the young man continues with his small tokens of generosity, asking nothing in return. In the end, he makes friends with these people. He sees the little girl cleanly dressed carrying a backpack, returning from school and running to her mom. He passes the now-thriving plant and watches the dog follow him home. The moving spot, with English subtitles, which explain the dialogue, explains that what he receives cannot be seen. It's happiness, friendship, love and beauty. The closing copy asks what you, the viewer, desire most. You might be surprised to know that this heartwarming spot was for Thai Life Insurance. The slogan magically portrayed: "Believe in good."

8. Portraying a Brand's Core Values

In one humorous 2013 Porsche commercial, the driver is struggling to parallel park. The spot continues with images of racing, trackside-pit-stop teams attending to the car. The message states that after more than 30,000 wins, Porsche drivers can only drive forward. That explains the parallel-parking problem in a funny way. It closes with just three words, which are superimposed against a black background: "Spirit. Principle. Vision." It's clear that the final message is a testament to the brand's core values (Figure 4.8).

Figure 4.8 How Embodying a Brand's Essence Reveals its Principles

Porsche created a short, commercial video, called "Reunion." In it, three childhood friends went back to their elementary school and relived nostalgic memories. These included their competitive spirits exemplified by them taking first, second and third place in a swim meet. It showed them mischievously hitting the teacher on the side of the neck with a slingshot. It also portrayed the teacher taking away one of the boy's magazines, being read under the desk. It turned out that it was opened to a Porsche ad. At the reunion, they see their teacher. The three friends each drive off in their Porsche 911s only to discover that the teacher has one, too. The spot explains that "It is our core values that define our strength. It's who we are." It not only reflects the core values of Porsche, but also of its owners. This is a clear, direct expression that's immediately understood by the audience. In addition, it especially resonates as a relevant and authentic message to all Porsche devotees.

Core value campaigns, of course, are not limited to car companies. Whole Foods Market showcased its brand-value message in several commercials, including its 2014 "Values Matter Anthem." The announcer said, "We are hungrier for better than we ever realized." She continued to discuss knowing the origins of the foods and how they were grown, raised and harvested in all the products the chain sells. Images showed fruit being picked in orchards, herds running in open plains and fish being netted. A few of the final spoken words were: "This is where it all comes to fruition. This is where it all matters." The visuals, music and copy beautifully depict the attention to the community benefits of judiciously overseen, ethically grown and quality-based nutrition as core values.

Be sure to notice the Thanksgiving Macy's Day Parade. Costing millions of dollars and countless hours of preparation, Macy's presents an iconic parade flying perfectly designed balloons, floats with major stars and marching bands from all over the country. It's wholesome America at its best. It presents Macy's as a symbol of grace, beauty, appreciation and wonder. It's a way for the brand to thank its loyal customers and bring people together in a harmonious, fun and exciting experience. Consumers celebrating Thanksgiving are drawn to watch the parade live or on TV to marvel at the spectacle. It closes with the arrival of Santa to welcome in the holiday season. Unforgettable and iconic, the parade embodies the wholesomeness of the brand.

9. Reinforcing Brand Positioning

Figure 4.9 How to Fortify Consumers' Opinion of Brand

Samsung began to gain traction with its "Next Best Thing" campaign. Some of the earlier commercials, such as the 2013 Super Bowl spot, used humor, storytelling and exaggeration strategies. Comedic film stars Paul Rudd and Seth Rogen portrayed apprehensive actors auditioning to be in the Samsung campaign. At first, they each believed they landed the part, only to find out they were called in to pitch ideas to decision maker, comedic writer/actor, Bob Odenkirk.

During the exchange, they suggested other talent. Thanked for their participation, they discovered that their comments talked themselves out of the gig. Another spot, featuring the same three actors, showed the continuing character and continuing story strategies. Here, they're discussing trademarked words they must avoid using. So Bob suggested "El Plato Primero" instead of the "Super Bowl," Paul offered the "Baltimore Black Birds" to replace the "Baltimore Ravens" and Seth asked to use the "50-Minus-Oners" for the "San Francisco 49ers." The campaign reinforced the "Next Big Thing" (Figure 4.9) and the actors convincingly played the tongue-in-cheek, creative advertising process in these memorable parodies.

Tempur-Pedic mattress campaigns have showcased its unique features for years. They explain what differentiates the Sleep Number mattresses from others. Consumers can set their side as softly or as firmly as they prefer by selecting their "sleep number." Without a doubt, mattress buyers can clearly understand the brand and how it positioned itself against its competitors. Shoppers with opposite mattress preferences could buy one mattress that satisfied both of them.

DirecTV positioned the brand with a humorous campaign that exaggerated what would happen if you had cable TV. For example, you would make bad legal decisions that would get the wrong man convicted. During his imprisonment he would focus on revenge and blow up your house upon release. The spot ends with the announcer warning, "Don't have your house explode. Get rid of cable. And upgrade to DirecTV." Each spot in the campaign showed another incredible life crisis if you had cable. Each spot was funnier than the other. However, the audience would still remember this simple notion: Cable is bad. DirecTV is good. In other words, DirecTV promotes the brand as the solution to preposterous problems.

To position Peeps as "the" candy of Easter, the brand created the "Brothers" commercial. It showed the older brother teaching his baby brother every inconceivable, and unrealistic way he could think of to enjoy Peeps. He listed: Peeps candles, tattoos, Pop Art, sheets, golf balls and T-shirts; Dutch chocolate Peeps cake; fried Peeps and so on. With the name "Peeps" repeated so often in the spot, the brand is etched in the consumer's mind, reinforcing it as the favorite candy choice for the holiday.

10. Changing Audience Perception

Figure 4.10 How to Create a Paradigm Shift

Dove discovered that just four percent of women define themselves as beautiful. Not just in America, but throughout the world. Wishing to change women's self-opinions, Dove created the Real Beauty Sketches campaign. This project invited a sketch artist to only draw from people's description, without seeing their faces. The first portraits were based on the women's descriptions. The second ones were from strangers' observations. The results revealed that the latter portraits were more flattering. Look how much this says about how inaccurately women see themselves. It proved the *universal truth*: "No one's harder on you than you are on yourself." The Dove website, which stated, "You are more beautiful than you think," was a way to reinforce and extend its earlier Real Beauty Campaign message (Figure 4.10).[14]

Consider how Dannon Oikos Yogurt addressed two different audiences simultaneously. Women, who were healthy and weight-conscious, ate yogurt as a low-calorie alternative to other unhealthy snacks. According to Michael Neuwirth, senior director of public relations at Dannon, they made up 65 percent of the yogurt audience.[15] As the mainstay of the yogurt market, women often chose lite and fit formulas. That is, until fitness-focused men became a new audience with a campaign that presented Greek yogurts, which had a higher level of protein compared to other, regular yogurts, as an "excellent source of protein." Now it could be considered just as nutritious as chicken, fish or eggs, and men could include it in their diets, without appearing to be calorie-conscious, as their female counterparts were.

With diverse, yet specifically targeted campaigns, Dannon could tap into the rapid rise in popularity of Greek yogurt and extend the brand's footprint.

11. Supporting a Cause

Many campaigns specifically address a cause. These could inspire support for critically and terminally ill children as in the St. Jude Hospital and Ronald McDonald House Charity, Joe DiMaggio Children's Hospital, SickKids and Make-A-Wish Foundation messages, to name a few.

Others battle hunger both nationally and internationally. These include America's number-one charities: Feeding America; Food Bank for New York City; California's Freedom from Hunger, Meals on Wheels and many others. Some international elimination-of-hunger associations include Action Against Hunger, the Hunger Project, World Hunger, Heifer International and Food for the Hungry.

Or abused animals as shown in various animal-rights promotions by the American Society for the Prevention of Cruelty to Animals (ASPCA), Humane Society of the United States, Farm Animal Rights Movement, Animal Defense League, Performing Animal Welfare Society, People for the Ethical Treatment of Animals (PETA) and numerous others.

Pay attention to these promotions and see which ones deliver the most powerfully persuasive and empathy-arousing messages. What impacted you the most? The images, the text (copy), the story or something else?

For example, in the SickKids campaign, each TV spot featured one child's story. Seeing them suffering through treatments helps viewers imagine what these children's lives are like. It shows them bravely facing each hurdle and pushing forward. Rather than being depressing, these spots generate empathy and compassion.

The World Hunger spots use statistics to impress upon the audience the urgent need to participate (Figure 4.11). One commercial stated these and other facts: 1) one in eight children under the age of 12 go to bed hungry, 2) 923 million people in the world go hungry,

Figure 4.11 Supporting a Cause

3) 183 million children are underweight for their age and 4) three billion people barely survive on two dollars (U.S. currency) a day. The images of skeletal-like children are heart-wrenching and difficult to see. However, they honestly depict the seriousness of daily starvation.

Unfortunately, when the images are too depressing, as in the SPCA commercials with Sarah McLachlan singing, they can unintentionally depress the audience and cause them to quickly change the channel. Instead of triggering donations from sympathy, these types of spots disturb and disengage the viewer.

12. Playing with the Audience

Unlike the SPCA spots, Saatchi & Saatchi created a viral hit with the Tui Brewery prank. The New Zealand video series, shot by 14 mini cameras, was so entertaining, that it generated more than 5 million views in seven days. How did they do this? They got several guys together to jimmy rig the plumbing in their friend's house. Beer flowed from every tap throughout the home. The videos captured the pranksters through every step of the process, even when they got dirty while going under the home to complete the task of hooking up the pipes to hidden beer kegs.

Guy Roberts, the creative director at Saatchi who helped develop and supervise the project's execution, had to make sure the plumbing didn't transfer beer into the city's water supply.[16]

In 2014, Coca-Cola replaced its logo on bottles, replacing with the most prevalent names, at that time, of teens and young adults. The campaign "Share a Coke" invited consumers to find bottles in select stores with their own, a friend's or relative's name and share photos on Instagram, via #shareacoke, on a campaign-related website and whatever other social media sites they use. For those with less common names, they could order a customized mini can online. In the Philippines, Coke took the campaign even further. It asked people whom they thanked most often in their everyday routine. They named the friendliest people they ran across. Grocery shoppers named the bag "boy." Commuters named the toll taker. Workers named the front-door, company greeters. When asked if they knew these cheerful people's names, they were embarrassed when they realized they didn't. As a way to personally thank ordinary service providers, customers brought them a personalized bottle of Coke. The surprised workers were delighted when they received a Coke and were touched that their customers knew their names.

What a nice way for Coke to recognize its audience as individuals, not just as the nameless mass. Also, what a great buzz-generating concept, which created more than 125,000 multimedia mentions.[17]

In London, McDonald's created an out-of-home game. Billboards with moving icons challenged passersby to use their smartphones to capture a picture of a sundae, a pie or a cup of coffee. Once they caught the required photo, they could go to a nearby McDonald's, show it on their phones and get one for free. With the images moving up and down, the billboards resembled app games. People were challenged, engaged and entertained. Then, they were rewarded with free menu items.[18] How much fun was that!

In Summary: Concept Strategies

One final word about conceptual thinking: To stretch your mental horizons, study the thoughts and actions of famous musicians, composers, painters, innovative entrepreneurs, inventors and other creative talents. Examine their philosophical beliefs. Learn how they problem solve. Read about their accomplishments. Allow yourself to become inspired.

Consider Steve Jobs, often referred to as one of the most influential figures of the century. He's frequently quoted for his inspirational messages.

In an internal meeting in 1997, he discussed advertising and asked this question to his team: "What does Nike do in its advertising? They honor great athletes and they honor great athletics. That's who they are and that's what they're talking about." Wanting to clarify his company's fundamental philosophy and core essence, he explained:

> *Customers want to know who is Apple and what do we stand for? Where do we fit in this world? Apple at its core—its core value—is that we believe people with passion can change the world for the better.*

His dream of being one of the few people to make a global change, he once again expressed that idea in the 1997 Apple commercial, "Here's to the Crazy Ones." It spotlighted other innovative thinkers, including: Albert Einstein; Bob Dylan; Martin Luther King, Jr.; Richard Branson; John Lennon and Yoko Ono; Buckminster Fuller; Thomas Edison; Muhammad Ali; Ted Turner; Maria Callas; Mahatma Gandhi; Amelia Earhart and Bernt Balchen; Alfred Hitchcock; Martha Graham; Jim Henson; Frank Lloyd Wright and Pablo Picasso. The inspirational spot ended with Shaan Sahota, a little girl, whose eyes are closed, perhaps imagining a breakthrough idea.

Originally, Jobs voiced the spot. In the final version, Richard Dreyfuss replaced him and delivered this unforgettable statement, summing up the power of new ideas:

> *The people who are crazy enough to think they can change the world, usually do.*[19]

In his final speech of the same title, but often referred to in the shortened version, "The Crazy Ones," Steve Jobs reiterated that sentence once again in this all encompassing message:

> *Here's to the crazy ones, the misfits, the rebels, the troublemakers, the round pegs in the square holes . . . the ones who see things differently—they're not fond of rules . . . You can quote them, disagree with them, glorify or vilify them, but the only thing you can't do is ignore them because they change things . . . they push the human race forward, and while some may see them as the crazy ones, we see genius, because the ones who are crazy enough to think that they can change the world, are the ones who do.*[20]

It is these kinds of comments that drive creative talents to dig deeper within themselves to find new concepts and novel approaches that they can integrate into new advertising strategies. Challenge yourself to be one of them.

Conceptual Strategy Exercises

Before beginning the exercises, let's review the twelve concept strategies listed in the chapter.

1. Engage the audience
2. Share humor
3. Spark an emotion
4. Reward the reader
5. Reflect the audience
6. Epitomize consumer opinions
7. Show compassion
8. Portray brand value
9. Reinforce brand positioning
10. Change audience perception
11. Support a cause
12. Play with the audience

Exercise 1: Search and find one brand that uses two concept strategies together. If you were extending the campaign, what other above-listed strategy would you choose?

Exercise 2: Name one campaign concept that promoted a cause. Answer these questions:

1. Do you think it was effective enough to motivate the audience to:

    a.   Make a donation?
    b.   Volunteer?
    c.   Promote the cause through co-ventures, events or other promotion-related efforts?

Exercise 3: Choose one digital product you personally use. Which strategy concept(s) would you utilize to target young professional techies?

Exercise 4: Which concept strategy would you use to reinforce brand positioning to a diehard, loyal audience?

Exercise 5: Name one campaign that shared humor. What universal truth did it demonstrate? (Refer to Chapter 3.)

Exercise 6: Which campaign made you "play" with the brand? (For example, the Doritos "Crash the Super Bowl," which offered the number-one-rated, consumer-created commercial a $1 million prize.)

Exercise 7: How could you create compassion for a cause you relate to?

a.   What strategy would you apply?
b.   What kind of message would you use?

Exercise 8: Besides the Cheerios "Gracie" (mixed-race family) commercial, which other one reflected the brand's audience?

Notes

1. Jack Neff, "Kleenex Builds Flu-Prediction Tool to Warn You When You'll Get Sick," *Advertising Age*, September 16, 2013: 7.

2. Visa, "NFL Fans Score with Visa Checkout—The Easier Way to Pay Online," https://twitter.com/Visa/status/509456305749102593, September 3, 2014 (accessed September 7, 2014).

3. Geoff Williams, "How to Use Humor in Marketing," March 11, 2009, Entrepreneur, April 2009, www.entrepreneur.com/article/200722 (accessed February 5, 2015).

4. Jacquelyn Smith, "The Most Unforgettable Ad Campaigns of 2013," *Forbes*, December 17, 2013, www.forbes.com/sites/jacquelynsmith/2013/12/17/the-most-unforgettable-ad-campaigns-of-2013/ (accessed February 12, 2015).

5. MRY, Case Studies, http://mry.com/work/sony-tweetsinger/ (accessed September 7, 2014).

6. Vinaya Naidu, "Eight Interesting Content Co-Creation Campaigns," *Content Marketing*, August 8, 2014, www.business2community.com/content-marketing/8-interesting-content-co-creation-campaigns-0969528 (accessed February 15, 2015).

7. Grace Chung, "Advertising Age Honors the Best Brand Storytelling at the 2014 Viral Video Awards," *Advertising Age*, April 1, 2014, www.youtube.com/watch?v=zIEIvi2MuEk (accessed February 5, 2015).

8. CNN Wire Staff, "Number of Interracial Couples in U.S. Reaches All-Time High," CNN, April 25, 2012, www.cnn.com/2012/04/25/us/us-census-interracial/ (accessed February 12, 2015).

9. Hansi Lo Wang, "Walking Down the Widening Aisle of Interracial Marriages," NPR, www.npr.org/blogs/codeswitch/2014/02/13/276516736/walking-down-the-widening-aisle-of-interracial-marriages (accessed February 12, 2015).

10. Cheerios. "The Breakfast Project: The Murphy-West Family," January 28, 2014, www.youtube.com/watch?v=4_saKni6HzM (accessed February 12, 2015).

11. MixedandHappy, "Cheerios Commercial: A Reply to the Racists and a Thanks to General Mills!" June 16, 2013, www.youtube.com/watch?v=8OtFRFgqHto (accessed (January 27, 2015).

12. Ann-Christie Diaz, "My, What a Beautiful Faucet You're Wearing," *Advertising Age*, September 16, 2013: 10.

13. Jilian Mincer, "Marketing to Millennials," *Sun-Sentinel*, September 25, 2014: 4D.

14. Jacquelyn Smith, "Most Unforgettable Ad Campaigns."

15. Mark Astley, "Dannon Touts Oikos Greek Yogurt to Protein-Hungry 'Fitness-Minded' Men," *Daily Reporter*, May 21, 2013, www.dairyreporter.com/Manufacturers/Dannon-touts-Oikos-Greek-yogurt-to-protein-hungry-fitness-minded-men (accessed February 15, 2015).

16. David Gianatasio, "Brewer Secretly Rigs Plumbing in Man's House to Make Beer Flow from Every Tap: Saatchi Stunt for Tui," *AdWeek*, September 25, 2013, www.adweek.com/adfreak/brewer-secretly-rigs-plumbing-mans-house-make-beer-flow-every-tap-152698 (accessed April 11, 2014).

17. Nathalie Tradena, "Coke's Personalized Marketing Campaign Gains Online Buzz," *Wall Street Journal*, July 15, 2014, http://blogs.wsj.com/cmo/2014/07/15/cokes-personalized-marketing-campaign-gains-online-buzz/ (accessed February 15, 2015).

18. Talia Eisen, "5 Interactive Campaigns that Engaged their Audiences," Aha Media Group, January 24, 2013, http://onlineitallmatters.blogspot.com/2013/01/5-interactive-campaigns-that-engaged.html, (accessed February 15, 2015).

19. MacBook, "Apple Confidential—Steve Jobs on 'Think Different'—Internal Meeting, September 23, 1997," November 5, 2013, www.youtube.com/watch?v=9GMQhOm-Dqo (accessed February 19, 2015).

20. Andrew Martin, "The Crazy Ones—A Steve Jobs Final Speech," http://youtu.be/2hZTpZrrDbY (accessed February 19, 2015).

5

VERBAL COMMUNICATION STRATEGY
Architectural Rendering

Although the expression "a picture's worth a thousand words" is true, what's also true is: "the right words can paint a masterpiece." So, what is the path to developing verbal, architectural rendering? How can copy walk the consumer through the strategy and draw an image? What are the elements that make up a well-structured message? What's the starting point? For every type of strategy, it all begins with the Creative Brief, discussed in Chapter 1.

In this section, we'll explore the following elements to serve as the underpinning structure that supports the core message and supporting copy:

1. Creative Strategy Statement (campaign direction)
2. Question five (consumer benefit)
3. Question six (brand feature that drives purchase)
4. Question seven (main brand message: slogan)
5. Question nine (brand's USP: unique selling point)
6. Question ten (brand's character or personality)

In addition, we'll apply writing practices to establish an apropos point of view, targeted tone of voice, memorable slogan, accurate brand character portrayal and meticulous word choice. We'll also examine the copy used in notable jingle lyrics: "musical slogans." We'll remind you how messages with an underlying universal truth resonate with authenticity and relevance. Now, let's start with the groundwork to establish a unifying theme.

One Unifying Exciting Message

After reading the Creative Strategy Statement, reconsider the audience's significant benefit and product feature that answers "why buy?" These two critical points will guide the solution. As you begin to design one multipurpose theme, think about how it will work the various touchpoints, platforms and media where it will appear. The core concept must become the structural support behind the headline, slogan, copy, jingle lyrics and relationship-building consumer interaction. A big idea transcends any writing-space limitations of different delivery vehicles, including mobile marketing, social media, out-of-home and transit.

Campaigns are built on a carefully designed foundation. Notice how the following series of headlines are interrelated and woven from the same conceptual fabric (Figure 5.1).

Figure 5.1 One Cohesive Message

Examine each campaign, one at a time. Spend a few minutes to digest and fully appreciate the brilliance behind the messages. The following campaigns were from Stephen Pollock's *The Hungry Copywriter* blog.[1]

1. De Beers Campaign:

    All the ads in one De Beers campaign featured one piece of jewelry, such as a diamond ring or bracelet, against a black background. The all-cap headlines, which were stacked, underlined and set in white type, were easy to read. As you read them, notice how they show an instant benefit to the diamond buyer. The messages, stated in a tongue-in-cheek manner, pointed out what diamond gift-givers would receive. First, a deeper understanding of how the recipients think. Second, immediate solutions to common relationship frustrations.

    *   "Getting Rid of Headaches since 1888." (Yes, an answer to the old excuse.)
    *   "Hey, What do you Know. She Thinks you're Funny Again." (She'll regain interest.)
    *   "Remember When You Got that Variable Speed Hammer Drill? It'll Make Her Feel kind of Like That." (How to relate this gift to something important to you.)

    Universal truth: The gift that keeps giving.

2. Porsche Campaign

    The ads in this campaign show the single driver behind the wheel of a sexy Porsche convertible, cruising down an open road. The sky above, the road ahead, the world behind. What an image! You can see yourself driving that sports car. Then, the words whisper what every Porsche lover feels while in the driver's seat. Take a look at the following headlines. Can you hear the owners and fans passion for the Porsche thinking out loud? Not needing any justification, the headline "testimonials" explain to others who can't comprehend this question: "Why a Porsche?"

    *   "The More Kids you Have, the More Practical it Becomes."

- "You Didn't Think it Got Better than Mile 8,453. Then Mile 8,454 Comes Along."
- "Calling it Transportation is Like Calling Sex Reproduction."

Universal truth: You can't explain. You have to live it.

3. Timberland Campaign

   This campaign's images are old, faded photos of Native Americans with an inset of a pair of moccasins and the headlines below. When you read the messages, think about the underlying honesty of these statements. Although candid, they are a real accounting of the era when the West was "won."

   - "We Stole their Land, their Buffalo and their Women. Then we Went Back for their Shoes."
   - "From the Days when Men Were Men. And So were the Women."

   Universal truth: Greed and power.

4. ABC

   To promote daytime programming, ABC presented an all-copy ad. It said everything in just five words. The headline, set against a yellow background, is ingeniously terse and witty. There's nothing left to be said. Not another syllable, word or phrase is needed. This encapsulates the kind of shows viewers could expect to see. (Try not to smile.)

   - "Marry Rich. Kill Husband. Repeat." ABC Daytime

   Universal truth: History repeats itself.

5. Zippo

   When you think of the basic Zippo lighter, you might think of focusing on reliability as the main idea. But that was where the campaign concept began. That thought may have led to the question: What kinds of things are reliable? Perhaps after brainstorming through several answers, someone may have offered this insight: best friends. Just by moving past a basic benefit, the campaign personified the product, making it seem human. As if anyone could have a "relationship" with a lighter. But, wait a minute. Could people actually feel so loyal to a brand that switching to another could make them think they're cheating? In reviewing the headlines below, notice how the campaign strategy embodied the emotional, brand connection.

   - "Don't Lose Your Zippo. Lifetime Friends are Rare."
   - "The $3.95 Zippo. Give it a Quick Try. Say . . . 35 Years."

   Universal truth: True friends are hard to find.

In each of the above campaigns, there's one underlying theme that unifies them and creates one clear, strategic message. Each headline supports the big idea and adds the support beams to solidify the structural engineering.

Targeted Core Audiences

Speaking directly to a specific audience requires language that can stealthily scoot in under their advertising "shield." The message can be so compelling that it cannot be ignored.

Even if it were negative, it would be hard for those particular people to look away. One such example is a widely shared campaign from the Lung Association. It presents a stark, all-type ad with the headline in gray, against a beige background. So bland. So concise. And so powerful. Could you possibly say more in few words? I doubt it.

"For More Information on Lung Cancer, Keep Smoking."

Universal truth: Experience is the best teacher.

Another classic, award-winning campaign, "Snow Plow" (Cannes Gold Lion, 1964), spoke to residents of cold, snowy climates who need a car that can get around in challenging, winter weather. Before the ATVs (all terrain vehicles) were popular, this Volkswagen message promised a specific benefit: reliability in all weather. The wintery, gray TV spot simply followed the driver from his garage, into his VW Beetle and to the snowplow. Shot from ground level, you never see the man, except for his feet. You hear the crunch of the snow as the car drives over it. At the end, he drives the snow plow past the VW, stressing the following point, which the voice-over talent delivered: "Did you ever wonder how the man who drives the snow plow gets to the snow plow? This one drives a Volkswagen. So you can stop wondering." It makes the assumption that people actually thought about that question. No one probably did. That's what made the question so unexpected.

The print ad, which closely related to the TV spot had a simple visual. It showed a snow-covered lawn in front of a home with the presumed owner getting into his car. This time, the car was a different model: a VW Rabbit. The headline just asked the same surprising question:

"How Does The Man Who Drives The Snow Plow Drive to the Snow Plow?"

Universal truth: Something you can count on.

No wonder this unforgettable campaign was celebrated. It was interruptive. It was smart. And it was honest. Anyone who owned a powerful, little Beetle, knew how tough and reliable it was. It took the creative team of DDB North America to put it into a relatable, authentic message. It didn't stop there. The campaign showed another model, which assured car buyers that all VW cars were dependable.

The Volkswagen "Don't Text and Drive" campaign demonstrated through a series of text messages what could happen in a second. These ads visually portrayed both the driver's texts and thoughts (in parentheses below). The use of the misspelled word, "drrving," made the campaign more authentic. Here are some of the ads:

"Hold on, drrving (I'm a moron)"
"One min, drrving (I'm about to crash)"
"Just a sec, drrving (I'm going to die)"

In a related ad series, unfinished texts appeared on white background. These showed the sudden impact of an accident interrupting the communications. Here are a few "unfinished" headlines.[2] Two possible choices completed the words: one predictable, the other prophetic.

"I'll see you n (now, never)"
"I'll be there in a wh (while, wheelchair)"

Universal truth: Better safe than sorry.

In a public service announcement (PSA), the National Highway Traffic Safety Administration also promoted no texting while driving. It showed teens in a car having fun. The driver looked at her phone, read the text and was getting ready to answer it. Without warning, an oncoming vehicle slammed into them. The images from inside the car showed everyone getting violently tossed around and sustaining injuries. The following type appeared on the screen closing with: #justdrive. The frank statement was hard to dispute.

"When you're texting, you're not driving."

Universal truth: You can't hide from the truth.

Obviously, targeting teens because of the casting, this PSA ultimately addresses everyone behind the wheel. It doesn't matter the driver's age, nationality, lifestyle or income. Any driver at any moment can get into a wreck. However, this campaign reminds the public that 26 percent of accidents are caused by cellphone use[3] (Figure 5.2). This means that one in four drivers will be in a car accident from recklessness behind the wheel.

In Chapter 4, we discussed a Zazoo spot that highlighted the impact of another kind of careless behavior: not using condoms. The commercial, "Screaming Kid" exemplified the result. Using another strategy, Durex condoms impressed upon the audience that safe sex meant protecting yourself against pregnancy and other serious complications: sexually transmitted diseases. With the clever use of few-word sentences, the campaign drove home what could happen. Just as some people may be symptom-free, that doesn't make them disease-free. Hiding in their bodies is an invisible disease that you'd hate to contract, even if you love the person. Notice in the examples below, how the disease is "ghosted back" (faded or grayed-back), just as if it were something that could haunt you later. The word "I" followed by a heart (to represent "love") and the person's name highlighted. Although

Figure 5.2 Speaking to the Core Audiences

the bold words state, "I 'love' Nancy," Amy, Phil or her, the full word represents the result of unprotected sex. Thanks again to Stephen Pollock and BuzzFeed for flagging this thought-provoking series.[4]

"I ♥ PREG**NANCY**"
"I ♥ CHL**AMY**DIA"
"I ♥ SY**PHIL**IS"
"I ♥ **HER**PES"

Universal truth: What you don't know can hurt you.

The beauty of this campaign is that it doesn't preach because no one listens to a lecture. Instead, it uses honesty. And it makes you think. Perhaps even rethink some of your life choices. That, of course, was the goal.

Headline Strategy Solutions

With all the messages bombarding consumers, finding one that actually gets through is a monumental accomplishment. However, it is possible and happens more often than you might expect. Why? Because a creative team found a way to say something that was impossible to ignore. It could have used humor, surprise, irreverence, curiosity, intrigue, fear, compassion, encouragement or any number of other emotional approaches. It could also have been informative, intimidating, newsworthy and so on. But most of all, it has to be attention-grabbing. There are many ways a headline can do this. Here are a dozen strategic solutions.

First, it can clearly explain the consumers' benefit, showing how their lives would improve. Second, it can entertain via playfulness, shock, surprise or humor. Third, it can highlight the brand or product's unique selling point (USP), such as "A Little Jiggle Wiggle from JELL-O." Fourth, it can tell a compelling story. Fifth, it can share news or make an announcement. Sixth, it can compare one brand to another. Seventh, it can feature results. Eighth, it can tease the audience by not revealing the advertiser until the end of the ad (blind headline) or until the final ad in a series (teaser campaign). Ninth, it can use a celebrity to endorse the product or act as a spokesperson. Tenth, it can share a testimonial. Eleventh, it can demonstrate how to do something. Twelfth, it can warn you of possible danger. This little chart overleaf will help you remember them (Box 5.1).

Multiplatform Writing

After you have digested the brief, analyzed consumer insights, developed an on-strategy concept and engaged in creative brainstorming, you can begin writing. Jumping ahead, perhaps from unrestrained eagerness, only creates rewrites. Right from the start of the writing process, you must consider all possible media, likely audience touchpoints and alternative platforms of delivery. This will help guide from inception toward relevant, strategically sound communication.

Always think about how and where the audience will receive the content. Is it on a mobile device? Online? On social media? In transit? In a unique location (ambient)? On TV? Out-of-home? Even on radio? On packaging? In snail mail? In an emerging medium? Considering where the audience and brand intersect will direct your thinking. You must take a moment

---

Box 5.1 Twelve Headline Strategies

1. *Highlight consumers' benefit*

2. *Entertain via playfulness, shock, surprise or humor*

3. *Showcase its unique selling point (USP)*

4. *Present a compelling story*

5. *Share news or announcements*

6. *Compare itself to another brand*

7. *Feature results*

8. *Intrigue the audience with a blind headline or teaser campaign*

9. *Use a celebrity as an endorser or spokesperson*

10. *Share a testimonial*

11. *Offer a how-to solution*

12. *Warn you of impending danger*

---

to picture the audience. What are their lifestyles, interests, hobbies, affiliations, cultural references, age-related perceptions and core beliefs? Some of these could be related to location, religion or social status. Social influences, even peer persuasion, are brand choice and purchasing decision factors.

For example, young Sneakerheads (hyper-fans of limited-edition Nike styles) communicate about the brand online. They meet at Nike swaps and are articulate about the different models. This audience would not be reached on TV or signage. They pride themselves on being diehard insiders to all the latest trends. Now, think about where to reach them. A few places could be Instagram, Pinterest, Snapchat, Pheed, WeChat, Bubbly, Vibr, LINE or KakaoTalk.

What if you were trying to speak to Yoga practitioners or New Age spiritualists, book club members, jazz lovers and so on. What media do they consume? Do they watch certain types of programs, follow popular bloggers or read interest-related publications? VALS and other categorizations are crucial to accurate message development. Why? Because different media have different size areas for information. Websites can hold more details than a taxi-top sign. Twitter limits comments to 140 characters. Billboards are most powerful with the fewest words. Ten is the most and seven or fewer is ideal. Packaging, table tents (foldable, standup signs) and shopping cart handles are limited to the space on the box, size of the paper or length of the grips. When the space is tiny, the message needs to be catchy and rewarding. Look at coupons. They may not be that creative, but for savers, they're invaluable.

Every consumer touchpoint is an opportunity to start a conversation. To spark interest. And to deliver a promise. But, you can't do any of these without reaching your audience. That means: knowing them as people, not numbers. What does it matter how frequently Millennials upgrade their devices if you don't know what platforms they prefer. You must know how they presently engage with each other, where they share their opinions, post their cool discoveries and interact with brands. It's not enough to superficially know your audiences. You must think as they do. Picture their needs. Listen to their concerns. Get a handle on their desires. And feel their passions. Gain a visceral sense of who they really are and what they care about. Then, finding their media and platform preferences will become more apparent to you (Figure 5.3).

When considering the medium, always realize consumers aren't dying to read an ad. They often have their radar up just to avoid being interrupted. Many feel advertising of any type is an actual intrusion: "Thanks, but no thanks. Don't bother me." That's true unless you're telling them something they want to hear. This could be information about a product they're interested in, or a hobby they love or a cause they support.

As mentioned earlier, messages that are relevant and authentic, not pumped up with hype, have a stronger chance to be read. This is why you must know as much as you can about them, as we just discussed. What are their lifestyles, what are their preferred platforms and what's important to them? Then, you also need to remember that if many people don't want to read a ton of text, how can you say less, regardless of the copy space?

You must condense the concept down to its core essence. Say what you have to say. Stay true to the brand, the audience and the strategy. Review the media options. Then, craft a message that can work (spin out) in all media. This approach will give the campaign structural support so that it doesn't have any weak areas. You want to create concrete concepts with sturdy, underlying construction. Think past word-count constraints and become resolute to design copy that's resilient, adaptable and well built. Don't allow yourself to be intimidated by tiny spaces or unusual media. Focus on the audience, the touchpoint and the key benefits. How will this brand, product or service make their lives better? See how the media can most effectively deliver that message.

Figure 5.3 Writing for Multiple Platforms

Later, in Chapter 7, we'll discuss media in more detail. Next, we'll examine how to determine the brand's unique personality.

The Brand's Character

Brands should be looked at as if they were like people with particular temperaments and individual dispositions (Figure 5.4). For a moment, imagine your favorite brand. If you were going to describe what you liked about it, explain how the brand "feels" to you. Is it friendly? Is it fun? Is it silly? Okay. Let's make it easier. What brand or industry tries to make you feel welcome? Well, Doubletree hotels give you hot cookies when you arrive. Some cruise ships hand you a glass of champagne as you board. Beloved characters say hi to you at the Disney theme parks. Didn't those experiences make you feel as if you were personally greeted like a friend, not a customer? These brands had a warm, welcoming personality.

In order to define a brand's character, you must see it in human terms: with traits and attitudes. The way to get there is to picture the brand in a three-dimensional way. Imagine if it were someone famous. It could be a TV celebrity, a famous athlete, a movie star or anyone that most people would know by name. Don't see these people as spokespersons who endorse the brand. They will never appear in a commercial. Instead, see them embodying the brand's spirit: a walking portrayal of the brand. Someone who personifies it.

You must ask what person seems most like this brand? If it has a friendly, fun personality, what famous person is like that? Perhaps Ellen DeGeneres or Cameron Diaz. Now, once you decide on one particular celebrity that best characterizes the brand, ask yourself: Who would this person be in my life if I actually knew them? Would she be a close friend, an affable neighbor, a loving sister or someone else? Carefully select the relationship she would represent to you. Don't rush this step. It's important. Now, visualize her speaking to you. How would she sound? Casual and easy-going? If that's how she sounds to you, then that's the tone of voice you'd use for the brand. That's how the brand would speak to the audience. It wouldn't be snobby or authoritative or cold. This step-by-step process is how you establish the tone of voice.

Use this visualization exercise every time you're writing any kind of promotional communication. It will accurately portray the brand. Now let's look further into tone of voice.

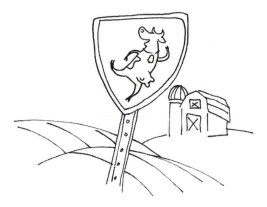

Figure 5.4 Finding the Brand's Character

Relevant Tone of Voice

Let's begin by studying how Harley-Davidson depicts itself. Is it comical or silly? Sophisticated or aloof? Of course not. That's not the brand's character. It's fearless, rebellious and cool. Like an action hero. Can you see Vin Diesel driving one? Does he depict the brand's nature? If so, who would he be to you? A daring and defiant friend?

There's one particular campaign that comes to mind. It used a blackletter Gothic font reminiscent of medieval times. The stylized type added horsepower to the messages. Take a quick look at some of these headlines and picture them in a Gothic font, set in white against a black background. If you get a chance to see all three ads at www.AdsoftheWorld. com, you'll quickly realize how they portray the brand's style and the HD fans' posture. Harley doesn't sell bikes. It sells a lifestyle.

> "The Book of Revelation warns of a beast. It fails to mention chrome."[5]
> "Some flirt with death. Others have their way with it." [6]
> "When the horsemen of the apocalypse arrive, we bet they won't be riding horses."[7]

When you read these headlines and see the Gothic type, they create haunting messages. In the face of danger, Harley-Davidson enthusiasts won't be worried. After all, they'll be on a Harley. Each ad closes with a "prophecy": The XL 1200 N Nightster is coming. The ads are commanding and formidable. Reminiscent of the archetypical image of the Hells Angels rider.

When you think of Ben & Jerry's, you wouldn't expect to hear an ominous tone of voice. Instead, you'd probably agree that the brand has an enthusiastic, fun voice. It's not imposing or serious. It's lighthearted. Because Ben & Jerry's personality is whimsical.

Knowing this, brand message developers create language that's playful and fun loving (Figure 5.5).

After all, when you picture ice cream, you feel happy and young. When you see a picture of it or hear the word, you're excited. That happens in one second, before guilt interrupts if you're on a diet.

Consider other brands, their personalities and their tone of voice. Look at Coca-Cola. It's brought smiles, happiness, life and more because it's the "real thing." The voice is cheerful

Figure 5.5 Creating a Relevant Tone of Voice

and enthusiastic. Messages are upbeat and joyful. Even the 1979 slogan, "Have a Coke and a smile" portrays the power of refreshment in the beloved "Mean Joe" commercial.

Every time you hear a commercial, read an online or mobile message or run into an ambient one, pay close attention to how you're addressed. Is the voice friendly? Informative? Empowering? Motivating? And so on. Don't allow yourself to be complacent when you see any form of advertising. Be alert. Take notice. Analyze. And above all identify, even categorize the brand, its voice and its target audience. Ask: Is it appropriate? Relevant? And memorable? Then ask: Why? The more you challenge yourself to be an astute observer and evaluator, the stronger your writing will become. Even without realizing it, you'll be honing your skills and enhancing your strategic thinking. You'll realize that using a humorous or edgy tone of voice just because it's entertaining is not sufficient. It must align with the audience, the brand and the message of the campaign.

Who's Speaking (Point of View)

Selected among the best print ads from 2013 to 2014 is one emotionally charged campaign for CVV/Emotional Support Hotline. It received the Cannes Gold Lion campaign award because of its unusual approach to a highly sensitive topic: suicide. The campaign helped emphasize the underlying hope beneath suicide notes. The innovative creative team at Leo Burnett Tailor Made, São Paulo, Brazil, rearranged victims' words in their good-bye letters. This repositioning reversed desperate messages into hopeful ones. Each ad in the series closed with an unexpected slogan: "Inside every suicide is someone who wants to live."

This campaign received great media coverage, including in online articles in *AdWeek,*[8] *Ads of the World, USA Today* and *Coloribus.* Although, the copy below is not from the actual ads, it exemplifies and pays tribute to the conceptual strategy.

Letter example #1:

Be kind to each other. Don't worry about me. I want to be happy. I'm not. We have to say good-bye.—R.G.

Rearrangement example:

Don't worry. I'm not about to say good-bye. I want to be kind. Be happy. We have each other.—R.G.

Letter example #2:

Not everything works out. I have no reason to live. What matters . . . I must go now.—A.G.

Rearrangement example:

Everything matters. I must live now. Not go. No reason to . . . What matters works out.—A.R.

Letter example #3

No joy. And just pain. Can't smile. Must rest. So much talk.—J.S.

Rearrangement example:

So much joy. Can't rest. No pain. Just smile and talk.—J.S.

Slogan Strategy Solutions

Of course, you've seen many slogan examples and most likely you know that they're a phrase that captures the brand's key message. There are many different ways to do that. In this section, we'll examine successful approaches to slogan copy and its development. Each one emphasizes a key point. It could be about a feature, a benefit, an invitation, a brand promise or something else. Most importantly, it should focus on one singular idea. It should be honest and credible. Promising a benefit that the brand can't deliver only alienates the consumer.

The slogan could also engage, entertain or entice. It could be stated with wit. It can even surprise the audience with an unexpected statement. Let's look at several of these slogan-building techniques one by one (Figure 5.6). A slogan can:

1. *Focus on a brand's feature.*

   Example: "The Citi never sleeps."—Citibank

2. *Identify a consumer benefit.*

   Example: "Save money. Live better."—Wal-Mart

3. *Address both attributes and benefits.*

   Example: "Better ingredients. Better pizza."—Papa John's

4. *Make it sticky.*

   Example: "Pizza! Pizza!"—Little Caesars

5. *Use dry wit.*

   Example: "If you want to impress someone, put him on your Black list."—Johnnie Walker

6. *Honor the consumer.*

   Example: "The customer is always and completely right!"—Marks & Spencer

Figure 5.6 Developing a Brand Message Strategy

CHAPTER 5

7. *Suggest a solution.*

   a. *Deliver a message.*

      Example: "Say it with flowers."—Interflora (FTD in the U.S., Fleurop in Europe)

   b. *Offer assistance.*

      Example: "You can do it. We can help."—The Home Depot

8. *State the brand's promise.*

   Example: "The next big thing."—Samsung

9. *Reinforce the brand's core belief.*

   Example: "Time is the new currency."—JWT (J Walter Thompson, ad agency)

10. *Speak to a specific audience.*

    Example: "Where a kid can be a kid."—Chuck E. Cheese

11. *Suggest a behavior change.*

    Example: "Think before you drink."—Miller Brewing Company

12. *Create an alert:*

    a. *Be unsettling.*

       Example: "Children of parents who smoke, get to heaven earlier."—Child Health Foundation

    b. *Point out consequences.*

       Example: "Smoking cures cancer."—Cancer Patients Aid Association (CPAA)

13. *Use a play on words:*

    a. To lecture with levity.

       Example: "Drive hammered. Get nailed."—Washington Traffic Safety Commission

14. *Show a reason to buy:*

    a. *Present a reward.*

       Example: "Get Met. It pays."—MetLife Insurance

    b. *Offer assistance.*

       Example: "You can do it. We can help."—The Home Depot

    c. *Promise an advantage.*

       Example: "An apple a day keeps the doctor away."—Apples

15. *Pose a question.*

    Example: "What's in your wallet?"—Capital One

16. *Give a simple order.*

    Example: "Spread the happy."—Nutella

17. *Use everyday speech (vernacular)*.

    Example: "You gotta hand it to 'em."—Handi-Snacks

18. *Establish trust*.

    Example: "Put your trust in us."—South Ottumwa Savings Bank (Iowa)

19. *Use rhyme for memorability*.

    Example: "A drop of Dawn and the grease is gone."—Dawn

20. *Redefine the brand*.

    Example: "United Problem Solvers" replaced "What can brown do for you?"– UPS

Companies that choose to reposition themselves often create a new slogan. As shown in example 20, UPS developed a new, global slogan that told consumers that it's more than a package delivery company. It should now be considered as a problem solver for businesses.

Reviewing Timeless Slogans

Several classic, even noteworthy, hundred-year-old slogans are based on brand's features. Ivory Soap, for example, was introduced in 1879. It's first slogan, "It floats," came out in 1891. By the year 1895, the famous slogan already appeared in advertising. You probably already know it: "99.44% pure." (Originally, it was "99 and 44/100% Pure.") It's used on packaging today with a slight modification. "99.44% pure clean and simple." The century-plus message now added a play-on-words. The idiom, "pure and simple" means absolutely, plainly so or no need to elaborate. So, "clean and simple" means what it does (clean) and, reinforces the product's absolute purity.

Even Morton Salt's slogan of 1912 has lived on and is in use today. The promise, 'When It Rains, It Pours," guarantees that salt will pour even in damp weather. The original copy read, "Even in raining weather, it flows freely." Although it expressed the key benefit, the company heads decided it was too wordy.[9] So, it was shortened to the iconic phrase everyone knows. This enduring declaration is as relevant now as it was more than a hundred years ago.

Who doesn't know the Wheaties slogan, "Breakfast of Champions"? This famous phrase dates back to 1927. The relationship between Wheaties and sports started in 1933, with Jack Armstrong named the "All-American boy." Throughout the decades, Wheaties has sported famous, elite athletes on its cereal boxes with the slogan. This established Wheaties as the cereal that reinforces the message.

Although the equally well-known, 70-plus-year-old Hallmark slogan hasn't reached 100 yet, it no doubt will. In 1944, C.E. (Ed) Goodman, the sales and marketing executive, wrote the famous line: "When you care enough to send the very best." He wanted to express the brand's core message and answer: "Why Hallmark stood above the rest?" While he was mulling this over, the slogan came to him.[10]

Brands aren't the only ones with time-honored longevity. Countries have also had a history of still-in-use branded messaging. Two in particular come to mind. One of the earliest ones, *Liberté, Egalité, Fraternité*," dates back to the 1789 French Revolution. This famous phrase translates as "Liberty, Equality and Fraternity" (brotherhood). It's found on many items that depict the spirit of the French citizens and of France itself.

The second one, "Keep Calm and Carry On," represented the British government during World War II. Designed to give courage to a population under siege, it's seen today on t-shirts, mugs and other items that promote the resilience evidenced by the United Kingdom's valiant stand against the then-imminent threat of occupation.

Examining Targeted Slogans

Slogans as familiar as the often-quoted one for Las Vegas "What happens here, stays here," show how the public can easily embrace a relatable phrase. Why? Because it's authentic. Many people go to Vegas to party. Sometimes with a little too much gusto. Their spontaneous actions might be outside their normal behavior. So, the phrase promises a sense of privacy and confidentiality. Many universal truths could apply, including:

- "We won't tell if you won't."
- "Have your cake and eat it, too."
- "Sometimes you get a break."

You get the point. Oftentimes, any number of universal truths will work because they have a similar message.

Other messages have a deeper meaning and greater social impact. One example is the forty-plus-year-old United Negro College Fund slogan: "A mind is a terrible thing to waste," created in 1971. This phrase was so deeply imbedded in consumers' minds that to abandon it would damage the hard-to-earn brand equity. Instead, it was revised in 2013 by extending it into: "A mind is a terrible thing to waste, but a wonderful thing to invest in."[11] This new slogan makes donors feel good, not just because they're helping someone else, but also because they're benefitting by knowing how this donation supported a deserving student.

This campaign has funded more than 350,000 students, supporting their dreams to go to college. Although many people may not know this, the NAACP, which dates back to 1944, is America's oldest minority scholarship program.

The earlier campaigns of the 1970s and 1980s used famous actors and celebrities. In 2013, a new approach was introduced. Now students who would benefit from the scholarships would also be delivering the messages. By showing how donations directly changed recipients' lives, the campaign also highlighted the gratifying benefit to the donors.

This campaign incorporated traditional media, including print, radio and TV. In one 60-second TV spot, a prospective scholarship beneficiary cleverly stated, "My name is Sidney, and I am your dividend." With a teenager telling a story, she presented herself as a personification of a stock. She introduced a new kind of investment for social change, which offered a high return for your investment: sending a student to college.[12] The closing line reinforced the core concept: "Invest in us and watch us grow." The call to action showed the donation site address (UNCF.org/invest).

The radio spots followed the same theme with a 16-year-old offering a stock tip. Print ads used a dark background with close-ups of young scholarship hopefuls and the slogan in yellow. This very cohesive, targeted campaign wrapped around the updated slogan.[13] (Visit www.npr.org/blogs/codeswitch/2013/06/14/191796469/a-mind-is-a-terrible-thing-to to view the campaign.)

Figure 5.7 Designing a Sticky Jingle

Lyrics and Musical Slogans

Some campaigns still use a musical signature. It could be a jingle, a few notes (sung or played), a famous song, or a new artist or popular group with original music (Figure 5.7). One recognizable "jingle" for Priceline Negotiator presented a seven-syllable music tag. Another one, was the pairing of the hit song, "Money, Money, Money" with H&R Block. Just as in slogans, the key principle is to make the song easy to repeat. For years, people were singing the McDonald's catchy jingle "Two all beef patties . . ." Created in 1974, it not only was fun to sing, it reminded consumers of the product. From 1971, McDonald's began to tell people, "You deserve a break today," with the restaurant items offering the reward. Still recognized today, the benefit-driven Alka-Seltzer slogan delivers on its promise: "Plop, plop, fizz, fizz. Oh, what a relief it is." It dates back to 1953, with Speedy, the character icon singing it.

According to a *Forbes* article, Linda Kaplan Thaler, CEO and chief creative offer at the Kaplan Thaler Group, today a jingle can extend its reach and longevity by being posted on YouTube. Invite people to create their own interpretations, even using their own lyrics. She said, "If you have something that is a real hook and you know, really is motivating to sell and people like singing and listening to, there are many more outlets where you can place that."[14]

The following two jingles for Apple and Chili's, included a popular Christmas song, a new jingle and the musical emphasis of one letter to promote the brand's name.[15] (View them at www.yahoo.com/music/bp/the-5-best-tv-jingles-ever-185240949.html.)

1. *2014—Apple*: The beloved song, "Have Yourself a Merry Little Christmas," appeared in a heartwarming TV spot: "Misunderstood." In it, a seemingly reclusive teen stayed inside while others went out and had fun in the snow. When everyone returned, he played the holiday video he just created that captured family members in love-filled moments. Suddenly, he was appreciated and became part of the group.
2. *2002—Chili's*: The then-popular boy band, NSYNC created their own version of the known jingle: "I want my baby back ribs." In the commercial, NSYNC group members were stranded on an island. Each one sang, "I want my baby back." Then, the tempo picked up and the last word was added "ribs." When they thought they were about to be rescued, by an overhead plane, a Chili's crate was dropped filled with baby back ribs. It was a funny, entertaining treatment of the jingle.

As discussed in Chapter 1, jingles have different applications and can draw attention to the brand, making it instantly identifiable. The more catchy the melody, the more easy it is to repeat.

Effective Writing Techniques

Before moving forward with copy, be sure that the concept can spin out (has legs) and work in all media. Then remember that the campaign's main concept, tone of voice, point of view, slogan and jingle must all align with the audience, the brand and the message of the campaign. Once you've double-checked that it does, the next step is to write body copy. This is where you can apply specific writing techniques to create effective copy. These will clarify, strengthen and drive home the message. We'll now examine some copy-enhancing methods.

1. *ABA*—repeating or referring to the headline in the final line of copy.
2. *Button*—an unexpected and entertaining last line that doesn't have to refer to the headline.
3. *Parallel construction*—reusing the same part of speech or word repeatedly, such as 'the one to know, the one to watch, the one to beat."
4. *Weave*—carrying one main idea from the headline throughout the copy.
5. *Alliteration*—using words with the same first letter or sound, such as the "h" in "have a happy holiday."
6. *Onomatopoeia*—including words that sound like what they are, such as "ding, dong" for a doorbell or "tick tock" for a clock.
7. *Connector*—including phrases that link one sentence or paragraph to the next, such as "besides" "in addition to," "in other words," "the point is," "more importantly," "in summary," etc.
8. *Contraction*—combining two words into one, such as "they are" becomes "they're," we are" becomes "we're or "you are" becomes "you're."
9. *Vernacular*—capturing everyday language, common phrases and popular idioms into the copy (when appropriate, not for medical facilities, for example).
10. *Mix up the sentence lengths*—writing in short and long sentences to keep the reader's attention.
11. *One-word sentences or phrases*—incorporating incomplete sentences or phrases, such as "Why?" "Why not? "Because" or "Oh, sure."
12. *Use punctuation to direct the reader's pace*—speeding up or slowing down the reader helps emphasize key points and can be achieved by using the eleventh tip (one-word sentences or phrases).
13. *Choose the active voice*—stating ideas with the subject and verb, such as "he stared at her," not "she was stared at" because that's the passive voice.
14. *Include relevant copy points*—including important features and benefits explains why consumers should buy.

Advertising copy should sound conversational and replicate everyday speech (Figure 5.8). Copy that sounds natural is easy to understand and sounds as if the brand is speaking to you. Breaking grammatical rules, such as including one-word sentences, moves the copy along and allows the reader to grasp an idea quickly. Writing copy that portrays dialogue

Figure 5.8 Effective Writing Techniques

is a skill that can be developed by applying the above list of techniques and reading aloud. When you listen to the text, you can hear if it flows or gets snagged. Don't worry about why it's hard to read. Just rewrite it. With practice, you'll get better. Honest. (Notice the one-word phrase, "honest.") Refer to the techniques as a guide when you're preparing your copy (Box 5.2).

The key to finding your own voice is to write, rewrite, read and reread your copy. Until it sounds natural. Be vigilant in your search. After practicing, start to mimic other writers. Then, compare how your voice differs. Become an active listener. Listen everywhere you are. Pick out great dialogue in TV commercials. Spot contrived or convoluted scripts on the radio, on videos or on podcasts.

Most of all, be proactive in your self-improvement. Be dedicated. Determined. Devoted. Remember . . . don't accept your first draft. Demand more of yourself. You're capable if you persevere.

Box 5.2 Four Writing Strategies

1. *Develop a Strong Message with Legs*

2. *Write the Way You Speak*

3. *Write to Your Audience*

4. *Utilize Great Writing Techniques*

In Summary: Verbal Strategies

Let's review the structural, verbal strategies that create well-constructed campaigns. First, you will develop one unifying message that has "legs" and is adaptable to all media. Second, you will specifically target your core audiences using authentic, relevant communication. Third, you will utilize strategic headline solutions. Fourth, you will focus on how to write fluently for multiple platforms. Fifth, you will determine the brand's character, its personality in human terms. Sixth, you will be careful that the tone of voice is appropriate for both the audience and the brand. Seventh, you will decide who's speaking and whose point of view is being represented. Eighth, you will select the slogan strategy solution for that campaign. Ninth, you will review timeless slogans to serve as an inspiration. Tenth, you will examine successful, targeted slogans. Eleventh, you will consider the use of music and lyrics as options to strengthen brand awareness. Twelfth, you will apply effective writing techniques to your copy.

Let this chapter serve as an architectural rendering that depicts your verbal foundation and supporting structure.

Verbal Strategy Exercises

Exercise 1: Identify one campaign with a single, unified theme.

a. List three related headlines in the campaign.
b. Write one more headline that fits into the campaign.

Exercise 2: Find one campaign that targeted a specific audience. Answer these questions:

a. What audience was targeted?
b. What message was used to speak to them?
c. What universal truth(s) supported the message?

Exercise 3: Name one headline strategy used in any weight-loss campaign. What other strategy could also work?

Exercise 4: Which multiplatform campaign used broadcast (TV/radio) and print? Where else did the message appear?

Exercise 5: What is the Disney theme parks' brand character?

Exercise 6: Whose point of view is represented in a testimonial campaign?

Exercise 7: Select a timeless slogan and explain why it has endured.

Exercise 8: Which familiar jingle is still used today?

Notes

1. Stephen Pollock, "Welcome to The Hungry Copywriter's Collection of Great Copy Ads." Best Copywriting Ads, August 9, 2011, The Hungry Copywriter, https://bestcopyads.wordpress.com/page/4/ (accessed March 5, 2015).

2. Stephen Pollock "10 More Great Ads that are Just Copy," BuzzFeed, September 3, 2013, www.buzzfeed.com/copyranter/10-more-great-ads-that-are-just-copy#.ffgYa1k5b (accessed March 3, 2015).

3. Gabrielle Krastas, "Phone Use Causes Over One in Four Car Accidents," March 28, 2014, *USA Today*, www.usatoday.com/story/money/cars/2014/03/28/cellphone-use-1-in-4-car-crashes/7018505/ (accessed March 14, 2015).

4. Stephen Pollock "10 More Great Ads" (accessed March 3, 2015).

5. Ads of the World, November 26, 2007, http://adsoftheworld.com/media/print/harley_davidson_nightster_beast (accessed March 24, 2015).

6. Ads of the World, November 26, 2007, http://adsoftheworld.com/media/print/harley_davidson_nightster_death (accessed March 24, 2015).

7. Ads of the World, November 26, 2007, http://adsoftheworld.com/media/print/harley_davidson_nightster_ horsemen (accessed March 24, 2015).

8. Tim Nudd, "The World's 17 Best Print Campaigns. 2013–14." June 23, 2014, *AdWeek*, www.adweek.com/news/advertising-branding/worlds-17-best-print-campaigns-2013-14-158466 (accessed March 6, 2015).

9. Morton Salt, General Company FAQS, www.mortonsalt.com/faqs/general-company-faqs (accessed March 15, 2015).

10. Hallmark Corporate Information, http://corporate.hallmark.com/OurBrand/Brand-Legacy (March 15, 2015).

11. Jane L. Levere, "College Fund Tinkers with its Slogan to Stress Investing in Students," June 4, 2013, *The New York Times*, www.nytimes.com/2013/06/05/business/media/college-fund-tinkers-with-its-slogan-to-stress-investing-in-students.html?_r=0 (accessed March 10, 2015).

12. Cory Weinberg, "United Negro College Fund Updates Its Slogan and Its Brand," June 16, 2013, *The Chronicle of Higher Education*, http://chronicle.com/blogs/bottomline/united-negro-college-fund-updates-its-slogan-and-its-brand/ (accessed March 10, 2015).

13. Gene Demby, "New Ads Still Warn a Mind is a Terrible Thing to Waste," June 15, 2013, NPR, www.npr.org/blogs/codeswitch/2013/06/14/191796469/a-mind-is-a-terrible-thing-to (accessed March 10, 2015).

14. Ken Bruno, "Best-ever Advertising Jingles," June 30, 2010, *Forbes*, www.forbes.com/2010/06/30/advertising-jingles-coca-cola-cmo-network-jingles.html (accessed March 10, 2015).

15. Amy Harrington, "The Five Best TV Commercial Jingles Ever!" August 18, 2014 Yahoo, www.yahoo.com/music/bp/the-5-best-tv-jingles-ever-185240949.html (accessed March 10, 2015).

6

VISUAL COMMUNICATION STRATEGY

Design Drawing

Design is conceptual strategy depicted in a visual way. It can instantly communicate an idea. When carefully constructed and tactically delivered, it will deliver a strategy-based message to a specific consumer. This is why it's crucial to be meticulous in your image choices. In the following section, we'll look at multiple approaches to visual development. Examine each one and prudently consider which would work best for a particular campaign. You may find blending several techniques would be the right solution.

We'll also discuss common mistakes in designing visual content. You'll find these useful tips to refer to while developing graphic solutions. Always check that the visual not only properly showcases the brand, but also fits well into the communication vehicle. At the end, we'll summarize the chapter for easy reference. Now, let's start with the development of one identifiable, graphic look.

One Unique, Strategic Visual

Regardless of which type of approach you choose, you still need to create one distinctive image that connects directly to the brand. As we will see below, not just icons, but also typography—even a single letter—can be visual conduits. Just think of the use of a lowercase "i" in these Apple products: iPod, iPhone, iPad and iBook. Just the "i" alerts the audience that the message deliverer is Apple. Or the word "Believe" in all script for Macy's. It appears in ads, on TV, online, even on its building in Manhattan, which "billboards" the message during the annual Macy's Thanksgiving Day Parade.

Often an identifying icon, makes the brand instantly recognizable. Once again, Macy's showed that the red star makes a visible footprint. Other brand marks also create a distinctive imprint. These include the MasterCard overlapping-circles logo, the Nike swoosh and the Apple apple. Think about the use of rotoscoping (a technique that converts realistic images into cartoon-like, animated illustrations for film), as in the Charles Schwab "Talk to Chuck" campaign.

The key is to create consistency and distinctiveness. Most importantly, any visual needs to strategically reflect the brand's positioning, personality and consumer promise. Strategy is everything. Just having an exciting image isn't enough. It needs to work on behalf of the brand as its ambassador. As Paul Biedermann, creative director and owner of re:DESIGN stated in an article by Chuck Frey, director of online training at Content Marketing Institute:[1]

Your visual strategy should not only be a reflection of your brand, but embody it.

Figure 6.1 One Strategic Message

Visual Elements

In seeking to create a specific and cohesive look, there are several factors to consider. First, it needs to look related to the brand's identity. For example, if you saw a corporate blog, it should be visually connected to the website and all the brand's social media platforms from the core four—Facebook, Twitter, Instagram and Pinterest—to Flickr, LinkedIn, Foursquare and others. As consumers move from one social network to another, the images should feel similar and recognizable (Figure 6.1). At no time, should consumers feel as if they walked into a different brand's space.

Just as retail, restaurant and resort chains have an instant familiarity, likewise the online presence should be visually analogous. If you placed a mobile message next to a blog or transit sign, it should be immediately recognized as comparable. That includes the use of typography; the kind of images (photography, illustration, bold graphics, diagram, info-graphic, etc.); the choice of color(s); the inclusion or omission of a decorative background; the integration of repeat graphic elements; the overall logo design and so on.

As with the development of campaigns, visuals need one strategic direction based on the Creative Brief. As you think through the graphic and pictorial options, review what your destination is and be sure you're on the correct course. Look at the logo. Check the textures you've used. Examine the shading or gradation of colors. Revisit the scope of graphic applications. In short, re-examine everything you've used for the brand and make sure whatever else you introduce, whether it's a new touchpoint, platform or medium, it coordinates with and supports your visual statement strategy.

Types of Visuals

Naturally, there are as many kinds of images as designers can create. These include everything from realistic illustrations to cartoons and abstract icons. When considering an image, whether a logo or a promotional visual, make sure it aligns with the brand's strategy and also connects to the targeted audience. The old saying "show it, don't just say it" is fine. However, an off-strategy or vague visual can also depict nothing if it doesn't create an understandable message.

Box 6.1 Quick List of Visual Techniques

1. *Image*

   a. Icon—Shell Oil
   b. Symbol—Olympic rings
   c. Emblem—Harley-Davidson
   d. Illustration—Apple
   e. Cartoon—Aflac Duck
   f. Visual depiction—Gerber Baby

2. *Color*—Yellow for Pedigree

3. *Signature campaign look*—Coke "Open Happiness"

4. *Celebrity rep*—Dennis Haysbert for Allstate Insurance

5. *Brand ambassador*—Animation of Garfield for Embassy Suites and Mr. and Mrs. Potato Head for LAY'S Potato Chips

6. *Identifiable word*—"Believe" for Macy's

7. *Typographic treatment*

   a. Letter mark—"f" for Facebook
   b. Stylized type (Word mark)—TAZO (tea)

8. *Combination of visual and typography*—Taco Bell

Always refer back to the Creative Brief. Check that your image is on-target and on-strategy. Consider variations to keep it fresh, but always be consistent. That icon, illustration, video, cartoon, etc., has to be the brand's spokesperson. With a unified, coherent visual voice.

Now, let's take a quick look at some possible visual solutions (Box 6.1). Think about which ones would work best and which ones wouldn't.

Notice, when aligned closely with the brand, how easily identifiable they are. Images that reflect the brand's core identity are instantly recognizable (Figure 6.2). Consider the mouse ears for Disney. The swoosh for Nike. The bold, red cross for the Red Cross. The panda for the World Wildlife Fund (WWF). The steering-wheel look to Mercedes-Benz. The "s" emblem for Superman. The multicolor, all-type Google name. The script form of Coca-Cola and Kool-Aid. The list goes on.

The point is, develop a critical eye so you can see what's effective and what isn't. Pay attention to all logos. See how they're being used. Which ones use typography as a graphic element, such as Oreo? Which ones have an icon, cartoon or brand depiction, such as

Figure 6.2 Variety of Visuals

iTunes? Which ones use a combination, such as Pizza Hut? Ask yourself: Why do they work? Also, notice those that don't. Identify the images that don't adhere to the visual strategy, align with the target audience or reflect the brand's personality. Challenge yourself to determine why the visual content is off-strategy, off-target or "off-brand."

Kinds of Visuals that Get Shared

One goal of visual content designers is to create visuals that generate more views. That means they need to know how to do that. In an article[2] on ROI Online, an Internet marketing company, author Steve Brown explained the importance of designing irresistible images, stating two key points about visuals and our brains: 1) we process visuals 60,000 times faster than text and 2) we absorb 90 percent of all content—from data and facts to ideas and information—as images. He emphasized:

Visual content is proven to generate more views, clicks and conversions. Therefore, it's imperative you use visual content to promote your business or brand.

Now that we understand its powerful influence, the next question is: Which types of visuals are shared more frequently? On social media, video reigns. Second in line are high-resolution visuals. These include graphics, infographics and other images. However, it's interesting to note that even simple, less polished videos can stimulate a response if they're interesting. For charts and infographics, the general rule is to make them vibrant, colorful and attractive. Avoid dull, statistical graphs. Brown suggested:

To make your business' visual content break through the clutter, make it attractive, quick and easy to consume, and most of all, memorable.

Also, keep in mind that branded emojis (cartoon characters and illustrations) and emoticons (use of type and symbols to depict people's expressions) are popular today. These visual icons have been used to promote apps, as in Tastemade (to see consumers' opinions of meals in different restaurants); movies, such as *Star Wars: The Force Awakens*; and products/services including 3-D-printed emojis created by 3D NYC Lab (http://3dnyclab.com/3d-printing/3d-printed-emoji/).

More social media networks, such as Twitter and Instagram, have also embraced these icons. It's interesting to note that research companies, including Amplify, are tracking the use and interpreting the meaning behind consumers' use of combined words and emojis/emoticons. This helps brands determine how audiences feel about their social media messages, advertising campaigns and promotions.[3]

Before you even begin to develop any visuals, you must determine the objective. What goal are they trying to meet? What type of visual will create that result? Next, revisit your audience. Does your intended visual content "fit" that target? Be sure there's a match. If not, change or modify it. Then, remember to incorporate a call to action. Yes, in the visual, as well as copy. What do you want the consumer to do after viewing your visual content? Share it? Like it? Click through to a website? Or click to purchase? For example, Pinterest added a "Buy" button to enable merchants to product sales. Last, determine where you plan to distribute the image. Will it be through a paid distribution channel? Or do you prefer to go "organic" and have your audience discover your message? Perhaps, you want a blend of both, paying first to create momentum and selecting "discovery" to continue the campaign.

The Power of Icons in Social Media

Advertising icons have been used to infuse personality into a brand and reinforce positioning similar to the way marketing content is currently used. Today, they need to work even harder because there are so many more media choices. They need to be as effective in touchpoints and packaging as they are in social media.

To learn how to apply traditional brand icons in new ways that engage the audience, let's turn to Lizetta Staplefoote. Drawing from her experience as a Rackspace marketing copywriter and an online-content blogger, Staplefoote offers the following tips in her article, "Nine Classic Advertising Icons and What They Can Teach You About Social Media."[4] Let's look at these one at a time, with the social media lesson highlighted at the end of each one. Check the list from time to time to jog your memory (Box 6.2).

1. *Reflect value proposition*—Show benefit. (Morton Salt: It pours even in damp weather. This answers the "what's in it for me" consumer question.)

   Lesson: Create easy-to-understand ways for customers to use the product or service.

2. *Be personable*—Humanize/personify the brand. (National Park Service's Smokey the Bear: Be responsible; animals live here.)

   Lesson: A strong brand personality that's lovable like Smokey or even irritating like Mayhem from Allstate Insurance engages and entertains the audience.

3. *Constantly evolve*—Update image, stay relevant, yet recognizable. (Kellogg's Tony the Tiger: Modified first from black and white into color, then to reflect society's fitness focus, he was a skateboarder, soccer player and a helmet-wearing football athlete. The message encouraged everyone that they could also be great.)

   Lesson: Although social media allow you to update the brand personality, remember, recognition and consistency are key.

4. *Flaunt your personality*—Depict positioning. (Planters Mr. Peanut: The top hat and monocle show a high-end product.)

   Lesson: Make sure the online content properly reflects the brand. If it's positioned as a sophisticated brand, be sure it maintains that image.

5. *Play to your audience*—Portray audience. (Cracker Jack's Sailor Jack: The image targeted kids.) (Figure 6.3)

   Lesson: Double-check that your message speaks to the correct audience. If you're targeting seniors, posts about Justin Bieber would be inappropriate.

Figure 6.3 Play to Your Audience

6. *Be conscious*—Revise if outdated or offensive. (Coppertone Girl: To reflect changing views of what could be construed as sexually suggestive and/or obvlivious to the dangers of skin cancer, the little girl's image was toned down, just showing the top of her back with a lighter tan.)

   Lesson: Be prepared to adjust your message. Sometimes, it may inadvertently offend consumers. Respond quickly if that happens.

7. *Be different*—Become distinctively identifiable. (Jolly Green Giant: His image was so imposing and recognizable, the company changed its name.)

   Lesson: To increase media post views, use images and video. For higher retention, add color. Keep your content fresh by varying your posts in social media. That keeps your followers interested.

8. *Leverage the familiar*—Create brand association. (Quaker Oats and "Larry" the Quaker Oats man)

   Lesson: Although Quakers were never involved in the creation of Quaker Oats, the indirect association builds trust and credibility. Notice trends in unrelated industries that might give you a way to highlight one unique brand characteristic.

9. *Have a story*—Use storytelling for emotional connection. (RCA's dog Nipper, paired with the famous line "His Master's Voice," depicted clarity.)

   Lesson: Allowing the brand to tell a story draws in consumers and builds rapport with them.

Box 6.2 Nine Key Lessons from Classic Icons—Lizetta Staplefoote[5]

1. *Reflect Value Proposition*—Show benefit

2. *Be personable*—Humanize/personify the brand

3. *Constantly evolve*—Update image, stay relevant, yet recognizable

4. *Flaunt your personality*—Depict positioning

5. *Play to your audience*—Portray audience

6. *Be conscious*—Revise if outdated or offensive

7. *Be different*—Become **distinctively** identifiable

8. *Leverage the familiar*—Create brand association

9. *Have a story*—Use storytelling for emotional connection

Visual Mistakes to Avoid from the Experts

According to the content experts in "Experts Share Visual Content Mistakes to Avoid," the same Chuck Frey article mentioned above, here is a list of the worst mistakes you can make.[6]

Seven visual content experts explain which mistakes to avoid. The advisers include:

- Paul Biedermann, creative director/owner of re:DESIGN, a strategic design and visual content marketing agency (www.redesign2.com/about-paul.html)
- Rebekah Radice, a social media strategist/digital marketing specialist and author of *How to Use Social Media to Virtually Crush the Competition* (http://rebekahradice.com/)
- Lisa Loeffler, publicity/promotions manager for social media guru Jay Baer and his blog: Convince & Convert (http://jaybaer.com/)
- Joseph Kalinowski, creative director of the Content Marketing Institute (http://content marketinginstitute.com/)
- Stephanie Diamond, prolific book author, including: *The Visual Marketing Revolution: 26 Rules to Help Social Media Marketers Connect the Dots* (www.contentmarketing toolbox.com/)
- Martin Shervington, a consultant/speaker/trainer and coach, specializing in Google+ and the community manager for Plus Your Business! (www.plusyourbusiness.com/)
- Donna Moritz, a social media marketing/visual content specialist and founder of the Socially Sorted blog (http://sociallysorted.com.au/blog/).

Now, let's take a look at the five most common mistakes. Keep the list handy so you can refer to it when you're determining the visual content.

The List of Five Visual Taboos

Refer to the following list of "don'ts" each time you're developing imaging for any campaign. Also, before approving a visual, double-check the guidelines below.[7] They will keep you focused and accurate.

1. Fail to Strategize

As mentioned earlier, if the visual just looks cool and enticing, but doesn't tie into the overall strategic direction, it doesn't serve the brand. There's no question that strategy precedes design. Always referring back to the Creative Brief will help you develop visuals and content that are both on-strategy and on-target. According to Biedermann:

> A *visual strategy is what brings your brand to life in all of your interactions and online engagements.*

2. Fall in Love

Sometimes designers and marketers get wrapped up in and swept away by a fabulous or unique image. They've fallen in love with it and are blind to the fact that this visual isn't working on behalf of the brand or message (Figure 6.4). It might even be so overboard that it's a distraction, leading the audience away from the key point. This, in turn, might not encourage viewers to respond by not taking any action at all. They could admire the image, but fail to follow up by contacting the company or making a purchase. Worst of all, they might not be able to even identify the advertiser. Moritz explained it this way:

Figure 6.4 Falling in Love

What do you want your fans to do when they view your image? Marketers need to think of their visual content as a doorway to great information. It's not about just catching the attention of fans with visuals but having them take action on your content.

One example of an attention-grabbing image, developed by the Swedish Pepsi-Cola division, showed a pin-covered voodoo doll. Designed to depict Cristiano Ronaldo, Portugal soccer superstar, the visual backfired. The campaign ran on Facebook ads; however the backlash from his devoted fans pressured Pepsi into an apology.

3. Think Universally

Marketers also forget to consider all media and social platforms when it comes to images. With varied specifications, visuals need to adhere to particular guidelines for maximum clarity. Each image must be customized to avoid a partial or distorted representation. Loeffler offered this advice:

> *Creating content that's highly shareable should be your top objective. Remember to take the time to step back from your personal creative lens and say, "If I was a fan of my brand, would this resonate and inspire me enough to share it in my social communities?"*

4. Don't Overstuff the Visual

Sometimes advertisers want to stuff as much visual and verbal content into one ad. If this sounds like some of your clients, the best and most shocking question to ask is this: "Are you going out of business?" After recovering from the unexpected question, they might say, "No! Where did you hear this?" To which you answer, "Oh, so if you're not, we can put some of this information in the next ad. With everything crammed into this ad, it seems like it's the last one you'll ever run."

An ad that's too busy looks as if you're trying to stuff fifty pounds of content into a five-pound bag. It just doesn't work. It confuses the audience. And, obscures the message.

5. Don't Grasp the Brand

One final blunder is inconsistency. A lack of a uniform image confuses the audience and prevents the brand from imprinting a specific look in the mind of the consumer. One consistent look reinforces the brand in every medium and touchpoint. The following quotes by Biedermann (former) and Radice (later) indicate that they concurred:

> *Only by presenting a strong, unified brand across all media touch points does a business stand any hope of gaining the traction it needs to be seen and understood.*
>
> *Maintain your brand's look and feel by consistently using its colors, fonts, and graphics.*

There's no question that consumers can more readily retain a consistent image, rather than a changing one. Just as people often shop for products by the packaging, such as white for

Ivory or orange for Tide, likewise they recognize brand by their distinctive look, from icons to colors.

Most Effective Visual Solutions

Now that you know what not to do, the question is what should you do to create images that deliver the visual content in a memorable way? The same seven experts once again share their experience and advice. You will see that several identify six successful tips that support material we've covered in earlier chapters. Be a perpetual student and absorb all the tips you find. The most important key point to remember is that graphics create the design structure of the campaign.

1. Expand the Horizon

Images should work on a broad scale. They should communicate a message from all platforms, media and touchpoints. They should be relevant and share a descriptive narrative. Shervington suggested:

> *Think storytelling. Take people on a journey through your content, linking each element back to another. Visuals can make content fly, but you need to know the direction in which you want it to go, and where it can land.*

2. Evaluate Preferences

For best results, Kalinowski recommends testing different visual approaches and then tweaking your images based on the engagement data. "We test to see how well the images in the CMI blog posts are shared. We keep tabs on what works and what doesn't," he says. But this requires a major time commitment, he warns: "It seems there are always updates to the different platforms that will affect how images are previewed."

3. Wear Audience's Glasses

Figure 6.5 See from Consumer's Point of View

It's crucial to see the images from your consumers' perspective (Figure 6.5). How they perceive the visual content may differ greatly from how you planned to project it. This is why you need to customize the message to fit each social media outlet. According to Moritz:

> It's important to step back and understand the nuances of each platform to see what type of content works best natively on that platform. Take off your marketer hat and step into the shoes of your fans. Then you will see that the styling and message of your visual content must vary from platform to platform.

4. Use Your Fans' Content

When your fans post their images, they're already partial to them. That's why it makes sense to reuse them. They enjoy feeling noticed and appreciated. Coca-Cola invites consumers to upload user-generated visuals to its Flickr page and then reposts them on its Pinterest boards. It integrates its brand color, red, to boost brand recognition.

5. Grow Your Talents

More and more marketers and marketing directors, not just designers, need to improve their graphic skill set. Why? Because so much of current messaging demands images to increase views, likes and shares. The faster they can put together a social media post with images, the more productive they'll be. By developing all the content, they'll be able to quickly package content, when they're pressed to get something "out." They'll be proactive in their to response to real-time content demands. Loeffler stated:

> The ability to conceive, design, package and showcase your visual content on the fly is the next set of skills that social media practitioners will need to possess.

Be proactive. If you need to improve your design abilities, do so. Ask someone talented to help. Go online and take a tutorial. Study great examples and try to copy them to learn how. Most of all, don't sit back when you can move forward.

6. Don't Jump

With the constant pressure to multitask and pitch hit when needed, today's markets are pressed to be deadline-responsive. However, speed doesn't always equate to quality. This is where top marketers realize they need to slow down to move their message ahead. Rather than settling for an easy-to-obtain visual, they might have to expect more from themselves. And, carve out the time to ensure that the visuals being used are the best brand representatives. Even if they don't think there's time for this, Diamond explained how:

> Look at what you're doing in your business and eliminate something that has no impact on the bottom line. Magically, time opens up when you strategically eliminate things that are not valuable to your audience or your business.

With all the handy and inexpensive visual tools available now, it seems too easy to just "grab anything." Biedermann warned against being too eager to move too fast and explained:

While these tools can be helpful, I think they work best only after an effective branding/design/visual strategy is firmly in place. That is too often the missing link; as a result, far too many businesses add to the visual noise pollution rather than cut through it.

Marketers must be careful that they follow all the corporate ID directives when using the logo image, brand color, typography and so on. They must double-check that all of these elements follow the guidelines and are up to "code." Accepting anything will lead you to think "anything is good enough." The result is . . . anything but!

Key Questions for Best Images

According to the experts listed above, the following key questions will force you to carefully consider your image choices to ensure they will be most effective. Notice how similar the questions are to those in a Creative Brief. It is the same strategic thinking that helps develop the Creative Strategy Statement, which guides the overall direction of the campaign.

1. Strategy

- *What are we trying to accomplish with our visual content?* This asks what is in the Creative Strategy Statement.
- *Who is our audience and what content do they crave?* Here you need to look into the psychographic profile of the audience: how they live, what they think, what brands they prefer and so on.
- *What problems do our organization solve?* Remember to think like the consumer: What benefit does the brand/product offer (Figure 6.6)?
- *How can we best position our business or brand and create a consistent look and feel?* Revisit positioning in the brief. In particular, what's the positioning in the mind of the consumer? What visual(s) can we use to stamp our brand for instant audience recognition?

Figure 6.6 Tool that Solves Problem

- *What is our clearly defined vision of who we are and what makes us unique?* Be sure to answer these two questions: What is the USP (unique selling point?) What differentiates this company/brand/product for its competitors?
- *How can we communicate those messages in a compelling way?* Here you're looking at creating strategic verbal and visual content that's unforgettable.
- *What metrics will we use to measure success?* Which terms should this image appear in search engine results? This question addresses measurable results. What campaign metrics or marketing analytics should you use?

2. Design

- *Is this content worthy of creating a visual?* Answer before you create it. Just because it might look cool or captivating doesn't mean it will work in a particular context. Or maybe, the message doesn't even need an image at all because it's strong enough by itself.
- *What graphics and visual assets appeal to our target audience and resonate enough to be highly shared?* Think relevance. What will feel authentic and relatable to your consumer? Remember the three Rs: "Messages that are Relevant and Resonate with authenticity are Remembered."[8]
- *Do the assets we plan to create adhere to our brand's graphic identity standards?* Check that whatever visual you design rigidly adheres to the brand's specific guidelines. Be exacting, not careless here.
- *How can we provide useful solutions and helpful hints and tips through graphics?* Use the graphics to convey the messages that reinforce product use and advice. Maybe use infographics, charts or other content-driven icons.
- *What do we actually want people to do with this content? What action do we want them to take? Should we include a call to action if that's important to our campaign goals?* Remind yourself to tell the audience what they should do: go to the website. Turn in a coupon. Post personal images or videos of them using the product. Create user-generated, product-related tips. Or vote for a favorite entry in a contest. Whatever action you're expecting, be sure to tell the consumer.

Although it may seem laborious, answering key questions will guide your visual-content strategy so your solutions will be most effective. This follows the same way of strategic thinking as in the development of the Creative Brief. Questions provide answers. Diamond explained:

> *There are so many visual choices that once you ask the right questions, you shouldn't be at a loss for ideas.*

The key point here is: be childlike. Keep asking questions!

Successful Visual Campaigns

Make it a habit to examine the award-winning campaigns. You'll probably find them an inspiration. You can find examples in graphic annuals, in articles, online on agency and other websites. Just look. There's a plethora of idea-provoking references. For instance, reporter Tim Nudd discussed the best print campaigns: winners of the Cannes Lion Awards.[9] Here are a few examples:

1. McDonald's

This print campaign showed a series of ads that portrayed morning moods at the start of the day. Every image depicts a particular mindset (Figure 6.7). One picture, depicting someone in a prickly mood, showed an overall-wearing cactus on the subway. A second one, indicating a fragile state of mind, showcased a blown-glass teacher. One more, reflecting an explosive mental state, featured an explosives-covered guy next to a copier.

In each ad, the message was clear: Regardless of how people wake up, they'll feel better after a breakfast at McDonald's.

Figure 6.7 Show Consumer's Mood

2. Buick

To emphasize the importance of obeying traffic signs, Buick designed an emotionally arousing campaign that featured victims with lifelong injuries created by recklessness. In each image, a victim held up the sign, to which drivers failed to adhere. One visual showcased a little boy in a wheelchair. He's holding a no-U-turn traffic sign. Another shows a one-armed juvenile girl, lifting a speed-limit sign. A third one depicts a young man on crutches with one leg partially removed holding up a wrong-way, no-entry sign. These disturbing images leave a permanent impression on the viewers, reminding them of the consequences of careless driving. No copy is needed because the images are so powerful.

3. Extra-Strength Bayer (AlmapBBDO, São Paulo, Brazil)

Another strong visual used the color red to indicate someone who's stressed. The image showed every office worker in green. The exception was the most stressed-out worker. He's the one who requires not regular Bayer, but extra-strength relief. Just showing one person in red allows the audience to identify not only who needs it most, but also to remember when they felt overwhelmed and frazzled (Figure 6.8).

Figure 6.8 Show Compassion

Spend time searching for persuasive and influential images. Keep a record of these for creative inspiration. This is an exercise that will pay you back with new ideas in the future. Collect new ones on a regular basis. You'll find excellent work can be an imagination catalyst.

More Excellent Visual Examples: Packaging

On Imgur, a visual sharing site, there are exceptional examples of graphic design. In one particular article by Epiz Hunter, "25 Creative Packaging Designs that Practically Sell Themselves," the package designs are worth your time to examine carefully.[10] Each one is visually compelling.

1. Gnome Bread Packaging

How intriguing! Picture this: French bread is packaged so that it sticks out of a bag with an illustration of a gnome on it. The tip of the loaf creates the gnome's pointed head. This is the kind of packaging that makes a brand stand out. The product and bag portray the name of the bread: Gnome.

2. Noté Headphones

For Noté headphones, the packaging used two musical notes to represent earbuds. These are set over music staff lines. Both note stems are tied together with the cords, creating eighth notes. This is a clever depiction of what the brand does.

3. Beehive Honey Squares

In this ingenious package, the cereal is visible through a clear section in the front of the circular canister. The image over the opening shows a bear with its mouth wide open, filled with Beehive Honey Squares. It sells the product in an adorable way.

4. NYC Spaghetti

Here one building in the New York City skyline is playfully featured. How? By using a vertical, square tube, which opens to reveal the spaghetti stacked to resemble Manhattan's landmark: the Empire State Building. This iconic image immediately epitomizes the name of the brand.

5. Smirnoff Caipiroska

Created as a direct-mail promotion to a select audience, Smirnoff packaged its new Brazilian-inspired drinks, a trio of beverages, in textured, peel-able bottles that feel and peel like the fruit flavors inside: lime, berries and passionfruit. They were sent together in a wooden crate that resembled the way fruit is shipped. How much fun was that to receive and peel open!

6. Pizza Hut: Pizza and a Movie

One more package design not included in the above list is this one: When Pizza Hut wanted to deliver pizza and a movie, it needed to redesign its delivery box to include a projector, stand and a short film. The package designers needed to create visuals that depicted myriad film categories or genres, including sci-fi, thrillers, action and so on. In addition, the box had to be reconfigured to hold everything listed above. So, they created two wings that would prop up the box and left an opening in the middle of the pizza to house the pop-out lens. Once removed and elevated, it could be placed in the front of the box, which acted as the projector. By using an app, customers could scan a code and play the movie from

---

Box 6.3 Strategic Visual Content Summary

1. *Visual Communication (Conceptual Strategy)*

2. *One Unique, Strategic Visual*

3. *Coordinated Visual Elements*

4. *Many Types of Visuals*

5. *Visuals that Get Shared*

6. *Power of Icons in Social Media*

7. *Five Visual Taboos (Mistakes to Avoid)*

8. *Six Effective Visual Solutions*

9. *Key Questions to Ask: Strategy and Design (Figure 6.9)*

10. *Successful Visual Campaigns*

11. *Excellent Packaging Examples*

Figure 6.9 Ask Questions

their phones. They only had to turn the image upside down before viewing, so it would project right-side up.[11]

What other amazing packaging have you spotted? Take photos and refer to them whenever you're looking for ideas. They'll probably spark your creativity and stimulate your imagination.

In Summary: Visual Strategies

Let's revisit the visual strategies that support well-designed campaigns (Box 6.3). First, remind yourself that visual communication is conceptual, as well as strategic. Second, check that you create one unique image. Third, integrate all the design elements in every medium and placement. Fourth, review the various kinds of images you could create. Fifth, be sure you're creating on-target, on-brand and on-strategy visuals that will trigger sharing. Sixth, strengthen the brand icon via social media. Seventh, learn the five visual content errors to avoid. Eighth, be inspired by brilliant visual solutions. Ninth, answer the crucial visual questions. Tenth, constantly scrutinize outstanding visual campaigns. Eleventh, examine exceptional package design examples.

Be an active observer and a keen, visual analyst. Dissect every visual that has the power to make you pay attention. Do this every day and everywhere you are: online, on mobile devices, out-of-home, on transit, on-site at retailers and so on. Then, ask yourself these questions: How did it work? How did it move you? What can you learn from this example? Developing effective visual content with on-strategy images sets the design foundation for your multiplatform, multimedia and multi-touchpoint campaigns.

Visual Strategy Exercises

Exercise 1: Identify one campaign with interesting visuals. Answer these questions:

a. What do you think the advertiser was trying to accomplish with the visual?
b. Did the image reflect the brand's personality?

Exercise 2: Find one campaign with a repeat graphic element (same type or style of visual). Answer these questions:

a. Where did you find the examples: in which media, platforms and/or touchpoints?
b. Did the image unify the campaign?

Exercise 3: Locate a campaign visual that featured the brand's USP (Unique Selling Point).

a. Did the visual depict what made the brand/product/service unique? (Did it showcase the Unique Selling Point?)
b. Did the visual differentiate it from its competitors?

Exercise 4: Describe one package design that made you take notice. Search on-site (at a bricks-and-mortar store) or online to find one. Why did it stand out? Was it the colors? The graphic design? The unusual package shape or see-through areas? Or something else?

Exercise 5: Name two campaigns that effectively used visuals to tell a story.

Exercise 6: Identify a campaign that reused fans' visuals as part of its branding, advertising and/or dialogue with its audience.

Exercise 7: List two visual taboos (mistakes to avoid).

Exercise 8: Besides Smokey the Bear, what other visual (icon or character) humanized the brand?

Exercise 9: Which visual did you share? What made you not only respond to it, but also send it to others?

Notes

1. Chuck Frey, "Experts Share Visual Content Mistakes to Avoid," January 16, 2015, http://content marketinginstitute.com/2015/01/visual-content-mistakes-to-avoid/ (accessed June 14, 2015).
2. Steve Brown, "Let's Get Visual: Visual Content Gets Major Boost in 2015," January 29, 2015, www.getroionline.com/small-business-internet-marketing-tips/lets-get-visual-visual-content-gets-major-boost-in-2015 (accessed June 16, 2015).
3. Garett Sloane, "I [Love in an emoji] Your Brand," *Adweek*, June 2, 2015, 12.
4. Lizetta Staplefoote, "Nine Classic Advertising Icons and What They Can Teach You about Social Media," September 29, 2014, http://blog.visual.ly/social-media-lessons-classic-advertising-icons/ (accessed June 7, 2015).
5. Lizetta Staplefoote, "Nine Classic."
6. Chuck Frey, "Experts Share."
7. Chuck Frey, "Experts Share."
8. Margo Berman, *The Copywriter's Toolkit: The Complete Guide to Strategic Advertising Copy* (London: Wiley-Blackwell, 2012), 116.
9. Tim Nudd, "The World's 17 Best Print Campaigns. 2013–14." *AdWeek*, June 23, 2014, www.adweek.com/news/advertising-branding/worlds-17-best-print-campaigns-2013-14-158466 (accessed March 6, 2015).
10. Epiz Hunter, "25 Creative Packaging Designs that Practically Sell Themselves," June 20, 2014, http://imgur.com/a/NdEz1 (accessed June 21, 2015).
11. Felicia Greiff, "Pizza Hut Delivers Dinner and a Movie," *Advertising Age*, June 1, 2015, 47.

7

MEDIA STRATEGY
Multi-Tier Application Development

If you know where the message will appear, you can immediately think about how to create media-appropriate and audience-relevant content. You must think multiple vehicles, not just one when developing the strategy. In fact, when it comes to the different vehicles, you probably will have to tweak and customize your approach. When Old Navy created a back-to-school promo, it considered the viewing habits of its targeted consumer: music videos. It used scenes from its TV spots with Amy Poehler and posted them as a video on YouTube. The music, "Unlimited," a custom-written song, featured the stress students feel when classes resume after summer. The first-day-back-tension-related lyrics stated a *universal truth*: "Day One" hurts.

The TV spots also aired as the back-to-school-days approached. The objective was to extend the "shelf life" of TV by customizing for other targeted media. Through the use of music, as a common denominator, Old Navy sought to interact with a younger audience much the same way as the Oscar-winning hit song, "Let It Go," did for Disney's animated film, *Frozen*.[1]

In this section, we'll examine digital and other media that can be used with traditional vehicles to extend the brand's promotional footprint. With new media options emerging frequently, these are suggestions that could accommodate modification and/or customization to provide a supportive structure for a multiplatform campaign. One important strategic point, according to an article by Nate Dame on the Marketo blog,[2] is that consumers are searching under topics, not keywords, and that content is driving what the audience is looking for. We'll now start examining various media, beginning with mobile marketing. Another point is to have cohesive tone, image and message, as with any campaign. Always remember that memorable media messages, especially social media content, are effective when they are:

1. Relevant
2. Beneficial
3. Authentic
4. Illuminating
5. Imaginative
6. Engageable
7. Entertaining
8. Prolongable
9. Memorable ("catchy")
10. Bloggable

11. Shareable
12. "Spinnable" (able to work or "spin out" in all media)

Consider each medium as another support beam for the next one. Think about floors in a building. You need each level below it to reach the 30th floor. The media choices serve as the building components to a multilevel campaign.

Mobile

The most interesting fact about mobile and messaging, according to a 2015 State of the Industry Survey, is that more than 63 percent of marketers use data signals to develop target-relevant ad content.[3] This is because advertisers are looking to choose media using the most effective and efficient methods. The way to achieve this is with specific analytics that maximize every platform's persuasive power. Therefore, both the delivery mechanism must not only match the targeted audience, but also the message must be tweaked for optimal performance.

Smartphones are already in consumers' hands, so interactivity is intrinsic. However, it can be entertaining, with animation and engagement, or just ordinary clicks. In the next chapter, we will focus more on interactivity. Let's look at some existing and new technologies that integrate into the mobile campaigns discussed in Allison Schiff's article on the AdExchanger blog.[4]

The Kargo Gyroscope utilized the phone's accelerometer in the Tic Tac app to create instant animation. This feature allowed users to watch the candies shake within their phones as if they're holding the package. As they moved their phones, the Tic Tac candies would slide from side to side, up and down and all around. They could also choose the flavor and click to open the cap. The colors changed from orange to blue, then to white with each swipe, matching the flavor choices. Not only was it fun, but it also reminded consumers of the different options they would have when buying.

The company, Innovid, and its iRoll product added a buy feature to video ads, which enabled users to shop instantly. Companies, such as Pedigree, Coors Light, Audi, Purina Beneful, Doritos, Nivea, IBM and others, have already integrated this shoppable technology into their campaigns. See more examples at www.innovid.com.

YouTube is also adding click-to-shop ads that send mobile users directly to websites for purchases. This feature quickly monetizes videos.

One more interesting feature Schiff mentioned was sound.[5] XAPPmedia created audio ads that permitted users to use their voice to initiate a call to action. These could include such choices as "download app," "watch now," "send e-mail" and so on. This in turn would generate an automatic dial, allowing consumers whose hands were busy driving, exercising and so on to take action with voice commands. The audio feature was driven by ClearVoice Research, which showed that more than 50 percent of all audio content is absorbed when consumers are already engaged.

Social Media

To increase your social media footprint, there are a few key tips to follow. First, have interesting, informative and shareable content. Second, post frequently. (Many marketers write several posts first and schedule them to appear later.) Third, establish your personal writing style and point of view. Fourth, expand your topic, so that one post can create many more. Fifth, connect to others in your area of interest. Sixth, share their info and give them credit. Seventh, ask for advice. You'll learn a lot, while growing your audience. Eighth, include graphics, images and videos. Ninth, use hashtags and try geotagging if a location is relevant to your audience. Tenth, offer free samples of your work, such as sample chapters of an app or book. Eleventh, check which times receive the most views. For example, Latergramme suggested that between 2 a.m. and 5 p.m. were the best times for Instagram. Twelfth, if you're promoting your clients, engage their audiences in user-generated content, contests, giveaways, puzzles to solve with prizes and more fun ideas. Just notice how much attention the Doritos Crash the Super Bowl has received. Each year, it has invited consumers to create commercials. Then, the spot that was voted number one in the "USA Today Super Bowl Ad Meter poll," won $1 million for its creator! Now, that's a press-worthy promotion.

Interesting to note, some visually driven networks have converted into promotional tools by adding "buy" and other click-through links. For example, ROI Online social media manager, Randi Hudson, stated:[6]

> I think Pinterest Advertising is a new medium people are not yet used to. The promoted pins are hidden so it's easy to advertise to people with. Also, it is obviously very visual focused.

She also mentioned SlideShare for campaigns and has personally found this a successful vehicle when it published "ROI Online Culture Code"[7] on this platform. Honored as one of the Top Slides of the Week, Randi added that a SlideShare campaign can be used as a different type of medium, stating that it's "not typically top of mind for everyone."

Being focused on strategy, ROI Online included in its presentation (slide 20), the following key point:

> We are here to deliver insights through strategy and to educate our customers and ourselves.

Figure 7.1 Social Media

In addition, create ads that are quick, easy and fruitful. One click works better than two or three. And, each ad should be seen as an opportunity to gather audience-contact information, such as e-mails. Make your direct-response mechanism or call-to-action step clear. Select multiple media channels/networks so they strengthen the message. Finally, monitor your social and other media through analytics.

Strategy, as you can see, is the structure that underpins every aspect of campaign messaging. Now, we'll focus our attention on six key points that strengthen online communication: 1) images, 2) videos, 3) music videos, 4) streaming videos, 5) consumer-created content and 6) emotionally driven content.

Social Media Influencer Campaign Tips

In another Marketo blog article, this one by Jeff Foster, there are several tips to create an effective campaign that generates press from influential bloggers. Although there are three key tips, there are several more that Foster discussed. This is invaluable information because influencers do exactly that: influence your audience. Maybe that's why 65 percent of all brands include influencers in their digital marketing.[8] The first three points are featured in the article and the last four are mentioned at the end. Be sure to read through the entire list because each one is noteworthy (Figure 7.1).

1. Identify Your Audience

Knowing your target market not only means knowing your consumer, but also which social media sites they prefer, what blogs they tend to follow and whether they themselves have blogs. You need to know this, as well as where the influencers are. Here are some key facts about influencers: 1) 86 percent have their own blogs, 2) 92 percent frequent Facebook, 3) 86 percent are regulars on Twitter and 4) 76 percent are busy on LinkedIn. Is this where your audience hangs out, too?

2. Select the Right Influencers

Just knowing the names of influencers won't work. You have to know which influencers would be the ones to reach your customers. So a golf-loving audience may not be a perfect fit for Beyoncé or Justin Bieber followers.

3. Give Influencers Reasons to Talk about Your Brand

Make it easy for influencers to cover your product or service. Go beyond sending samples and a basic product description. Provide them with captivating images, clear videos, infographics, news exclusives and intriguing facts. Modify and follow Jerry McGuire's advice: "Help them, help you!"

4. Listen to Influencers' Product Feedback

Pay attention to any comments they make about your product/service. These may be invaluable to making it more marketable to your specific audience.

5. Observe Their Cultural References

Absorb every nuance, cultural reference and figure of speech the influencers use because this is the language that also resonates with your audience.

6. Stay in Contact

Don't be an infrequent guest, become a familiar visitor. Follow their blog, make comments, participate and show interest. Establish a relationship.

7. Ask Them to Guest Blog for You and Pay Them

When you discover some excellent influencers, ask them to be your firm's guest blogger. Your readers will gain deeper insights. The blogger, on the other hand, will feel appreciated by receiving remuneration and will bring their audience to yours.

Online Images and Videos

1. Images

Apple used actual photographs taken by the iPhone 6 to showcase the quality of the camera's images. Many images were like works of art, including one that captured the layers created by frozen bubbles on a Canadian lake. Others included natural shadows, which created a line of stripes down the back of a dachshund and colorful Thailand fields of glorious sunflowers, or sunlight peeking through trees. The images are an indisputable way to exemplify the impressive photos taken by the iPhone 6.

2. Videos

To target a younger market, the Farmers Insurance Open golf tournament at Torrey Pines used a video. It needed to create something fresh, so it turned to two companies: Skratch TV, a PGA-tour content provider, and Bedrocket, an online, multiplatform/multichannel video creator and provider. What they created was an under-two-minute video of Jason Day receiving his trophy by a parachutist who landed on the 18th hole to deliver it live. The idea was to create a video that would be "shareable and snackable," according to Bedrocket founder, Brian Bedol.[9] That is key because 65 to 70 percent of the videos his company produces are designed for mobile viewing. The stunt video was promoted on YouTube to reach its targeted audience: Millennials.

3. Music Videos

The Ad Council wanted to create a paradigm shift in those with prejudicial beliefs by creating a music video, "Diversity and Inclusion," using the song "Same Love," by Macklemore and Ryan Lewis, featuring Mary Lambert.[10] In the video, two or three people were dancing and kissing behind a black screen, appearing as skeletons. This image hid their age, gender, nationality, race, disability and religion. Only when they stepped out from behind the screen could the audience see who they were. Some were same-sex couples. Others were best friends of different races and loving sisters, with one having Down syndrome. Some others were an elderly couple and best-friend neighbors wearing different religious garb. Shot on Valentine's Day, the images were accompanied with copy that under - scored the point: Love has no labels.

4. Streaming Videos

The key to streaming video is quality. Any hesitations or freezes instantly turn off the viewer. This is why it's critical to carefully select the best companies when using this medium. Each year, various online firms evaluate them. StreamingMedia.com developed an alphabetized compilation that included the company's chief officer's name, as well as the year it was founded in "The List of the 100 Companies that Matter Most in Online Video." It's worthwhile to checkout the websites and the services they provide. A few of the top streaming video companies included Highwinds, Octoshape and Wowza. Of course, with a list of 100, there are many more. Take a moment and look for the highest-rated streaming video companies of the year.

5. Consumer-Created Content

Although, we will discuss this in the next chapter on interactivity, let's take a quick look at one exceptionally creative campaign in which Belkin teamed up with Lego and integrated Instagram. As mentioned in an article by Alan Cassinelli on the Postano blog,[11] consumers who bought iPhone cases with a Lego baseplate back, covered with the little nubs, chose them so they could decorate them however they wanted. Then, they'd post their masterpieces on Instagram, with #LEGOxBelkin. That way other future shoppers could be inspired and realize what they, too, could create. It turned past customers into a sales force! This was a brilliant cross promotion that featured consumer-created content.

6. Emotionally Driven Content

One wonderful example of emotional content, as discussed in Chapter 4, is exemplified in the Thai Life Insurance commercial "Unsung Hero."[12] The lengthy spot shows a humble, young man doing small, seemingly insignificant good deeds every day. He helps an old street vendor lift her cart over the sidewalk curb. He feeds a stray dog his hot lunch. He moves a dying plant so it could receive rainwater. He gives a donation to a women and her child, who are begging in the street holding a sign that reads "for education." He offers a young woman his seat on the bus. He hangs a bunch of bananas on his elderly neighbor's door. Throughout the video people scoff at him, as if he's wasting his time. Each day he repeats his acts of kindness, receiving "nothing in return." The commercial closes with the dying plant blooming. The dog following him home. The elderly street vendor selling more food. The little street beggar coming home from school in her uniform. The neighbor hugging him for the daily bananas. And, the spot wraps up showing the young man in his meager apartment with his loyal dog and the beautiful plants he nursed back to health. Why did he do this? Because what he received was something that was priceless: making his little world a more wondrous place.

Low- and No-Cost PR Media Tools

Although the next ten tips were listed as indispensable PR tools, they're equally applicable to advertising campaigns. See how easily they relate to both disciplines and how they can be used interchangeably and/or simultaneously. These wonderfully strategic guidelines, offered on the Big Ideas Machine blog, were written by Amie Smith.[13] One of the most important skills is organization when you're trying to run a multiplatform, multimedia campaign. Each of these online methods will help facilitate that.

1. Google Apps for Business

For those of you who favor Microsoft products, Google's Apps for Business drives productivity. By keeping all data on the cloud through Google Drive and accessible/editable on all devices using Google Docs, both clients and agencies can work together. Plus, the Gmail accounts save all correspondence for easy reference.

2. PRMax

Although in the UK, PRMax is a handy media database that makes accessing key contacts simple. (As a personal side note: In the USA there are a few that have been frequently mentioned as low- or no-cost, including Hey Press, Muck Rack, Anewstip, HARO [www.helpareporter.com], Profnet and Flacklist. Those that charge higher prices included Cision, MYPRGenie, Pressat Media Database, and Anewstip Pro Plan. (Twitter was also a great media reference tool.)

3. Yet Another Mail Merge

This Google Apps for Business downloadable app can work with Google Sheets. For a minimal annual fee, it sends out and personalizes e-mails and press releases, by using first or last names.

4. Talkwalker

Rated one of the top social media monitoring tools of 2014 and 2015, this instantly notifies you of all blog posts of every size from tiny blogs to major publications in real time, keeping you current. Best of all, at no cost!

5. Facebook

This social media network goes beyond family photos. It connects to important news within agencies, groups, industries and journalists specializing in particular areas of interest. It can offer support for special events, including those for nonprofits.

6. Boomerang for Gmail

This allows you to schedule e-mails to and from anywhere, so you don't have to stay late. Have a mass mailing? It's taken care of with mail merge.

7. Flipboard

Using Flipboard allows you to both collect and organize clippings from every topic, as well stay abreast of trends and keep your clients updated by sharing.

8. *Twitter*

Twitter has moved from personal updates of daily activities to an important tool for news and information. Today, journalists turn to Twitter as another form of communication with agencies because everyone's e-mail boxes are jammed-full.

9. *Crowdfire*

This handy tool has many features, some for a fee. It streamlines some of your social media challenges. It recommends whom to follow, lets you copy (your competitors') followers, helps you decide whom to unfollow, makes it easy to have several accounts, offers location and keyword searches and more.

10. *Coverage Book*

Although this is the highest price in the list, it is an invaluable time-saver. It works hand-in-hand with Talkwalker as follows. Once you receive the coverage from Talkwalker, you then copy the links into Coverage Book. This tool, in turn, not only reviews the press, but it also estimates and summarizes the views and shares, making it simple to send to the client. It's in your interest to familiarize yourself with each of these and apply them to both PR and advertising and all marketing campaigns, as they are applicable to all.

Ambient

Finding unexpected images and messages surprises consumers and instantly draws their attention (Figure 7.2). What better way to sell Natural Bliss Coffee Creamer than to have actors portraying baristas and customers in their natural state only covered in body paint?[14] That's exactly what Nestlé did in 2016 when it converted Irving Farm Coffee Roasters, a Lower East Side coffee shop in Manhattan, into Natural Bliss Café. Unsuspecting, regular customers walked in for their regular, wake-me-up morning coffees and got much more than that as their eye opener. Surprised and startled by the skimpy, but artfully painted, clothing-look-alike coverage, they asked what was going on.

When the baristas welcomed them to the Natural Bliss Café' and explained how the new Natural Bliss Creamer listed the all-natural ingredients, most coffee lovers needed to "rewind" the reply. Groggy and visually distracted, they couldn't quite grasp what they were seeing or hearing. Once they understood, customers had a good laugh and took selfies with the actors.

What an ingenious way to introduce a new product. It drew press, and the stunt clearly aligned with the product. It was just a funny prank. Yet, it was one that had a strategic connection to both the brand and its message. That's an example of an impressive ambient campaign that instantly went viral.

Other examples of ambient advertising introduce art installations in everyday settings. For instance, in 2013, Dutch artist, Florentijin Hofman, created a giant inflatable, 54-foot-tall, yellow rubber duck. As it floated in Hong Kong's Victoria Harbor, it generated plenty of photos by residents, tourists and press members.

Figure 7.2 Ambient Messages

Out of Home

There are many types of out-of-home (OOH) messages. These include pop-up stores, mall kiosks, bus-side shelters, oversized and undersized objects in odd places, marks on pavements or sidewalks and more. Billboards, for example, have become eye-catching and memorable, especially with the use of 3-D imagery; special effects; moving images; and real, live people. Just because these oversized road signs have been around for decades, doesn't diminish their impact on motorists. That is, if they're graphically and verbally spectacular. Let's look at a few of these before moving to other types of OOH campaigns.

One gold Clio billboard was for the Kansas City Royals. It showed a player sliding into base with such force that he pulls back the "grass" background, revealing the billboard's behind-the-scene scaffolding. The image appears to have movement and makes viewers feel as if they're actually watching the action live.[15] Other hard-to-miss billboards included real people. One showed beautiful, live models in a pop-up billboard to promote Johnson's World of Softness at the Westfield Shopping Centre in West London.

A few other exciting billboards include the Coop's Paints wallscapes that have buckets of paint that "spilled" down building walls over parked cars. A billboard that encouraged smokers to quit simply stated: "quitplan.com." However, a vertical cigarette butt, not a signpost, supported the board, creating a compelling image. It was a clever and clear explanation of the product's benefit: to snuff out the habit. Another outdoor sign replaced its post and used a giant fork to hold up a juicy bite of steak. The message stated that the flavor was the actual size, a nod to many mirrors stating that images may appear smaller. The advertiser was www.shopbloom.com, which comes up online as www.FoodLion.com. This was a delectable way to depict its high quality line of meats.

For a quick look at other OOH traffic-stopping campaigns here are some not to miss (Figure 7.3).

1. *The Flower Council of Holland* changed red emergency boxes into love symbols in Paris. The glass had a message printed in white that read, "In case of love at first sight, break glass." Inside was one beautiful, red rose.

Figure 7.3 Out-of-Home Messages

2. *Coca-Cola* promoted its new Mini Coke with baby-size, soda-vending machines and micro-street vendor kiosks. Instantly, passersby would notice the tiny size of the "dispensers" and then realize these miniature structures reflected the new, little Coke bottles.

3. *Oldtimer* promoted its all-you-can-eat, rest stop buffet with a giant wallscape draped in front of a mountain tunnel opening. The image hanging over the entrance showed a lady with her mouth wide open. As cars drove into the tunnel and past her lips, it demonstrated that Oldtimer was a nonstop, fill-you-up restaurant.

4. *Oreo* had a "wonderfilled" campaign in Times Square, New York. It integrated 12 digital billboards that were 22 stories tall showing animated, whimsical illustrations of people passing, sharing and dunking Oreo cookies from building to building in a mesmerizing display. What a playful way to show what people do with one of America's favorite cookies!

5. *Webjet*, a discount travel site, placed an enormous, bright-red suitcase next to a bus stop and used the front as a message board. It reminded commuters to use webjet.com.sg to book their holiday air travel plans.

6. *Dumocalcin* demonstrated the bone-building benefits of its chewable calcium supplement by constructing giant bones as bridge columns in Jakarta, Indonesia. These mammoth bone-shaped supports reflected the kind of structural reinforcement your joints would receive from Dumocalcin.

Transit

In busy cities, with people on the move, transit is another influential vehicle to carry a message. Unusual visuals and thought-provoking copy are still tools that can drive a message directly to the viewer. If you were driving along and saw what appeared to be a bridge paved with Lego bricks wouldn't you share it? Instead of using its actual bricks, Lego painted an image of multicolored Lego pieces across the entire bridge. It's possible that people even got out of their cars to double-check what they were seeing.

Bus and subway straps, "straphangers," have been used to promote many products in many ways. Big Pilot watch bus straps wrapped around people's wrists as if they were trying them on. Pepsi-Cola created a two-part bus handle display. The bottom part was a clear handgrip, which wrapped around a Pepsi can with a straw. The second part connected the straw to a pair of feminine lips resting on the handrail. It looked as if someone were drinking a Pepsi. Bus straps have also been popular. To show the grip and durability of its products, Hankook Tires placed mini tires as bus straps. To remind people to work out the Fitness Company created mock, workout weights along the handrails to replicate barbells.

Television

As with many media, six key elements strongly contribute to effective TV spots: 1) storytelling, 2) consumer benefits, 3) message relevance, 4) universal truths, 5) sound and 6) exciting visuals, such as intriguing graphics, vibrant colors, cartoon characters, beloved celebrities, etc.

Let's look at examples of the six, above-mentioned techniques, one at a time.

1. *Storytelling*—Sponsored by Keep America Beautiful and the Ad Council, "The Recycling Campaign" stood out because of its endearing story. It spoke through the personified voice of ordinary trash that wanted to be recycled. One plastic bottle, for example, explained in a female voice, how she was told she was nothing but trash. And, that's all she would ever be. It was as if she were recalling the demeaning comments of an emotionally abusive parent. Yet, she dreamed to be more. Until finally, someone picked up the bottle and placed it in a recycling bin. At which point, she stated that she finally arrived where she always knew she belonged. A touching story that reminded everyone to recycle by humanizing the items we simply toss away, often without giving them any thought.

2. *Consumer benefits*—A wonderful example of this is the Maytag Man as the personification of all the kitchen and laundry appliances. As he plays every role, he explains how each appliance solves problems, such as the fast-cooling refrigerator, perfect-temperature-controlled oven and high-powered cleaning dishwasher. The spots also demonstrate key benefits including reliability, dependability and functionality. In one spot, all the appliances are whistling to demonstrate how they work in harmony to facilitate housework.

3. *Message relevance*—A commercial that focuses on message relevance is Iams "Welcome Home." Told in a story (as explained in Chapter 3, under "storytelling") Rocky, the Irish Wolfhound, races out to greet his returning home soldier "mom," Dawn. He showers her with affection on the driveway. They go inside and she feeds him Iams to demonstrate her love for him. For pet owners, who believe they are feeding family members, not animals, this spot resonates with them. It connects with the care they show their pets by choosing the best food.

4. *Universal truths*—In the Home Depot "Tree House" commercial, a dad overhears his son bragging to his friends how his dad can do anything, even build a great tree house. Now the dad is under pressure to perform. He races over to Home Depot and confesses he knows nothing about building tree houses. The sales assistant walks him through the necessary building materials and procedures, reassuring the dad. The next scene shows an amazing tree house with the dad, his son and friends having a sleep out. *What's the universal truth?* My dad's a hero.

5. *Sound*—The "Blueberry Fart" commercial for Mr. Sketch Scented Markers instantly comes to mind. It shows a blueberry slightly shaking and then emitting a blue gas, which

is captured in a tube, carried along and deposited into a marker. The message is that scented markers make coloring even more fun. For children who are often fascinated with body function and odor, the commercial is a tasteful, yet humorous spot. The tiny sound released by the blueberry adds to the lightheartedness.

6. *Exciting visuals*—Progressive Insurance has created a distinctive campaign with Flo, the quirky recognizable spokesperson. Everywhere she appears, consumers instantly connect her to the brand and recall its promise of unbiased pricing-comparison. Her attention-demanding persona allows Flo, the character, to appear in different scenarios and guises, without losing her unique identity. For example, in one commercial, she portrays all the members of one family. As a character actress, Stephanie Courtney, is a humorous and unique brand ambassador, who doesn't overpower the brand's message: We tell you the honest-to-goodness prices of our competitors so you can choose.

Another other visually compelling campaigns are the Tide-To-Go "Talking Stain" commercial. Often referred to as the "Interview" spot, a job candidate is in the middle of an interview when the stain on his shirt starts speaking indecipherable comments that "out-shout" the interviewee's voice. The possible employer is so distracted by the "talking stain" that he can't concentrate on what is actually being said by the candidate.

A third example was mentioned in Chapter 3: the Febreze "Noseblind" campaign. The visuals show how people become used to scents in their homes and cars. In short, they've become "noseblind" to them. A car transforms into a giant sheepdog. A couch in a cat-filled house becomes one huge cat. A teenager's room turns into a locker room. (Figure 7.4).

Figure 7.4 Television Spots

Radio

There are several reasons to still consider radio. First, almost half of all listening time is spent during the daily commute. Second, 56 percent of drivers who are at least 18 years old most frequently listen to AM/FM radio, as compared to 11 percent who prefer satellite radio.[16] Third, many commuters are loyal listeners with stations preset to their favorite music genres with longer tuned-in spans. Fourth, they are "trapped" in their cars with fewer other media options. Even subscription-based, satellite listeners have the option to go back and forth between public to paid stations. Therefore, both groups are exposed to commercials in that medium.

Radio commercials have evolved. Change is a key strategy. Just notice how relevant this quote is by Charles Darwin in the *Origin of Species*.

It is not the strongest of the species that survives, nor the most intelligent; it is the one that is the most adaptable to change.

Memorable radio spots still work. There are a few basic strategies to keep in mind when developing an all-audio message. The most important ones to master, whether for a product, brand or service, are these 1) determine the most appropriate audience for the product/brand; 2) be sure that the brand aligns with the audience's needs, interests and core values; 3) write relevant content that offers a benefit and solution; 4) use appropriate and ear-catching sound effects and music; 5) cater to the listener's ear, then create lifelike visuals through descriptive copy; and 6) cast carefully because talent can transform a commercial to one that's impossible to forget or hard to remember.

Some of the long-running radio campaigns, such as Motel 6, have used the same voice-over talent: Tom Bodett. This makes the brand instantly recognizable as soon as listeners hear his distinctive tone and deadpan delivery. One of its spots, "Smartphone" received the best radio spot to air in the 2014 Super Bowl. Yes, you read that right. Radio spots run during the big game and all ears are listening up because everyone expects to see the commercials. Westwood One Super Bowl Sound Awards named Poo-Pourri the 2015 winner for its "'Before-You-Go' Toilet Spray spot. The other four 2015 honorees that made up the top five winners were Motel 6 (two spots), Subway and Exergen.

Other celebrated campaigns that have received press attention are the Old Spice "Smell like a Man, Man," with Isaiah Mustafa and the famous line: "The man your man could smell like." Although it also ran on television, online as a viral campaign and in print, the radio spot embraced the medium with superbly visual copy, excellent delivery and perfect timing.

Go Outside magazine created a "mosquito-repellent" commercial: "Go Outside Repellent Radio." It interrupted regular programming with a message that told listeners they could enjoy the outdoors again without getting bit. It emitted a sound wave that was barely audible to humans, yet threatening to mosquitos. That was because the 15kHz frequency replicated the dragonfly's "voice," the mosquitos' natural predator. Notable, however, was the identifiable buzz of mosquitos that drove home the point of how disturbing these tiny biters were.

Some radio spots effectively tackle social causes. For instance, one anti-bullying public service announcement (PSA) radio campaign, "Be More than a Bystander," left a strong impression on the audience. Created by the Ad Council, it included downloadable scripts, actual live-announce and pre-recorded spots.[17] When young talents voiced the commercials, they made these how-to-stop-bullying messages even more authentic.

In one spot, a young girl talked about all the things she learned in school that day. Discussing her self-worth-crushing experiences from one class to the next, she mentioned how she learned that she was fat, and stupid and ugly. Using parallel construction, the comments took the form of, "In chemistry, I learned. . . ." "In gym class, I learned . . ." Each statement ended with a negative statement, such as "I learned I'm disgusting." Such harsh words would be internalized forever, leaving indelible, emotional scars on her. The commercials ended by encouraging listeners to be proactive and not just observers. The direct response, closing-line sent them to the website, www.stopbullying.gov, where they could learn what to do.

One classic radio campaign definitely worth your listening time is the Bud Light "Real Men of Genius" series. Each spot uses the same writing style, same voice talent and same inflection (type of "read"). This cohesive and humorous campaign shows the impact great copy can have on the audience. It also demonstrates how this medium creates pictures for people to imagine and why it's accurately referred to as the "theater of the mind."

Be sure to search the Internet for unusual radio commercials so you can hear for yourself why they worked. Analyze them. Was it the talent, the story, the sound effects, the surprise, the humor or something else? Could you see what you were hearing? Visit several sites for examples, including YouTube for examples and NextRad.io. Look for informative blog posts, podcasts and online discussions, such as this one by Claire Bowen from the UK Radio Advertising Bureau (RAB)[18] for some tips and guidelines.

Podcasts

Podcast consumption has grown steadily. The 2014 Infinite Dial from Edison Research[19] pointed out some interesting statistics that support this fact. These include the following: Thirty percent of the 12-and-older U.S. population has listened to a podcast. One-fifth of weekly listeners have tuned in to six or more podcasts each week. In one month, a record-breaking 39 million people have heard a podcast.

Podcasts present a win–win for all: the hosts, listeners and advertisers. There are many benefits, as discussed in a SwipeStation blog article by Ceren Has.[20] For the creator, podcasts are free, easy-to-develop and can be polished with a few online lessons by experts, such as Dan Benjamin. For the listeners, they're accessible, with the majority of them on iTunes, which are portable on mobile devices and updatable with new episodes automatically replacing those already heard.

Most importantly, for the advertisers, podcasts are void of "stop sets," which are the three-and-a-half minutes of commercial breaks. Instead, the podcasts' hosts integrate the advertising messages into their broadcasts, tweaking them to appeal to their specific audience. The key point here is that their audience is really listening, not using the program as background noise.

Whether you're delivering or advertising on the podcast, always consider how you can help your listeners by teaching, solving problems, directing them to solutions and engaging them through informative, exciting and/or inspiring content (Figure 7.5). Unlike other audiences, this one is opting to tune in.

Figure 7.5 Podcasts

Print

Although the power of print may have declined, magazines are still read. There are some exciting ads in the form of pop-ups, inserts and double-truck (two-page spread) ads that are still being used.[21] For example, Nha Xinh Furniture created a campaign of pop-up ads that folded flat when the magazine was closed. Each one featured a specific piece of lightweight, foldable furniture the store carried. So, the ad actually demonstrated how the furniture folded. One was a folding chair. Another ad was a folding bookshelf. A third was a folding table. It was a brilliant use of the medium because consumers could see how easily the furniture could be stored and put away.

For years, Hallmark has used inserts to display its greeting cards and its magazine of the same name. Some ads describe how cards target audiences. Others show how the sound chips work. Several boast about the magazine circulation increase. Knowing that magazines have a shelf life and are shared with others, Hallmark uses them as one of its go-to choices.

One double-truck ad by DHL included the use of a clear acrylic sheet with printing on it between the pages. On the in-between page was the DHL delivery person holding a package. As you turned the clear page, he delivered the package from one person on the first page to another on the second page and vice versa. What an innovative way to show what the company does: deliver.

Another simple, yet highly effective ad is the Hawaiian Tropic no-copy, two-page spread. The left page is pink. The right page is tan. The logo appears on the bottom right of the second page with one line of text: "Enjoy the sun." This same double-truck ad appeared using reflective paper on both pages. Readers would use the ad as sun reflectors to get a better tan. You could consider this a type of interactivity with the brand.

Direct Mail

To create a "must-open" direct mail piece, create something surprising. Tantalizing. Intriguing. Make consumers inquisitive. First, they must notice it before they'll open it. Ask yourself: What would make you tear it open? There was one example I saw in an award book that I never forgot. It was a small box with one line of copy on the outside. "How to fit an elephant in a box." Once opened, the box held a faux-ivory bangle bracelet. Emotionally heart wrenching, it instantly made the "save our elephant" point vividly clear.

Therefore, always be on the look out for terrific direct mail campaigns like the following examples. One company, Griffiths, Gibson and Ramsay Productions, sent such a popular direct mail piece to agencies, that they received requests for more copies to give the agency recipients' children. What was it? A working, record-playing turntable made from foldable cardboard, with a record included. The easy instructions were printed on the cardboard.[22]

Skype sent a small square box with sealing label displaying its recognizable logo, encouraging recipients to open it. Inside, they found a Rubik's Cube illustrating Skype's benefits. This fun and interactive direct mail piece, instantly engaged the audience.

In London, Kit Kat sent out a postcard that resembled an unable-to-deliver card the post office leaves, complete with the recipients' name and address. The red color and prominent Kit Kat logo drew the audience's attention to read on. It stated that it couldn't deliver the package because it was too "chunky" to fit in the mailbox. All readers had to do was to go to a nearby newsstand to pick up their free Kit Kat "Chunky" chocolate bar. Motivating, isn't it?

Here's another example of "gotta-see-if-this-is-for-real" innovative ideas. In celebration of World Water Day, the Green Belgium Mailing service sent out a piece that could only be visible when held under water. The message was that "without water, knowledge can't flow." When a mailer prompts curiosity, it already has done more than most. It stimulated the reader to figure it out. It's hard to resist a message that you have to work to read. This piece turned reluctant consumers into active participants.

One final example that challenged innate problem-solvers: college engineering students. To recruit this particular audience, Australia's Defense Force developed a recruitment direct mail campaign for the Air Force. It challenged these natural "builders" to make a radio. They received all the parts needed. The only thing missing was instructions. They themselves had to figure out how to build a working radio. Once assembled, they could tune into the Air Force FM station. What was the goal? To target the students with the initiative to complete the task. Once they accomplished it, they were invited to start a mentally stimulating career.

Take a little time to search online for more innovative direct mail campaigns (Figure 7.6). You'll be delighted by many of the terrific examples to discover.

Figure 7.6 Direct Mail

Direct Response Marketing

This can occur in all media from television to print to out of home to direct mail and so on. Direct response is a call-to-action message that drives recipients to do something: make a donation, call a phone number, ask their doctor or pharmacist or make an appointment, etc.

You have seen many commercials for Save the Children, St. Jude's Hospital, the Humane Society, Breast Cancer, as well as other noble causes. These are all direct response, marketing examples. They all ask for your participation. Whether it's through donation, pet adoption or event support, as in walkathons.

Greenpeace New Zealand developed a "Polar Bear Video" direct response television (DRTV) campaign, which raised almost $25,000. The heartbreaking spot featured a homeless polar bear in London. In one, it walked alone through the streets, pawed through trash for food, sniffed exhaust car fumes, wandered into a park, slowly collapsed and died under a tree. The closing message asked for you to help save the arctic. The video appeared on social media in e-mails and online blogs.

Although social media might not be the first as a direct response vehicle that comes to mind, today's search engine optimization (SEO) strategy should also think about content and shareability. These two factors help build, reward an audience and enable readers to share valuable information. According to an article on a Marketo blog by Nate Dame,[23] the following tips will strengthen any SEO strategic plan.

1. Be prepared on your key topic to provide solutions to your audience's questions and optimize your content by choosing synonymous, related keywords.
2. Guide your readers in how-to tutorials, enabling them to take action on a purchase or learning a new skill.
3. Avoid a keyword "overkill" by overuse.
4. Be sure all of your content is clearly related to all keywords, main topics and secondary subjects, posts and sub-sections.
5. Watch what generates a fair amount of social shares. These validate both the quality of your information and quantity of audience interactivity.

In short, don't dismiss any medium when it comes to direct response engagement. Keep in mind what you want your audience to do and invite them to do it, whether it's replying, sharing, liking, calling or visiting a website. We'll talk more about interactivity in the next chapter.

Cross Promotion

You've probably seen many cross promotions over the years. Most recognizable might be the McDonald's movie tie-ins. The fun, yet criticized for promoting high-calorie foods, "Happy Meals" included children-size portions and little toys like Looney Tunes characters. Other well-known promotions team up beverage and snack items. When combined, they showcase savings, coupons and rewards. Even hotel and airfare packages come to mind.

You may want to find more exciting ways to marry two brands into one happy-to-say-I-do promotion. Sometimes, marriages are unexpectedly and financially successful as these timing-was-right pairings: 1) Reese's Pieces and the film *ET*, 2) Budweiser Select and Emerald Nuts 2006 Super Bowl and 3) Monster drinks and the Triple Crown winner at the 2015 Belmont Stakes. The jockey not only wore a cap with the Monster logo, he also was drinking the beverage just after he won. This was a historic moment because no other horse had won this three-race event for 37 years. The immediate exposure for the brand was incalculable. It had coverage during the event and in many newscasts for days afterward.

Some cross promotions are short-lived and specifically targeted to high-traffic, high-visibility areas. Times Square, New York, with its giant, world-famous billboards has been selected for endless cross promotions. Monster chose this venue for a two-month run when it featured its products and the film *Southpaw*, occupying the G-Tron bi-directional board.

Other cross promotions have presented appealing offers, such as popcorn and a movie. One example was the free three-pack Orville Movie Theater Butter popcorn when consumers bought the movie *Rio 2* at Walgreens. Although consumers always appreciate savings, some promotions work even harder. They remind shoppers of product benefits, even on simple promotional items like logo-covered cozies or beverage holders or cups.

Although coffee sleeves were not new, Wrigley's Orbit's "Coffee on the Go, Clean Teeth on the Go" campaign was. Tag 8 teamed up with DDB to create a coffee sleeve that housed

Figure 7.7 Cross Promotion

a small package of gum that would sit on every Seattle Coffee Co. cup sold. The idea of solving a consumer problem, coffee breath, by offering free gum with each cup they bought also reminded them about Wrigley's Orbit as a brand option. This is an imaginative use of a frequently used medium.[24]

When thinking about a cross promotion, give it some energy. Make it exciting and enticing (Figure 7.7).

Multimedia Summary

Review the entire list below and refresh your memory wherever you need strengthening (Box 7.1). Always think about projecting the core values of your brand and audience, solving consumers' problems, addressing their needs and desires, engaging their imaginations, providing a clear call to action. These include responding and sharing; developing valuable and relevant content; presenting an authentic voice; creating unique messages in unexpected, but audience-present media; creating a campaign that has longevity; and generating memorable promotions.

Box 7.1 Multi-Tier Media Summary List

1. *Multimedia*—Establish campaign concepts that are sustainable and supportable.

   a. Relevant
   b. Beneficial
   c. Authentic
   d. Illuminating
   e. Imaginative
   f. Engageable

---

g.   Entertaining
h.   Prolongable
i.   Memorable ("catchy")
j.   Bloggable
k.   Shareable
l.   "Spinnable" (able to work or "spin out" in all media)

2. *Mobile*—Attract and activate influencers.

a.   Images
b.   Videos
c.   Music videos
d.   Streaming videos
e.   Consumer-created content
f.   Emotionally driven content

3. *Social Media Influencer Campaign Tips.*

a.   Identify Your Audience
b.   Select the Right Influencers
c.   Give Influencers Reasons to Talk about Your Brand
d.   Listen to Influencers' Product Feedback
e.   Observe Their Cultural References
f.   Stay in Contact
g.   Ask Them to Guest Blog for You and Pay Them

4. *Low- and No-Cost PR Media Tools*—Search for and adopt effective technology.

a.   Google Apps for Business
b.   PRMax
c.   Yet Another Mail Merge
d.   Talkwalker
e.   Facebook
f.   Boomerang for Gmail
g.   Flipboard
h.   Twitter
i.   Crowdfire
j.   Coverage Book

5. *Ambient*—Surprise and intrigue consumers in innovative places.

6. *Out of Home*—Implement eye-catching, special effects like 3-D, live people, movement.

7. *Transit*—Reach people on the move by attention-demanding ideas.

8. *Television*—Develop memorable, targeted message, using multiple senses.

    a.   Storytelling
    b.   Consumer benefits
    c.   Message relevance
    d.   Universal truths
    e.   Sound
    f.   Exciting visuals (intriguing graphics, colors, characters, celebrities, etc.)

9. *Radio*—Engage listener's imagination + where they're listening: most often in the car.

    a.   Determine appropriate audience
    b.   Align brand with the audience's needs, interests and core values
    c.   Offer a benefit and solution
    d.   Use ear-catching sound effects and music
    e.   Cater to the listener's ear
    f.   Cast talent carefully

10. *Podcasts*—Discover this medium: a win–win for host, listener and advertiser.

11. *Print*—Use exciting ads in the form of pop-ups, inserts and double-truck (two-page).

12. *Direct Mail*—Create a "must-open" direct mail piece.

13. *Direct Response Marketing*—Design a call-to-action to do something.

14. *Cross Promotion*—Create power couples.

Media Strategy Exercises

Exercise 1: Identify one multimedia, multiplatform campaign that generated shares and press coverage. Now, describe the following:

a.   The types of media used.
b.   Name the types of social shares it stimulated.

Exercise 2: Find one out-of-home campaign that used visual effects, such as movement, 3-D visuals, live people, or oversized images. Answer these questions:

a.   Name the advertiser.
b.   How did that effect strengthen the brand's message?

Exercise 3: What radio campaign was an excellent use of this medium with a clever mix of talent, sound effects, music and delivery?

Exercise 4: What social media campaign did you share? Explain what motivated you to send it to others?

Exercise 5: Name one low-cost or free PR tool you could apply to advertising.

Exercise 6: Go to YouTube and find three Doritos "Crash the Super Bowl" consumer-created commercials that received the $1 million award. List the names of the consumers who created the winning TV spots.

Exercise 7: Cite two TV commercials with instantly relatable universal truths. How did these truths drive home the brand's message?

Exercise 8: What exciting cross promotion made you buy the product?

Notes

1. Ashley Rodriguez. "'Backbone' of Back-to-School Campaign is an Online Music Video," July 31, 2014, http://adage.com/article/cmo-strategy/navy-cmo-aims-lessen-brand-s-reliance-tv/294404/ (accessed August 19, 2014).
2. Nate Dame, "Here's How to Create a Modern SEO Strategy that Works," July 13, 2015, http://blog.marketo.com/2015/07/heres-how-to-create-a-modern-seo-strategy-that-works.html (accessed July 15, 2015).
3. Celtra, "Using Data to Inform Ad Content," *Adweek*, March 30, 2015, M4 and www.adweek.com/sa-article/celtra-using-data-inform-ad-content-163695 (accessed March 30, 2015).
4. Allison Schiff, "A Banner Year for Innovative Mobile and Digital Ad Units," January 5, 2015, http://adexchanger.com/online-advertising/a-banner-year-for-innovative-mobile-and-digital-ad-units/ (accessed July 14, 2015).
5. Schiff, "A Banner Year."
6. Randi Hudson, personal correspondence, June 29, 2015.
7. ROI Online, www.slideshare.net/GetROIOnline/roi-online-culture-code (accessed June 29, 2015).
8. Jeff Foster, "Three Steps to Executing a Flawless Influencer Marketing Campaign," May 11, 2015, http://blog.marketo.com/2015/05/3-steps-to-executing-a-flawless-influencer-marketing-campaign.html (accessed June 29, 2015).
9. John Paul Newport, "Courting Millennials, with YouTube," *The Wall Street Journal*, February 21–22, 2015, A9.
10. Ad Council, "Diversity & Inclusion," March 3, 2015, www.youtube.com/watch?v=PnDgZuGIhHs (accessed July 20, 2015).
11. Alan Cassinelli, "Ten Great Examples of User-Generated Content Campaigns, April 21, 2014," www.postano.com/blog/10-great-examples-of-user-generated-content-campaigns (accessed July 19, 2015).
12. www.youtube.com/watch?v=uaWA2GbcnJU.
13. Amie Smith, "10 Low Cost/Free Online Tools No PR Professional Should Be Without," June 26, 2015, www.bigideasmachine.com/10-low-cost-free-online-tools-no-pr-professional-should-be-without/ (accessed July 4, 2015).
14. Tereza Litsa, "Nestlé Uses Nude Baristas to Sell Coffee Creamer," July 21, 2015, www.creativeguerrillamarketing.com/guerrilla-marketing/nestle-uses-nude-baristas-sell-coffee-creamer/ (accessed July 20, 2015).
15. Clio Sports: Gold Standard," *Adweek*, July 6, 2015: 29.
16. Edison Research, "The Infinite Dial 2014 from Edison Research and Triton Digital," March 5, 2014, www.edisonresearch.com/the-infinite-dial-2014/ (July 25, 2015).
17. Ad Council, "Be More than a Bystander," http://bullyingprevention.adcouncil.org/radio/ (accessed July 25, 2015).

18. Claire Bowen, "The Top Five Most Unusual Radio Commercials and Trails," October 25, 2012, www.youtube.com/watch?v=m4HUilNBOKU (accessed July 25, 2015).

19. Edison Research, "The Infinite Dial."

20. Ceren Has, "Casting Call for All Pods," July 23, 2015, www.swipestation.co.uk/casting-call-for-all-pods/?utm_content (accessed July 24, 2015).

21. Designzzz. "50 Brilliant Magazine Print Ads," August 8, 2013, www.designzzz.com/magazine-print-ads/ (accessed July 17, 2015).

22. Urbanriver, "Ten Creative Direct Mail Campaigns," www.urbanriver.com/10-creative-direct-mail-examples.html (accessed July 17, 2015).

23. Nate Dame, "Here's How."

24. The DieLine, "'Coffee on the Go, Clean Teeth on the Go' Direct-Marketing Campaign," July 9, 2014, www.thedieline.com/blog/2014/7/7/coffee-on-the-go-clean-teeth-on-the-go-direct-marketing-campaign (accessed July 17, 2015).

8

INTERACTIVE STRATEGY
User-Centered Design

Create a Relationship

The point of audience engagement is not just to have fun with the audience, but also to build a solid rapport. When consumers interact with the brand, they feel a true kinship to it. They feel emotionally connected. As the brand–consumer relationship grows, so does the loyalty and trust. Sometimes the bond results in a zealous passion for the brand.

One example is the Nike Sneakerheads. They are so passionate that they'll wait in the street for hours until a store opens with a limited-edition model. Others vigilantly scour the Internet to spot the newest, most sought-after or unusual designs. Nike carefully fueled and harnessed the fervor behind this group of devoted loyalists. It created events, an e-commerce site, blogs (www.sneakerhead.com/blog/), exhibitions, shows, contests and giveaways. These didn't just occur in the USA, they took the brand events overseas. As a build up to the soccer frenzy of the World Cup, Nike created the "Risk Your Soul" campaign in London. It pitted five teams of sneaker retailers against one another. Each team selected one pair of Nike to go against another team's pair. Fans voted online for their favorite styles. Then, the five teams had to demonstrate their athletic prowess in a team-against-team football match. Timed perfectly, the sneaker battle occurred just prior to the 2014 World Cup.

Continuing its soccer celebration, Nike featured its latest football sneakers in Madrid. Then, in France, it exhibited its most visually exciting and Paris-inspired designs in the Nike Phenomenal House. Displayed individually in glass-enclosed pedestals, the shoe presentations resembled a museum exhibition.

These kind of exciting events energized and rewarded its staunchest devotees.

Entertainment as a Brand Builder

McDonald's introduced a memorable and shareable interactive campaign. In London, it showed a billboard with moving menu items. It invited passersby to capture a shot of a sundae. Their reward? A free coffee. Pedestrians had to stand there, waiting to see the sundae, while viewing all McDonald's menu items. It wasn't just about the free coffee. It was the fun of catching a shot of a moving image. The board also showed the nearest location. People were looking for the billboards so they could interact with it and get a free cup of Joe.

Coca-Cola teamed up with Shazam to create its "Drinkable Coke Zero" campaign. It introduced the first "drinkable" billboard. Equipped with a giant, swirly straw, Coke Zero poured out, serving thousands of amazed participants. Other billboards invited people to make believe they were drinking from their smartphones. As they "consumed" Coke Zero,

Figure 8.1 Interactive Print

the billboard bottle amount decreased showing how much they drank. When they "finished" the bottle, they received a coupon for a free Coke Zero.

The idea revolved around the ability to "drink" the beverage from all devices and media. To engage as many consumers as possible, the campaign utilized a wide range of media from print, flyers and billboards to television, radio, social media and more. TV spots through Shazam technology "poured" Coke Zero directly into viewers' phones using digital straws. They could play anywhere they were, at a game or on their couch at home. Print ads became cups once they were pulled out of a magazine. Flyers turned into straws. Radio spots and 140-character tweets used the sound of the soda being poured. So all audiences could join in. Just by showing the smartphone coupon to retailers, everyone who played got a free Coke Zero.[1]

This campaign demonstrated the effectiveness of cross promotion, multiplatform delivery and conceptual cohesion among all media.

Remember, as mentioned in Chapter 7, all media can interact with the audience. For example, Bubble-Gum chose to use a print ad. It could be blown up and make a bubble, reminding people how much fun chewing it is. The bubble would expand when people blew into the pop-up ad (Figure 8.1).[2] (See www.designzzz.com/magazine-print-ads/.)

Fun Engagement and Rewards

Taco Bell created buzz before the introduction of its Cool Ranch Doritos Locos Tacos by tempting its fans with its "Speakeasy" campaign under the "Viva Mas" slogan, describing its latest creation. Exuberant fans were so intrigued that they not only tweeted about it, but also banded together in protest, refusing to eat there until the new sensation arrived. In response, Taco Bell invited its most ardent fans to be the very first ones to taste it.

But, it didn't just serve the Cool Ranch Doritos Locos Tacos (DLT). It drew fans into a "find the answer" type of game. It engaged businesses in major cities to play along. It placed an old-fashioned phone with a sign outside each establishment. For example, in New York, it involved a florist. Fans were told to go to specific addresses. Also, people who were just walking by would read the sign next to the blue bouquet, which read: #COOLRANCHDLT.

WAS HERE. They would pick up the phone, hear the phrase and were told to go inside and ask for it. For example, the florist's phrase was "blue bouquet." People who repeated the phrase were given a free Doritos Locos Tacos. Of course, the business staff would tease them by showing them various blue floral bouquets. But, fans kept asking and were finally rewarded. They had so much fun, they tweeted to their friends, using the hashtag #COOLRANCHDLT, to go the florist, say the phrase and get the free new taco, too. Soon hundreds of people were lining up outside the businesses to join in the free giveaway.

In Dallas, they worked with a barbershop and had fans go to the fourth barber and ask him to "make them look cool." Playful stylists replied with funny comments, implying it would be really hard to do that. Finally, the "clients" received their free Cool Ranch Doritos Locos Tacos on a silver platter, which, of course read: #COOLRANCHDLT WAS HERE.

In Los Angeles, it set up its Taco Speakeasies in a parking lot. Valets were there waiting to hear passersby say, "It's the blue one." Once they said it, a beat-up van pulled up. Then, the doors opened to reveal an all-blue interior where blue angels served them a free Cool Ranch DLT. The light blue license plate read: #COOLRANCHDLT WAS HERE (Figure 8.2).

The campaign resulted in selling a record-breaking number of its new taco the first day it was introduced: 1.5 million! In addition, its eight videos, posted on the Taco Bell YouTube channel, generated four million views.[3] The beauty of this cross-promotional campaign was its tight integration and cohesive concept that effectively "spun out" in multiple media and platforms. These also included Virgin Airlines planes with exterior-painted messages, tray tables and free passenger samples; pop-up street vendor kiosks, "Taco Trucks"; an Uber app that had drivers deliver the taco to your location; and even drones or "TacoCopters" to fly in yours.[4]

Some brands repurposed user-generated content showing its fans that it used their contributions. For instance, Starbucks asked consumers to share images of them with friends and family enjoying their favorite beverages. Then, Starbucks created eight-piece collages of the photos and posted them on Facebook. People could see their pictures as part of a cultural montage. (See an example at www.facebook.com/Starbucks/photos/a.10150362709023057.369892.22092443056/10150906911398057/type=1&permPage=1.)

Figure 8.2 Fun Engagement

Big-Reward Contests

Doritos "Crash the Super Bowl" contest, as mentioned in Chapters 3 and 7, isn't the only company offering $1 million prizes for consumer-created content. Frito-Lay's potato chips joined in and developed its own "Do Us a Flavor" contest. The 2015 winner, Temple University surgical nurse Meneko Spigner McBeth, concocted the new flavor using the Lay's kettle-style chips and adding wasabi and ginger. The new flavor, "McBeth's Wasabi Ginger chips," will be sold everywhere Lay's is available.[5]

With giant-size prizes, creative consumers are excited to take on the challenge, even if their chances of winning are minuscule. They might be thinking, "After all, someone has to win. Why not me?" They're right because McBeth's recipe beat out 14 million other flavor submissions and won.

Pillsbury has run its famous Annual Bake-Off contest for almost fifty years. In 2014, the forty-seventh $1 million contest winner was Beth Royals for her Peanutty Pie Crust Clusters recipe (Figure 8.3).

When a brand can ignite that kind of participation, it wins in several ways. First, it creates "talk value" through the contest itself. Second, it ties the "assignment or challenge" closely to its brand. Third, it draws national attention to its winners and their creative ideas. Fourth, it gives out exceptionally high rewards for a relatively easy-to-play contest. Fifth, it creates anticipation, with people wondering who and what idea will win next.

Other brands also develop $1 million contests; however some require a high level of skill in a specific field. For example, the Chrysler Million Dollar Film Festival recognizes up-and-coming filmmakers who compete for the prize at Cannes, France. Once there, the top ten competitors, with scripts in hand, cast the talent from local actors. The films must reflect Chrysler's devotion to sleek design and auto innovation and be shot, edited and completed in just a few days with the help of Avid Technology. Then, the films are viewed and critiqued by a panel of ten, top filmmakers. The film that best exemplified the brand's styling and breakthrough technology was by SungPae Kim from Vaughan, Ontario.

Netflix challenged techies to find or create software that performed at least 10 percent better than its in-house, favorite-film picker: Cinematch. Teams consisted of skilled

Figure 8.3 Big-Reward Contest

statisticians, computer engineers, machine-learning experts and more, who were working with more than 100 million movie ratings. A daunting challenge, the two winning teams tied. The winner? The team that turned in its solution first. It turned out to be BellKor. A 20-minute difference separated the losing team, The Ensemble, from the $1 million prize.

The brand–consumer-engagement contests mentioned earlier arouse more interest in the general public because "anyone" can play. However, more complex, expertise-required contests eliminate most of the population and look to reward the few individuals or teams capable of participating. With that said, brands looking to engage more of their audience members would do better to create inclusive contests.

Branded Apps and Audience Engagement

With the endless number of new, brand-centric or branded apps, just developing an app isn't enough. It has to reflect the core message, entice the audience to "play" along, reward participants and gain new market share. In other words, an app that's not fascinating won't generate a response. Plus, creating an app with multiple digital applications deepens the audience's interactivity.

The apps that connect with the audience and create excitement are the ones that get noticed. Take, for example the Oscar Mayer consumer-created app contest, "Wake Up and Smell the Bacon" (Figure 8.4). Winner of the Best Use of Technology Shorty Award in 2015, it stimulated 67,000 app downloads and generated 520+ earned media impressions. This is the kind of interactive campaign that creates talk value and generates mass appeal. The Oscar Mayer contest enticed 300,000 entrants to participate.[6]

What made this contest so inviting? It used the consumers' imagination paired with their sensory memory of bacon's mouthwatering aroma. Oscar Mayer gave the participants several digital tools. It offered the first-ever alarm clock app and scent-deliverable device. Together, this technology allowed people to actually "Wake Up to the Smell of Bacon." How? Through an app they could use on their smartphones as their wake-up call, while reinforcing Oscar Mayer as the brand to buy.

The challenge was its pricing: above day-to-day bacon brands, while below gourmet. By making the app fun and sensory, Oscar Mayer presented its product worth the slightly higher-than-ordinary-brand pricing. Using social media to gain consumer insight, Oscar Mayer realized that bacon über fans enjoyed sharing their thoughts. So, it monitored them. One

Figure 8.4 Branded App

main point it discovered was how bacon was the favorite morning comfort food, steeped in hard-to-ignore flavor-and-scent nostalgia.

When you examine interactive campaigns, notice which media were used and how they challenged, teased and/or enticed the audience to "play." Always think about what makes the engagement fun and rewarding. It's not always the size of the prize. Often, it's the excitement of the contests and their like-minded competitors.

One example of this is the way Coca-Cola tapped into athletic fans for the 2012 London Olympics. As explained in an article by Giselle Abramovich,[7] Coke featured musician, Mark Ronson, in a video documentary. He went around the Olympic village and chatted with athletes, letting their comments inspire new musical ideas. He integrated sounds from athletic events such as gymnasts flipping, ping-pong balls bouncing, etc. and used them to establish an underlying beat. Teen fans of Mark, who were the targeted audience, could download the Coke app, along with Ronson's pre-recorded beat, and create their own music, remixes and so on. Then, the app users could share what they created online.

Ask Questions First

Before developing a branded app, you must think backwards. What are you trying to achieve by engaging the audience? How can you depict the brand's philosophy? What type of app would be relevant and entertaining? How could the app tie in to the consumers' lives and everyday routines?

Asking questions is one tested way to effectively guide the app's development. With all the expense up front, it would be wise to follow the experts' advice. According to an article in the "Points of View" blog series by Millward Brown, a global brand and advertising consultancy, there are five key questions and sub-questions that compose a strategic metrics for a successful branded app.[8] These include those listed in Box 8.1 below.

Box 8.1 Millward Brown: Metrics for Branded App Success

1. Is the app engaging? Does it draw users in and provide them with an enjoyable experience?

2. How does the app perform from a usability perspective? Is it intuitive? Can consumers find what they're looking for?

3. How does the app perform from a technical perspective? Is it reliable? Does it do what users want it to do?

4. What is the brand's role in the app? Does the app leave users with a compelling impression that is linked to the brand?

5. Does the app encourage users to continue using the brand or to take some specific action?

Brand Gamification Engagement Benefits

More than 63 percent of marketers use data signals to develop target-relevant ad content.[9]

That applies to all media, including gamification. The challenge for brands is to set a clear strategy based on the objectives they wish to achieve. As you've noticed every type of interactivity is based on a specific strategy and not just designed for "fun." Even though games, by their very nature, are entertaining, branded games need to work much harder to embrace and promote the brand's philosophy, core values and message. Once again, the best approach is to check with experts in gaming and digital marketing campaigns. One article by Cormac Reynolds, which was posted on the B2BMarketing blog, listed five important benefits of gamification.[10] These were:

1. Collect and examine consumer insights.
2. Use crowdsourcing to help solve complex business challenges.
3. Make gaming an educational tool.
4. Enable gamification to support local communities.
5. Focus on consumer relevance.

Even after applying these five tips, continue to discover more answers as technology changes. Here's an article by Velly Angelova, posted on Website Magazine's blog, with other insights into the reason why brands create games.[11] They can "boost customer loyalty, employee performance, sales growth and more" in these ten ways:

1. Raise brand recognition.
2. Expand customer base.
3. Deliver in-depth engagement.
4. Increase sales.
5. Keep in-time analytics.
6. Provide entertainment and a polished brand experience.
7. Incentivize customer interaction.
8. Deliver immediate feedback and helpful real-time analytics.
9. Create stronger loyalty bonds to the company.
10. Motivate employees and boost productivity at workplace.

She also reminded us that games must be innovative to instantly deliver brand messages when they connect with consumers on their go-to device: the smartphone. This actually is the most direct channel, which makes it an important digital platform to tap for their attention. It enables brands to target, interact with and continue to engage with a specific audience.

As with all media vehicles, it's your job to learn what campaigns work and why. Look for exceptional examples as references. Make this search a part of your regular routine.

Gamification examples

Keep a close watch for new gamification with brands. Every year, another technology extends apps' capabilities. Successful, branded games deserve your attention. Review articles and blog posts to see what's breaking through and creating talk value. One article by Yu-Kai

Chou, a gamification pioneer offers excellent examples.[12] "Top 10 Marketing Gamification Cases You Won't Forget."

1. Nike+ Fuelband, plus Accessories

The brand message of Nike—fitness and performance—is typified in its gamification. Instead of just staying as a basic app, Nike modified its 2012 design into a friend-to-friend game. By incorporating the Fuelband technology, which monitors wearers' movements, the Nike app allowed fans to follow and trace their activities. They could compare their workouts, as well as their friends', to study the energy expended and calories burned. This allowed users to reach their fitness goals while competing with their earlier performance or that of their "friendly" competitors.

The reward for reaching their fitness goals was a streak or a cartoon character that would enthusiastically cheer their achievements. As users gained more points, they moved up on the scoreboard. But more importantly, they became more physically fit.

This app aligned closely with the brand's and audience's core value. In addition, it added a social interaction among users, making Nike a part of the individual's and group's daily activities; thus integrating the brand into the consumers' lives.

2. My Starbucks Reward

Basing this app on its customers' service focus, Starbucks rewarded its customers with points for each purchase. The points appeared as stars. Once enough points were gained, the stars filled in to become a coffee cup. Customers would eventually reach the highest, or third, level and win prizes. Rewards included free items: food, beverages, birthday gifts, an extra cup of Joe and more.

This app encouraged more visits and purchases by enhancing the standard loyalty reward programs. It enticed consumers to stay longer at its ambience-filled settings, collect more points and enjoy the accomplishment of receiving free rewards.

3. Heineken's Star Player Game

As a brand that has generated exciting online experiences, Heineken combined its official sponsorship of the Champions League game with a branded Star Player Game. To heighten the sports fans' engagement during live games, it encouraged them to interact with the app and predict various possible outcomes. Whether enthusiasts were at home or at the game, they could anticipate and react to plays in real time. Questions that elicited fun predictive responses included: Will the player score the goal by foot? Will the penalty be saved? Will they score within 20 seconds? If players got the right answer, they gained points. More right questions during the game earned more points. Everyone likes to call the "shots." Now they would be rewarded when they made an accurate prediction

Gamification has become another vehicle to execute a brand's marketing and creative strategy. It engages consumers, develops fun interactions among individuals and groups, reinforces the brand's message and drives product sales. When done well, gamification creates a rewarding experience for consumers and an impetus in generating revenue (Figure 8.5).

Figure 8.5 Gamification

Tips for Irresistible Interactivity

In an article by Jared Flamm on the Convince & Convert blog, "Three Ways to Create Amazing Interactive Content," he detailed three specific techniques to develop brilliant, interactive content.[13] He explained its importance like this:

> *It's time for marketers to wake up and learn that if you are not interacting with your audience, you will be ignored.*

It seems simple enough, but it requires innovative ideas to lure the audience into clicking, choosing, leading and following along myriad story lines. When it comes to videos, today just watching isn't enough. You want to invite the viewer to participate. Here are a few examples of how to do it.

1. Interactive Video Marketing

When you invite the viewer to do something, be sure what they're doing is exciting. You can add any of the following.

a. *"Interactive hotspots"*—This technology lets you insert different images, from people to inanimate objects. There are "tags" that are driven by motion. You've probably seen them on websites, apps and games. You click on a door and it opens. You scroll over a tin can and a big garbage bag tumbles out. You brush the cursor over a cat and its hair stands up. How does this connect to the brand? By connecting the clicks to a product benefit. For example when the door opens, it could reveal decorative front door designs. When the garbage falls and the bag doesn't break, it could be advertising a sturdier plastic option. When the cat's hair spikes, it could link to brushes to tame your little "lion's" mane.

Interactive hotspots are fun. They can also be a strong selling tool, as well as a way to boost your audience's brand engagement.

b. *"Tell a story"*—The difference here and in other media, is that you can create multiple situations and consequences, depending on the viewers' choices. First, you need to decide what you want to feature. Then, build scenarios around that. And last, invite the audience to pick and choose different options.

One example is the "Designed to Play" video by Philips. In order to showcase various grooming tools for men, the site started with a story. A guy's shaving, as he's looking into his bathroom mirror. He can't remember what happened the night before. But, he sees lipstick marks on his cheek and neck. Trying to figure out the events, stating that he only remembers himself shaving, he invites the audience to pick a style or "look" for him. Choices include him with a beard, mustache, chin curtain, stubble, clean-shaven and so on. Then, depending on the one they picked, he would transform into the character. Using different accents—Southern, Spanish, French, etc., he would relate what took place. Of course, each style shows him using a Philips shaver to create it. There's also other interactivity that shows all the possible styles with one click, demonstrating the product's versatility. (See it at www. play.philips.com/en/#click-and-style.)

Another fun example is the Agency Pizza Maker site. Immediately, you see a welcome from Gus and Joe. Then, some choices appear. You can "See the menu" or "Make your own pizza." Around the home page are five-star ratings and testimonials. It looks like a real pizza shop. As soon as you click on a choice, an old-fashioned record player appears on the upper right. The "record" spins, with the needle on top, and "plays" authentic Italian songs. The scratchy sound resembles a vintage 78-rpm recording. You can stop the sound whenever you want. Then, the needle moves off of the record and rests on the side.

In the menu section, you see different pizza recipes with the toppings listed. You can "share a pizza" by clicking on the red bar and you're sent to Reddit. In the make a pizza section, you see instructions and then a pizza appears, waiting for you to add toppings. Just click on your choice and click to place that ingredient on top. You can make designs, images and whatever else you want on your pizza. Then, a pizza paddle places it in the oven. You can hear the pizza baking. Just hit "OK" and the paddle takes it out. You then can choose sauces to top it off. It's so much fun, you want to keep making pizzas (Figure 8.6). (Play along at www.agencypizzamaker.com/.)

But, the site isn't selling pizzas. Instead, it's a pitch for two creative talents to get an agency interview. The home page mentions a free delivery for a lunch meeting with two creatives. But, the type is light and so small you don't notice it. Then, at the end, when you "Click here for more info," you "get it." The ah-hah moment hits and you realize you're being invited to see their portfolios and contact them. Without question, this is an innovative way to get an agency job in the creative department. It demonstrates strength in conceptualization, social media, design, sound and interactivity.[14]

In this case, the brand is a creative team that "branded" itself as the Agency Pizza Maker. Who are they? Two art directors from Sweden: Gustav Hedström and Joel Utter. More impressive than the website is that they developed it in 2010!

Figure 8.6 Interactive Tips

Key point: Jump into creative video interactivity or you'll be left behind. Be proactive. See what's out there and include new technological touchpoints. Find ways to wrap interactivity as you design your campaigns. Think of new methods to entice your audience.

2. Reveal-Based Marketing

Some intriguing techniques are those that have a "slow reveal." That means that the consumer has to figure something out or take some action to see the "answer." This approach draws the audience in by stirring their curiosity while delaying their gratification. The result is a lured and challenged consumer who is ultimately rewarded in an exciting way. Review the following types of reveal-based marketing.

Games—These include different rewards. The consumer participates by doing something before seeing what they "won." They might scratch to reveal the "prize," spin something to see the discount or play a game to discover the promotion.

Problem Solving—Here, consumers are challenged to demonstrate their skills by figuring out puzzles, riddles or drawing pictures (Figure 8.7).

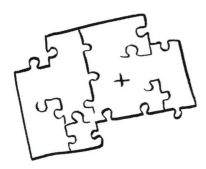

Figure 8.7 Problem-Solving Game

Motion Interactions—These are particularly intriguing because they ask people to shake, move or tilt to see the deal.

Key point: Apply technology to deliver the message, including online via e-mail, mobile and social media interactions.

3. Polling

Why would they polls work? Because they 1) solicit feedback from your target; 2) create a dialogue with the consumer, demonstrating your (the brand's) interest in their opinion; 3) expand the interaction by reaching the audience twice. First, in the poll and second, in the results. If the poll is enticing enough, it might result in the Holy Grail of campaigns: going viral. Here are three types of easy-to-adopt polling tools:

a. *Polldaddy*—a quick-to-learn software survey that lets you create not only polls, but also surveys, quizzes and ratings.
b. *Wedgies*—an interactive tool that enables you to embed it into your blog.
c. *Poptip*—a real-time polling method that allows you to develop and evaluate polls on two social popular social sites: Twitter and Facebook.

Key point: Polls give you the ability to create a consumer–brand dialogue in a fun, easy and valuable manner.

Above all, if you're not engaging with your audience, some other brand is. Why make it that much easier to lose touch, or even worse, to lose your target?

Stay Current on Winning Strategies

It's not enough to just have an understanding of interactive strategies. You need to keep abreast of the trends and which tactics (media choices) are working. One way to do this is to read through industry-related trade publications, such as *Adweek* and *Advertising Age*, as well as online websites and blogs for exceptional examples of effective and award-winning work. One place to keep informed is on content-deep blogs that discuss these campaigns. Check out the Shorty Awards for the Best Use of Social Media, Apps and Video[15] and the Cannes Lions Award. Here's one recognized example.

The Domino's emoji celebrated campaign let consumers place their favorite, pre-saved orders by tweeting the pizza emoji (icon). This time-saving idea showed the impact of "word of web" and hashtags' shareability. Having the "cool factor" encouraged people to share the fun. The campaign also expanded the way Domino's received orders, impacting its mode of operation. By making it easier to order from Domino's, it resembled other one-click online orders from major companies, including Amazon. It won a Titanium Grand Prix Cannes Lions Award.[16]

If you know where the message will appear, you can immediately think about how to create media-appropriate and audience-relevant content. You must think multiple vehicles, not just one when developing the strategy. In fact, when it comes to the different vehicles, you probably will have to tweak and customize your approach. When Old Navy created a back-to-school promo, it considered the viewing habits of its targeted consumer.

More and more brands are finding ways to create a brand-specific strategy that can work in myriad social media settings. In addition, they're using videos as a way to engage their audiences in interactivity. They're also connecting digital and offline platforms into an interrelated campaign. Smart marketers are customizing messages to directly reach their core markets. Finally, they're utilizing consumer data to mold their strategic direction.[17]

More about Innovative Mobile and Digital Uses

Following blogs that discuss trends will help you develop a reference of inspiration from which to spark your imagination. For example, Allison Schiff brought to light some of the most innovative and interactive campaigns of 2014[18] on the AdExchanger blog (http://adexchanger.com). She showcased unforgettable, creative and strategic ideas. First, the demise of the banner ad is mentioned because it hasn't evolved past its origin in 1994. Without any animation and interactivity, it's just a print ad that's online. However, when it offered "shoppability," as in number one below, it moved into the digital age. Now, marketers who understand the importance of consumer–brand interaction are dominating through the application of technology. Here are a few examples. (For all eleven examples, go to http://adexchanger.com/online-advertising/a-banner-year-for-innovative-mobile-and-digital-ad-units/.)

1. Shopbeam: Shoppable

This interactive capability called Shopbeam is often referred to as "AdShops." It allows the advertisement to become a type of shopping cart (Figure 8.8). So viewers can make purchases without leaving the website they're currently on. This prevents customers from being sidetracked by landing on another site to buy.

Figure 8.8 Shopping Links

2. True[X]: Mid-Roll Replacement

With this technology, you'd see the same high-definition clarity as on a normal TV spot. But, you'd have a choice of an ordinary two-and-a-half-minute commercial or a 30-second interactive one that returns you to the show you were watching. Many people would choose the spot because that option is engaging and shorter. It might include a short survey about the brand. For example, if the ad were for a cereal, the short survey would allow the advertiser to learn about the tastes and shopping preferences of that particular viewing audience. It might show visuals of different breakfast items and ask: Which one would you choose if you were dieting?

3. Kargo: Gyroscope

Designed to specifically run on a mobile device, it allows users to see various types of animation depending on whether they tilt, rotate or shake their digital device. We've already discussed how Tic Tac integrates this tool.

4. mNectar: Playable

The benefit with this tool, which accesses streaming technology, is that mobile users can use the app or game without having to be bothered with downloading. It serves as the modern-day free trial or "try-before-you-buy" sales technique.

5. Klick Push: Music

With this technology, brands can add music to their ads. Created from the music-focused Klick Push, ADjams lets users download their music choice from pre-selected free songs. All they have to do is provide the advertiser with their e-mails. The songs are then sent to their e-mail addresses, where the recipients are redirected to the brand's website. Consumers get free songs that they've personally chosen and brands get an opportunity to converse with potential customers, as they learn which songs users preferred.

6. betaworks/Tapestry: Storytelling

For Tapestry, part of betaworks studio, the name embodies the consumers' action. They should "tap" to continue. The beauty of this type of engagement is that it allows the brand to tell its story and show how the product works. Colorful visuals are paired with simple instructions. All users have to do to learn more is to keep tapping the screen. This model is particularly helpful for brands that want to teach or share information. This would include step-by-step recipes that clearly show how to make a favorite food like quiche. Tapestry boasts that more than half of engaged consumers (54 percent) go through all the steps, spending an impressive three minutes on each ad.

The reason you want to keep studying the market is that you'll find out about exciting and innovative mobile ad applications. These examples, in turn, will help spark novel ideas. Continue to examine and notice which of these and other new technologies are driving strategic solutions. These strategies can and should be considered in future campaigns you develop. Don't stop today. Keep on challenging yourself to create unique advertising opportunities by blending traditional and interactive media both in online and off-site brand messages.

7. Zumobi: Immersive

Creative consumer–brand interaction was the heart of the Zumobi experience. Consumers could share the fun with their friends. For example, while they planned parties together, they could also view and decide on snacks, discover and download drink recipes and save all their activities to their mobile home screen in the app (Figure 8.9). One successful example was for Sauza Blue Tequila, which garnered a five percent click-through rate and a 74 percent consumer–ad engagement.

Figure 8.9 App and New Technology

In Summary: Interactive Strategies

Brands are connecting to customers where they are: on Instagram, Snapchat, Twitter, Vine, Pinterest, Tumblr, LinkedIn and elsewhere.

In looking at these digital campaigns, realize that consumer connectivity is the heart of the strategy (Box 8.2). More and more marketers recognize that the Internet of Things (IoT) will grow in the future. Today, it's computers, smartphones, tablets and wearable devices. People are connected to their homes' electricity, appliances, security devices, etc., and to their cars' alarms, directional devices, smartphones and more. Soon, all electronics will be connected to consumers so they can access any "thing" anywhere in real time.

Box 8.2 An Overview of Interactivity

1. *Create a relationship between brand and consumer*

2. *Use entertainment to build the brand*

3. *Engage and reward audience*

4. *Consider big-reward contests*

5. *Develop strategic-driven, branded apps*

6. *Ask questions before app development*

7. *Examine the benefits of brand gamification*

8. *Collect excellent gamification, app, digital, social media and other online and offline campaign examples*

9. *Review tips and key points for irresistible interactivity*

10. *Stay current on successful campaign strategies*

11. *Learn how new technologies apply to interactivity*

Interactive Strategy Exercises

Exercise 1: Select one interactive campaign and use it in another interactive media. Be sure that it:

a.   Is relevant to the audience.
b.   Is rewarding and fun.
c.   Is able to tell the brand's story, principle or core value.

Exercise 2: Find one branded app that targeted a specific audience. Answer these questions:

a. How did you know which audience it targeted?
b. How did it engage the consumer?
c. What was the audience's reward for using the app?

Exercise 3: Identify one brand that used gamification successfully. What specific elements made it work? For example, it replicated the brand as in the Tic Tac "Shake It." It encouraged individual goals and group engagement as in the Nike+ Fuelband.

Exercise 4: Which multiplatform campaign used broadcast (TV/radio) and print? Where else did the message appear?

Exercise 5: What campaign excelled in multiple platforms, such as digital, social media, gamification and so on?

Exercise 6: Find an example of an online and digital campaign that focused on consumers' real-time engagement, such as apps that tie into sporting events.

Exercise 7: Select an app that went beyond frequent-user rewards, such as My Starbucks Reward.

Exercise 8: Name another example of a campaign that created a "wow" using digital and traditional media, such as Cool Ranch Doritos Locos Tacos.

Notes

1. "Coke Zero: Drinkable Billboard," June 5, 2015, www.youtube.com/watch?v=jdvteFAmG_k (accessed July 28, 2015).
2. Designzzz. "50 Brilliant Magazine Print Ads," August 8, 2013, www.designzzz.com/magazine-print-ads/ (accessed July 17, 2015).
3. Book of Button, www.bookofbutton.com/Taco-Speakeasy (accessed January 25, 2015).
4. www.bookofbutton.com/Cool-Ranch-Doritos-Locos-Tacos (accessed August 14, 2015).
5. Kelly Roncace,"Wasabi Ginger Chips Winning Lay's $1 Million Prize is 'Biggest Blessing,' N.J. Woman Says," *South Jersey Times*, October 21, 2014, www.nj.com/gloucester-county/index.ssf/2014/10/westvilles_meneko_mcbeth_is_the_winner_of_lays_do_us_a_flavor_chip_contest.html (accessed February 22, 2015).
6. Kristina Monllos, "Check Out 2015's Shorty Award Winners for the Best Use of Social Media, Apps and Video," March 23, 2015, www.adweek.com/news/advertising-branding/check-out-2015s-shorty-award-winners-best-use-social-media-apps-and-video-163627 (accessed August 11, 2015).
7. Giselle Abramovich, "The Coke Mobile Way," January 17, 2013, http://digiday.com/brands/the-coke-mobile-way/ (accessed August 2, 2015).
8. Millward Brown, "What's App with Your Brand, Branded Apps," December 2013, www.millwardbrown.com/Insights/Point-of-View/Whats_App_with_Your_Brand/default.aspx (accessed August 24, 2015).
9. Celtra, "Using Data to Inform Ad Content," *Adweek*, March 30, 2015, M4.
10. Cormac Reynolds, "Five Benefits Gamification Can Bring to Your Marketing Business," June 19, 2015, www.b2bmarketing.net/blog/posts/2015/06/19/5-benefits-gamification-can-bring-your-marketing-business (accessed August 13, 2015).

11. Velly Angelova, "The Real Reasons Brands Gamify," www.websitemagazine.com/content/blogs/posts/archive/2015/04/29/the-real-reasons-brands-gamify.aspx (August 14, 2015).
12. Yu-Kai Chou, "Top 10 Marketing Gamification Cases You Won't Forget," www.yukaichou.com/gamification-examples/top-10-marketing-gamification-cases-remember/#.Vc5e90Wi1TU (accessed August 14, 2015).
13. Jared Flamm, "Three Ways to Create Amazing Interactive Content," August 26, 2014, www.convinceandconvert.com/digital-marketing/3-ways-to-create-amazing-interactive-content/ (accessed June 30, 2015).
14. Margo Berman, *The Copywriter's Toolkit: The Complete Guide to Strategic Advertising Copy* (London: Wiley-Blackwell, 2012), 273.
15. Monllos, "Check Out 2015's."
16. Jack Neff, "It's Simple: Tweet Emoji. Get Pizza Delivered. Win Grand Prix," June 27, 2015, http://adage.com/article/special-report-cannes-lions/simple-tweet-emoji-a-pizza-delivered-win-a-titanium-grand-prix/299255/ (accessed June 28, 2015).
17. Greenspace, "Five Interactive Advertising Trends for 2015," January 15, 2015, www.creativebloq.com/advertising/interactive-trends-2015-11513901 (accessed July 1, 2015).
18. Allison Schiff, "A Banner Year for Innovative Mobile and Digital Ad Units," January 5, 2015, http://adexchanger.com/online-advertising/a-banner-year-for-innovative-mobile-and-digital-ad-units/ (accessed July 14, 2015).

9

CAMPAIGN STRATEGY
Architectural Model

Every campaign combines all of the strategies discussed in previous chapters. Each is a block that builds and braces the overall design. Step one is the development of the creative strategy you plan to use. You determine this by reviewing the client research, its competitors and the core audience. Then, you decide on the tactics you'll use to execute the creative strategy. The tactics appear as the touchpoints or places where you'll reach the audience, including online, offline and through brand-centric social media vehicles. Summarized in the Creative Strategy Statement and spelled out in the Creative Brief, these structural beams support the entire campaign.

The campaign "structure' begins with the foundation laid out in the brief. Without this base cemented into place, the campaign will not be structurally sound. Go back and review Chapter 1, if you don't fully recall the questions outlined in the brief. In fact, take a moment to browse through Chapters 5, 6 and 7, which discuss verbal, visual and media strategies. Every campaign combines all of the strategies. So, let's take a look at some of the ways to group myriad media to facilitate the creative solutions.

Groups of Media Choices

With online, offline, on-air, digital, interactive media, blended and earned media, let's identify which ones fall under these seven categories (Box 7.1). This list will help you think through your options more quickly. In addition, notice the strength in blending both traditional and ever-changing new media. Realize that now, many messages include a way to purchase via 800 numbers, click buttons on social networks, QR codes, mobile coupons and so on.

1. *Online*—This includes videos, consumer-created content, podcasts, websites, animated and the now-less-popular banner ads and Internet radio and talk shows.
2. *Offline*—This covers out of home, transit, print, direct mail, point of purchase, ambient, signage, etc.
3. *On-Air*—This consists of radio and television.
4. *Digital*—This appears on mobile devices, such as smartphones, tablets and yet-to-be-invented portable tools.
5. *Interactive*—This consists of social media (Twitter, Facebook, LinkedIn, Instagram, Pinterest, blogs, etc.), branded apps, brand-sponsored social media, games, contests, yes, even direct response (Figure 9.1).

6. *Blended*—This combines traditional and engaging media, as in cross promotions that might blend interactive billboards with smartphones, branded social media, apps, as well as on-air and other traditional media.
7. *Earned*—This occurs when the campaign generates free publicity through press coverage, social media shares and viral buzz.

Box 9.1 Seven Media Groups Review

1. *Online*

2. *Offline*

3. *On-Air*

4. *Digital*

5. *Interactive*

6. *Blended*

7. *Earned*

Figure 9.1 Interactivity Between Brand and Consumer

Many campaigns use combinations of media choices, customizing each message to target a specific audience. Astute strategists create relevant content that engages their audiences on their favorite platforms. Always recheck if you have the same audience(s) and if these consumers have changed how and where to access content. As new touchpoints develop, audiences have more options, dwindling time and limited attention. Therefore, they are confronted with the onslaught of more than 10,000 daily media messages and the challenge to keep up. Brands that connect to and engage with their audiences create that emotional bond that welcomes a two-way conversation.

Expertly crafted and branded content, such as apps, games, contests and other interactive vehicles, can not only entertain and engage the audience, they can also inform and influence them. When considering how to create this relationship, examine as many effective campaigns as you can. Then, deconstruct them to discover the strategy or strategies used and the universal truths, which we discussed earlier in Chapters 1, 3, 5 and 7.

For each strategy, you want your audience to notice, remember, interact with and share the brand communication, think of these six "R" words:

Only *relevant* content that *resonates* with authenticity gets *recognized, recalled, responded* to and *"recycled."*

Seven Types of Powerful Campaign Strategies

The Creative Brief acts as your blueprint for each campaign. In addition to determining the audience, tone of voice, point of view, visual and typographic design, media vehicles and specific touchpoints, you also need to consider what specific type of strategy you want to use (Box 7.2). Refer to these as the foundation of the campaign.

Box 9.2 Seven Campaign Strategy Categories[1]

1. *Consumer-focused*

2. *Brand-centric*

3. *Savings-driven*

4. *Emotional appeal*

5. *Storytelling*

6. *Interactive engagement*

7. *Combination of strategies*

Here are explanations of each category with easy-to-recall examples.

1. *Consumer-focused*—These campaigns are easy to identify because they stress consumer benefits, such as weight loss, workout equipment, health foods, vitamin and nutritional supplements and so on. They could also focus on safety, such as car tires, childproof-cabinet locks, home-security and smoke alarms.

2. *Brand-centric*—These messages center on brand and/or product features. They might talk about selection, award-winning construction, durability, portability and strength, etc. Examples would be the many products at Wal-Mart, car models recognized for their design, Duracell batteries for longevity, tablets for their light weight and Super Glue for its stickiness.

3. *Savings-driven*—Think about coupons, sales and special promotions, BOGO offers, frequent shopper rewards, time-limited savings and so on.

4. *Emotional appeal*—These quick-to-recall campaigns impact viewers on an emotional level. They might feel sympathetic, sad, inspired or entertained. Many famous Super Bowl commercials fit here. The beloved Volkswagen "Darth Vader" spot, as discussed in Chapter 3, takes viewers from disappointment to amazement. A little boy, dressed in costume, tries unsuccessfully to show his powers on items in the house—the washer and dryer, exercise machine, his sister's doll and even his dog—through outstretched arms. Then, he goes outside and reaches out to the family car. Dad, watching from inside, hits the remote and starts the car. Surprised, the little boy believes his powers really worked! (This spot also fits under the seventh category "combination of strategies," because it tells a story.)

5. *Storytelling*—These campaigns take the audience on a journey. Often, emotional appeal is used. One funny commercial is the 2008 Heineken "Closet" commercial. Friends are over at a couple's home. The girls go into the hostess's new, dream closet and all her girlfriends scream with excitement. Meanwhile, the host takes the guys downstairs to show them his "dream," wall-to-wall beer room and they start shouting enthusiastically. Each group hears the other's screams, but can't figure out why. No women would get thrilled over a ton of beer and few men would care that much about a closet. There's the irony. So, there's an emotional appeal strategy, too (Figure 9.2).

6. *Interactive engagement*—Campaigns that create an interaction between the brand and the consumer build a stronger relationship. As we've already mentioned, these can include games, apps, contests, social media, interactive billboards and more. The next time you're involved in participating, ask yourself: "What made me join in?" This act of self-observation will heighten your awareness of consumer motivations.

7. *Combination of strategies*—Many campaigns do this; however, the Budweiser Clydesdale spots are irresistibly heartwarming (emotional), tell a little story (storytelling) and

Figure 9.2 Storytelling as a Campaign Strategy

are usually voted the fan-favorite Super Bowl spots. The ones that use anthropomorphism (assigning human emotions to the non-humans) are perfect examples. Check out these spots and see how they use many strategies. "Hank" (2008), "American Dream" (2010), "Brotherhood" (2013), "Puppy Love" (2014) and "Best Buds," (2015) are particularly adorable.

Storytelling: A Valued Strategy

Found in all media, storytelling, when expertly designed, can create talk value, earned advertising (free press), consumer sharing and more relationship building between the brand and consumer. These little mini movies, or vignettes, can generate positive responses, profitable outcomes and memorable impressions.

Often rich in universal truths, fortified with emotional content, stories that deliver brand messages, as in other types of advertising, are frequently tested for their effectiveness. Various techniques are used. One of these is pre-testing or copy testing. Researchers ask people in focus groups their opinions and reactions to the copy before it is used in a campaign. Their responses indicate the impact of the story or other type of message. Does it sound believable, authentic and relevant? Was it clear or confusing (ad consistency)? Did they like or dislike it (general impressions)? Did it trigger an emotion (emotional effect)? Would they share (tell others about) the story? Would they respond to, interact with or use the brand, product or service (usage effect)? Would they consider making a purchase (overall ad appeal)?

Copy testing is used as a predictor of its future performance. Before executing and distributing the message, you want to know the answers to these and other questions. Does it create:

1. Audience attention?
2. Brand awareness?
3. Purchase motivation?
4. Emotional response?
5. Ad recall?
6. Clarity of message?[2]

Gaining consumer insight into what makes them take action after seeing the copy (Figure 9.3), in a storytelling or other type of ad, gives you the tools to construct a solidly built campaign.

Figure 9.3 Purchase Motivation

According to Sarah Walker, solutions director at Millward Brown, a global brand and advertising consultancy:

If done right, storytelling can make your communications more engaging, more impactful, and more motivating for your brand.[3]

Well-designed stories, which build one scene upon another, are persuasive brand communicators that impact, influence, engage and motivate an audience (Figure 9.4). To measure a storytelling ad's overall effectiveness, Millward Brown uses global neuroscience techniques. These monitor, record, interpret and code the viewer's facial expressions. The consumers' response to key questions shows how well the ad performed. If it worked, fine. If not, it is revised to improve its success. Storytelling ads created more facial reactions, increased attention, heightened enjoyment and higher recall. Walker also commented:

The most successful messaging occurs in stories where the brand's role is necessary, believable, and integral to the plot.[4]

Brand stories can also work as a trigger that connects the product to a consumer experience. Many products "cue" the consumer to think of another. Holidays like Thanksgiving often become a cue to buy all ingredients related to the "feast." Many seasonal campaigns, especially supermarket messages, deliver little stories with families gathered around the festive, holiday table. These serve as reminders to shop for everything at once. For example, visuals of the famous String Bean Casserole prompt people to buy Campbell's Condensed Cream of Mushroom Soup and French's French Fried Onions, while they're picking up string beans.

Remember to think about how to inject "cues" into ads to stimulate a subconscious connection to the brand and its uses (Figure 9.5). Blending these reminders into the story helps solidify the message in consumers' minds. Walker stated that there are three main points and key takeaways when using storytelling in a campaign.[5] These were:

1. Stories can help brands to engage people.
2. Facial coding can determine if storytelling is working for the brand.
3. The stories told need to be appropriate to the brand and its objectives.

Figure 9.4 Storytelling Ads

Figure 9.5 Brand "Cues"

One important fact to know is that not all story ads are stronger than non-story ads. Without a clear and integral connection to the brand and its message, storytelling narratives can fail to register with the targeted audience. The story and the brand must work in harmony, with one supporting the other.

Symbiotic and supportive relationships are equally important between the message, the platform and the audience. Today, recognizable and remembered promotions engage consumers by creating multiplatform, in addition to multimedia campaigns.

One Core Idea with Many Stories

One storytelling example is the Subaru campaign, reviewed in Chapter 3: "Love. It's What Makes a Subaru a Subaru." Told in several media, including print and TV, each story reiterates the common theme: love.

The stories demonstrated relationships, including touching father–daughter scenes, such as: 1) the "Baby Driver" spot where the dad realizes his baby is growing up and 2) "Cut the Cord" commercial with the dad watching his little girl boarding the bus for the first day of school. They demonstrate the dad's feeling of protection and love as he watches her go away.

To target dog lovers, Subaru also created humorous multigenerational, dog scenarios, such as these: 1) "In the Dog House," where the male dog is eyeing a pretty poodle crossing the street when he gets a growl from his dog "wife." 2) "Road Trip Convenience Store," where the family of dogs on a trip, stop by to pick up a few snacks, use the rest room (naturally, to drink out of the toilet) and blow dry their "hair" before they leave.

The "Love" campaign is just that: lovable.

There have been many print ads that are connected to the "Love" campaign. Some used the entire slogan. Others didn't. One with the slogan showed two Subaru drivers parked next to each other, holding hands. The other, without the slogan, used the word love in the headlines. Here are a few examples: "Share the Love Event," "A Lot to Love Event" and "Pack In More of What You Love."

Even though you might notice the "Love" ads, it's the TV spots that might come to mind first. Maybe it's because television engages two senses not just one: sight and hearing. Online videos spark a third: touch. The focus is: love of family. These included father–daughter and people with their family dog. Another campaign, which showed the word "love" in animated form, closed with a different slogan: "Confidence in Motion." Again, it built stories around the families. Some of these included various family members. Others featured the Barkleys, a family of Golden Retrievers, with the key phrase: "Dog Tested. Dog Approved." At the close of one spot, a brand-new car was immediately assaulted with wet-dog "head shakes"; spilled dog-food bags; and kids' dirty socks, shoes and diapers. It ended with this sad-but-honest promise: "You don't have to put up with that new-car smell for long."

In short, all of the "Love" campaigns were relatable and endearing. Take a quick look at some of these touching commercials.

1. *Love. It's What Makes a Subaru a Subaru.*
    a. "Father–Daughter"(2010)—www.youtube.com/watch?v=6F3-InOdMP4
    b. "Dream Weekend" (2015)—www.youtube.com/watch?v=tmuwxUnKOlI (Music: "My Buddy, My Pal, My Friend" by Willie Nelson)

2. *"Love" and Confidence in Motion.*
    a. "New Car Smell" (2013)—www.youtube.com/watch?v=i8EBm9VXhxM
    b. "Road Trip Convenience Store with the Barkleys (2014)—www.youtube.com/watch?v=VDut1RkQP_s&list=PLJ4EyrO-Ww7YggzptiCnoKe4-l7F19aqW

Of course, this campaign uses the combination strategy: incorporating many types of above-mentioned strategies:

• Consumer-focused (the benefits of owning a Subaru)
• Savings-driven ("Love" events at dealers)
• Emotional-appeal (family ties)
• Storytelling (various family-centric stories).

In addition, it used several universal truths:

• *They grow too soon*—"Father/daughter" stories
• *Love conquers all*—"New Car Smell" spot
• *Your happiness is my happiness*—"Dream Weekend" commercial
• *A penny saved is a penny earned*—"Love" events

Of course, you could think up other universal truths for ads. Those unspoken messages resonate with everyone. Parents seem to turn around and their daughters and sons go from toddlers to brides and grooms over night. Dads who once cherished the "new car smell" for as long as possible, acquiesce to the it-doesn't-last-at-all reality of life with kids and pets. Dog lovers can't spoil their pets enough. And, the universal-yes question: "Who doesn't like to save money?"

At the core of every conceptual and media strategy, are key reasons why they were successful. Analyze why. Remember to review how the audience-relevant messaging, media choices and platform selections worked in harmony to depict the brand with authenticity, while emotionally engaging the consumer.

Multiplatform Campaigns

Knowing where consumers access content is key to selecting the appropriate platform(s). These platform-specific vehicles are touchpoints where the brand and audience intersect. These constant "collisions" result in interactions. The most powerful "impacts" generate more interactivity. The more relevant the content, the stronger the emotional bond. The following campaigns exemplify strategically targeted platforms.

Notice how each one embraces both where the consumers follow their areas of interest and how brands create venues where they can interact in an enriching and entertaining way. These can entertain, inform, persuade, reward and of course, engage consumers.

1. Foot Locker—"Horse with Harden"

Foot Locker teamed up with NBA expert shooter, James Harden to generate excitement and a real-time experience. During a one-week period, fans were invited to tweet and upload videos of their coolest shots on Instagram (@Footlocker #horsewithharden). They were challenging superstar Harden to a game of Horse, played on courts around the country. Players dare one another to beat each other's best shots. As each shot gets harder than the previous one, the contest demands escalate.

In this interactive, multiplatform campaign, Harden demonstrated the best shots and attempted to top them. Playing in an undisclosed location for a few hours, he posted the scores and tweeted the results live. Fans could follow along and see how their shots measured up. This event not only replicated the thrill of being at a live game, but it made fans feel as if they were playing against a basketball legend (Figure 9.6).

Figure 9.6 Engage with Idols

Through social media, Foot Locker reached NBA sports enthusiasts, engaging them in on-target platforms, wherever they were, using any of their mobile or digital devices.

During the weeklong event, the Foot Locker challenge generated an increase of 300 percent in its YouTube channel subscriptions. In addition, it attracted press attention, from national news and top sports blogs to numerous websites. Combined, they represent an audience of around 61 million.[6]

2. Virgin America—"Free Love Field" (Advocacy Campaign)

Wanting to promote fair airline competition and create a vehicle for consumers to voice their opinions, Virgin America used traditional, digital and social media. This was a novel multimedia and multiplatform campaign. Driven both by PR-type events including a seem - ingly spontaneous press conference and tours. Even Richard Branson led a "pep rally" to promote the idea that healthy competition relieves consumers' financial travel pains. The campaign spread through social media, driven by a single change.org petition and www.freelove.com microsite to integrate all of the airline's social media engagement touchpoints: Twitter, Facebook, Google+ and Instagram. By incorporating easy-to-share images, charts and infographics, Virgin clearly explained the competition-related consumer benefits.

To reinforce its point, Virgin America created special "Love Field" gates at Dallas airport. There, travelers to and from this location would enter or exit these gates and become more aware that open-market competition is in their best interest. They would have more travel options paired with reduced fares at "Love Field." In short, the campaign portrays the famous motto: "When airlines compete, consumers win." (See the video at www.youtube.com/watch?v=je6-h8DPmUM.)

3. Airbnb—"Is Mankind?"

The provocative question is posed: Is man kind? This simple phrase is a play on words that really asks "Is Mankind?" but, meaning all of humanity. Who are we? Are we compassionate? Welcoming? Open? Well, as children—here used as a metaphor for travelers—we don't know. What will we find in a new city or country? How will we be received?

Many travelers feel scared and isolated, as if they are not part of this new place. Airbnb plans to change that. It wants people to discover other cultures, stories and insights from the locals. To feel as if they belonged there. To feel welcomed everywhere they'd go. To not feel like a stranger, but instead, like a member of the universe of mankind. To feel kindness, especially from those we just met. To travel and feel the acceptance of "mankind." Travelers were invited to share their stories of the kindness they found in the world. They were encouraged to become part of the dialogue "kindness exchanges" at #Mankind. (See the video at www.youtube.com/watch?v=2xegsh1CmPU.) This campaign used TV, social media and consumer–brand interactivity. Through the photos and comments of travelers around the world, the campaign depicted how people can feel connected and welcomed wherever they are.

Ambient and Interactive Campaigns

Brands that surprise their audience with a unique and inviting experience can garner instant attention, participation and shareability. The first flash mobs did that. Then, once they became popular, they lost their initial intrigue. Creating an equally exciting "event" is challenging and rewarding.

1. Reebok: "Run the Movie"

Unsuspecting audiences at movie theaters in Seoul discovered an ambient, interactive invitation. Expecting to just sit down and watch an action film, they were surprised when the movie suddenly stopped and two treadmills were spotlighted in the first row. Within a few minutes, curiosity overtook a few moviegoers. They got up from their seats, sat down on the treadmills and they started pedaling (Figure 9.7). Immediately, the film started to play again. Other members of the audience realized that the only way they were going to see the entire movie was to keep the treadmills moving.

The audience had fun, got a workout and helped each other finish the show. Reebok found a way to engage a normally passive audience to become part of the "action." The event attracted press coverage, shares and buzz.[7] (See the video at http://creativity-online.com/work/reebok-run-the-movie/43046.)

Here's another successful, ambient and interactive Reebok campaign.

Figure 9.7 Run the Movie

2. Reebok: "Get Moving, Get Pumped"

Again in South Korea, Reebok "woke up" robotic, daily commuters with a surprise. They looked up and saw their faces projected on a large screen. Once, they noticed it, they saw a message that asked them to play along by pushing a start button. They hear "one, two, three" and they jump into action. Suddenly, they find themselves thrust into the middle of a game. They automatically engage and find out the winner would get a free pair of Reebok ZPump Fusion sneakers. Catching the audience off guard quickly converted ordinarily reserved commuters into one-on-one "gamers." This gave the brand a chance to deliver a message: the introduction of another model, while rewarding successful players.[8] (See videos at http://eugenianazarova.com/?p=472.)

3. Google: "Words-into-Poetry" Billboard

Google created an interactive billboard, with 17 LED panels and microphones, to showcase its Google Speech Platform.[9] It launched at King's Cross, a London train station adjacent to Google's headquarters. The Poetics project invited commuters to say whatever they wanted into the microphones. Using its voice-to-text technology, Google Speech, it translated the words into spontaneous, unrelated lines of poetry.

Designed by the winners of London's Central Saint Martins School of Art competition —Laura Ventura Ricart, Yunqi Cai and Emily Kimura—this innovative campaign engaged students and commuters through Google technology. Campaigns that introduce and remind consumers of new inventions or products in a fun, entertaining way establish unforgettable brand moments through "edutainment."

4. Hugh Acheson: "Endangered Eats—Save the Flavors"

Using a seemingly offensive message is risky. However, when the campaign reveals and a different meaning, the audience's first negative impression is replaced and rewarded with a positive, brand-focused one.

This is the approach that Hugh Acheson, celebrity chef, used. Looking to demonstrate that almost-extinct vegetables should be revered as much as extinction-threatened animals, the chef invited guests to eat endangered animals on a one-day event at Empire State South, an Atlanta restaurant. The uproar from PETA and other environmentally conscious gourmands spiked the attendance of curious attendees.

As the people were about to begin their lunch, Acheson informed them that they would only be tasting the Cherokee Purple heirloom tomato. He wanted to highlight soon-to-be-gone fruits and vegetables in a "Save the Flavors" concept. Surprised guests learned how, just like the world's animals, the plants are also on a path of no return. They were reminded that by saving them from extinction, consumers are also preserving their unique flavors.[10] (See the event at www.youtube.com/watch?t=27&v=V2kAU4EDcAA.)

Social Change Campaigns

These promotions are designed to affect the consumer. They can change public perception, shift core beliefs, influence behavior, initiate action, spark controversy, as well as generate participation and support. Let's see how the following campaigns changed their audiences.

1. PG Tips Tea Bags "Monkey"

The PG Tips Tea two-per-brew idea campaign consisted of many components. It began by introducing its tea bags in the shape of the number 2." Each package included several kettle stickers to remind tea drinkers to count to 2 for each "cuppa" (cup of) as they fill the kettle.

The problem was how to stop 75 percent of Londoners from wasting two million liters (half a million gallons) by overfilling their kettle when making tea. Currently, Londoners consume 11 million cups of tea ("cuppas") per day.[11]

Two-second messages appeared on YouTube, TV and radio, with Side Kick, a sock "Monkey" puppet, voiced by comedian Johnny Vegas, delivering them. He appeared on TV and videos wearing pajamas and a white, terry-cloth bathrobe. After he sang a two-second chorus, he challenged viewers to make their own two-second videos using the "2" tea bags. Monkey would recreate each one. Then, the most popular submissions became TV ads with sock Monkey acting out the suggestions. For example: Monkey "Ice, Ice, Baby."

Figure 9.8 Save Water

The campaign also used print ads in London's free newspaper with the slogan, "Saving the world. So easy a human can do it." Posters appeared all along the walls next to the escalators. Each two seconds, the ads would "fill up" in color, reminding commuters to count to two when they prepare their morning "cuppa" (Figure 9.8).

Social media invited people to have someone else make them a "cuppa." They'd receive a customized message from Monkey. Counting to two per "cuppa" would change the way millions of Londoners would prepare their tea, which currently uses 11 million cups of water per day. That would save enough energy to power half of London's streetlights for one entire year.

2. Subaru: "Share the Love"

Since 2008, Subaru has run its annual "Share the Love" campaign. Within a set time frame, these charities, ASPCA, Make-A-Wish, Meals on Wheels Association of America and National Park Foundation, would receive a $250 donation from Subaru for each new or leased vehicle. Customers would pick where the donations should go. Retailers, also, could add a local charity for which they wanted to raise funds.

The TV spots, "How it Feels," launched the promotion. It showed images of grateful recipients, including elderly people enjoying their meals, shelter dogs being petted after their rescues, Make-A-Wish children smiling after having their wish granted. Supported by broadcast and digital media, the campaign was a feel-good, pass-it-forward experience. It reminded consumers that while they're getting a new car, they could be part of giving back to those in need.[12] (See the spot at www.youtube.com/watch? v=W7fPJuGL5tA.)

3. UNICEF: "The Photo Speaks for Itself"

Although many companies want consumers to "like" them on Facebook, UNICEF explained in a conversational tone, "Hey, a 'like' does nothing. So donate." One ad showed children getting vaccinated and stated:

Like us on Facebook, and we will vaccinate zero children against polio.

This clear statement shows how ineffective a "thumbs up" is to address hunger, poverty, disease and other life-threatening challenges. The copy said that for only four euros, twelve children could get a polio vaccine. That's another way to reinforce the idea that donations help. Likes don't.

Here, UNICEF took a brave stand. It was daring and risky. However, the message made you rethink how little more it took to make a big difference. A "like" isn't enough, but just four euros are.[13]

4. Water is Life: "#FirstWorldProblems"

With so many companies, brands, nonprofits and so on, trying to create a video that goes viral, very few do. When it happens, everyone agrees that it worked. When it doesn't, it's difficult to say why. The Water is Life campaign launched with a provocative video that started out as something difficult to watch. Then, it revealed how silly many of our everyday complaints really are. The video showed scenes of impoverished people living in shambles, without running water or safe roofing, stating petty, unrelatable annoyances that start with "I hate it when . . ." Here are a few examples. "I leave my phone in the bathroom." Or, "I tell them no pickles and they still give me pickles." Or even, "My mint gum makes my ice water too cold." Some were people in tattered clothes. Others were children in a room with rows of bunk beds. Several more were adults in broken-down, rubble-strewn homes. These images were a bleak contrast to what we call "problems."

Picture a man standing in front of a one-room-in-need-of-repair shack quietly stating with a smile, "I hate it when my house is so big, I need two wireless routers." This scene points out the incongruity between the visual and verbal content.

The videos were so gripping, they instantly went viral and spread the word via social media, using #FirstWorldProblems, to support one cause: clean water. Viewers and sharers were asked to donate at http://waterislife.com/donate to help bring fresh water to those without any. (See one video at www.youtube.com/watch?v=fxyhfiCO_XQ.)

Strong Single-Medium Events/Campaigns

Some brands create a one-time event, focus on a single medium or establish brand awareness with a specific vehicle or platform to deliver the message. This doesn't mean it only uses that one exclusively. It just means that it's easily recalled. Think about the effectiveness of the "1984" Apple commercial. Or the pre-recorded beat app in the 2012 Coca-Cola sponsorship of the Olympics (in Chapter 8). Or the instantly recognizable Oscar Mayer Wienermobile. Keep in mind that one event or even stunt might be a consideration when planning a strategic campaign. Here are a few examples to use as a handy reference.

1. Netflix: "Orange is the New Black" Parisian Stunt

Sometimes one single event creates interest in a specific location. For example, Netflix chose Paris for its stunt to promote another season of the popular TV series *Orange is the New Black*. The entire front of a building was transformed into a multi-floor, outdoor prison. The top floor was painted in orange with the show's title.

The "prisoners," who replicated the cast from the show, arrived in a bus, wearing standard incarceration-wear: orange jumpsuits. Escorted by "policewomen," they disembarked and climbed up the metal steps to their cells. Once there, the female prisoners interacted with each other and the crowd of onlookers, who gathered to take pictures. The "Orange is the New Black" signage explained to the crowd what was going on: a promotion of the show.[14] (See the video at www.youtube.com/watch?t=17&v=dyC6lsZ7l2M.)

Mainly Mobile Campaigns

Some campaigns primarily use mobile messages. These allow brands to directly reach their audience where they "reside," as well as to offer interactive, entertaining engagement. Mobile campaigns can, as we mentioned earlier, employ games, apps, virtual experiences and so on. Let's look at a few of these up close.

1. Guess: "Virtual Sunglass Try-Ons"

What do most people do before buying sunglasses? Try them on, of course. To solve the problem of not being able to do that online, Guess created a mobile ad that let consumers see how the glasses looked by taking a selfie of themselves. It also guided them by suggesting which frames looked best on various face shapes from round and oval to square and oblong.

With the tech help of Kargo, the "Try On" ad accessed the phone's camera and connected it to the mobile ads and videos. Millennials, the target audience, just had to click on the "Tap to Explore" link to open the ad. Instantly, they could try on different styles and do what they do best: share their selfies on social media (Figure 9.9).

Not only did this ad let people play with the frames, it made it easy and convenient. They didn't have to wait for someone to open a case and show them the frames. Or wait their turn at an optical store. Or feel rushed. They could take their time and try the frames on over and over to compare their photos as often as they wanted.

This was a consumer-focused strategy. It was all about the benefit of shopping on consumers' time. In the privacy of their mobile "home": their preferred platform.[15]

Figure 9.9 Try on Guess Sunglasses

2. Triscuit: "Trial for Limited-Edition Flavor"

When Triscuit introduced its new flavor, Toasted Coconut & Sea Salt, it created native ads (designed to specifically work in that platform) and increased its mobile engagement. To drive a trial for its first limited-edition Triscuit flavor, it first teamed up with Martha Stewart and then focused on 1) developing native mobile ads on Facebook and 2) connecting to Pinterest through promotions placed on the boxes. To encourage consumers to try the limited-edition flavor, it did three things. First, it offered recipe tips. Second, it explained ways to create new snacks ideas. Third, it showed a Triscuit box beside images of possible ingredient combinations on the crackers. The everyday party techniques and recipes served as inspiration for creative pairings. The link to Triscuit on Pinterest made the purchase doable with one click.[16]

3. Schick: Interactive Mobile-Optimized Videos

To push its Xtreme3 razors, Schick USA invited its male audience to list their three indispensable everyday comforts. Choosing from a list of ten, such as coffee, smartphones and Xtreme3 razors, "players" had the chance of winning them all. Lutz, the oddball video host from "Comfortopia," reacted in a silly way to their choices. By sharing their picks on social media, they would be eligible to win. When they picked one of Schick's razors, Lutz would describe its advantages and someone in the background would perform a stylized dance. The mobile-designed video was shown as one of Onion's dedicated microsites (www.comforts ofman.com/video). This humorous approach tied into Onion's satiric tone of voice and resonated with its comedy-loving fans.[17]

4. Google Cardboard

Teaming with digital production firm, B-Reel, Google developed a pick-up-and-play prototype: Google Cardboard for Nexus 5 and 6. Once downloaded, players would find themselves in a virtual reality setting, where they would have the hands of George, a 160-foot giant. Now, they were stuck with huge, oversized hands in a Lilliputian-type world. Everything was almost impossible to do because his "big, stupid hands" always got in the way and destroyed whatever they touched. Just as King Kong could knock down buildings, now players could, too. All they were trying to do were simple, mundane tasks like picking up a brother from school or playing soccer with buddies.[18] With the easy-to-use app, gamers had a great time dealing with this challenge.

Just as in all the examples above, brands optimized the mobile medium to create instant interactivity with their markets. Participants had a lot of fun, while being introduced to or reminded of the brands' features.

Rebranding Campaigns

Sometimes brands have a difficult time bouncing back from having lost market share, image and/or appeal. Companies like Cadillac and Hush Puppy shoes have reinvented their brand images and attracted new audiences. Both were perceived as stodgy, old-fashioned brands. Today, they're cool and popular. So how do brands turn themselves around? Here are a few ways.

1. *Product redesign and improvement*—enhanced Gillette razor models.
2. *Appeal to a new audience*—Cadillac.
3. *Recapture a former audience*—Lego.
4. *Produce a product-centric movie*—Federal Express in *Castaway*.
5. *Personalize the brand's products*—custom labels in Burberry products.
6. *Introduce a fresh brand ambassador or embrace an unplanned one*—Michelle Obama wearing American and other designer brands from Michael Kors and J. Crew to Jason Wu and Jean Paul Gaultier.
7. *Incorporate social media to engage the consumer*—Domino's Pizza Emoji ordering campaign.
8. *Update the packaging everywhere: on- and offline, including retail sites*—new store designs, menus and advertising at Wendy's.
9. *Develop an upscale version or limited edition with an imported label*—Apple watch with Hermès design and logo.
10. *Adapt to social attitude changes*—e-cigarettes.

Now, let's look at a few examples of big-name rebranding campaigns. Notice the specific techniques they used to achieve their image.[19]

Figure 9.10 Branded Movie

1. Lego

You may not realize that the beloved Lego blocks would be losing their ground. What's gaining traction against this more than 100-year-old, classic toy? You probably already know. Kids now are entertaining themselves with video games, apps and social media.

Almost in bankruptcy, the brand rebuilt itself in the late 1990s and it never stopped looking for opportunities to boost its appeal. The popularity of its 2014 release of *The Lego Movie* restored its top-of-mind awareness (Figure 9.10). How? By reminding adult fans of their childhood passion: building anything they could imagine with Lego bricks. Suddenly, the movie reawakened their memories and they wanted to share their favorite pastime with their own children.

Through social media channels, such as Facebook, Twitter and Pinterest, Lego attracted almost 300,000 Twitter followers. The ongoing consumer engagement and shares generated more and more fans, resulting in the resurrection of the brand. It repurposed consumer-created content. It also rekindled in yesterday's fans the excitement they had when they showed creations to family and friends. This was reminiscent of their childhood exclamation: "Hey, look what I made!" Now, their children are saying the same thing.

2. Burberry

To make the brand seem fresh again, it bought back 23 right-to-use product licenses with other companies to regain quality control. Plus it focused on 1) customization, 2) technology and 3) cool brand reps, such as movie star Emma Watson and super model Cara Delevingne.

One often-mentioned campaign, "The Art of the Trench" (http://artofthetrench.burberry.com), features images of fashionable people wearing the timeless design. The celebrated trench has morphed into different colors, lengths and details, but it still remains the indisputable, go-to coat.

Recognizing the trend for personalization, people can order a coat off the runway and have their names or initials added to the label. Burberry knows how to engage its audience both on runways, websites and social media.

3. Old Spice: "Does Your Man Look Like Me?"

As mentioned in Chapters 3 and 7, Old Spice really spiced up its outdated image. Once considered the aftershave scent for granddads, it immediately replaced that image in 2010 with a half-dressed, perfectly built athlete: former NFL player Isaiah Mustafa. It went from musty to must-have in a viral second. How could it not? Mustafa was either atop a horse or dripping with water in a shower.

The campaign had Mustafa look into the camera and invite women to look at their man, then back to him. It resonated with a younger audience and sparked millions of online views and social media shares. The fact is that sales of Old Spice Body Wash increased by 11 percent within a year of the campaign's launch. It was listed as one of the ten most successful rebranding campaigns in history on www.businessinsider.com.[20]

Campaign Strategy Summary

Campaigns execute the Creative Strategy Statement that is detailed in the Creative Brief. Together, they created the underlying support to all conceptual, audience-related, verbal, visual, media and platform strategies. Media choices can be grouped into these seven basic solutions.

Seven Media Groups Review

1. Online
2. Offline
3. On-Air
4. Digital
5. Interactive

6. Blended
7. Earned

In addition to these media choices, there are also seven core campaign strategy categories. These will help refine your creative solutions. They'll remind you of possible options that would work best to build a foundation for relevant, brand–audience communication. They are listed here.

Seven Campaign Strategy Categories

1. Consumer-focused
2. Brand-centric
3. Savings-driven
4. Emotional appeal
5. Storytelling
6. Interactive engagement
7. Combination of strategies

When looking to test your copy before releasing it, you can use these questions to help predict if your message is resonating with the audience. Keep these questions handy as you develop your campaign. They will help you focus on how to strengthen your promotions.

Ask Yourself if Your Campaign Prompts . . .

1. Audience attention?
2. Brand awareness?
3. Purchase motivation?
4. Emotional response?
5. Ad recall?
6. Clarity of message?

As you move through your decision process, consider using the storytelling strategy. Remember, it must both tell the brand's story and relate to the audience. You may want to add facial coding to determine the viewer's reactions and guide you in tweaking the message. Adding product "cues" to your message will ignite the consumer's desire to save time and shop for several items at once. The truth is that storytelling ads only rate higher when the brand and story work in unison.

Three Key Points to Remember

1. Stories can help brand to engage people.
2. Facial coding can determine if storytelling is working for the brand.
3. The stories told need to be appropriate to the brand and its objectives.

In summary, reference the previous chapters and integrate those principles into your campaign structure. Then, consider how they could all come together in one cohesive brand message. Always remember to think about where the consumer accesses information. Determine which touchpoints would work best as media intersections. Continue, in your development steps, to set building blocks that will offer solid support, with one reinforcing the other. Messaging should be an exciting and engaging two-way exchange.

Campaign Strategy Exercises

Exercise 1: Find one campaign that uses interactivity in an innovative way. Explain the following:

a. How it engaged the audience.
b. The type of interactivity: game, app, interactive billboard, contest and mobile, etc.
c. Whether the audience shared it on social media.

Exercise 2: Discover one campaign that generated media buzz, resulting in earned media. Answer the following:

a. What is the brand or product?
b. What made it outstanding?
c. How did it reinforce the brand?

Exercise 3: What Super Bowl spot used an emotional appeal strategy?

Exercise 4: Name a campaign that motivated you to buy the product? Where did you see the message: online, on your smartphone, TV, radio, magazine ad, out-of-home, etc.?

Exercise 5: Identify one brand-centric campaign. Answer these questions:

a. In which media did it appear?
b. Did it use social media? Which ones?

Exercise 6: Go to YouTube and find two campaigns for two different brands or companies that used a storytelling strategy. Answer these questions:

a. Did the stories portray the brands' messages?
b. Were they relevant to the target audience?

Exercise 7: Cite one campaign that used both traditional media, interactive and social media with instantly relatable universal truths. How did these truths drive home the brand's message?

Exercise 8: Identify one campaign that expressed a universal truth. Answer these questions:

a. What was the brand?
b. What was the universal truth?
c. Did it make the campaign stronger and more memorable?
d. Why? (For example: It spoke to a specific audience. It showed a consumer benefit. It highlighted a unique feature.)

Notes

1. Margo Berman, *The Copywriter's Toolkit: The Complete Guide to Strategic Advertising Copy* (London: Wiley-Blackwell, 2012), 18-23.
2. Margo Berman, *The Copywriter's Toolkit: The Complete Guide to Strategic Advertising Copy*, 11.
3. Sarah Walker, "The Power of Storytelling," June 2015, www.millwardbrown.com/Insights/Point-of-View/The_Power_of_Storytelling/ (accessed August 13, 2015).
4. Sarah Walker, "Power."
5. Sarah Walker, "Power."
6. Shorty Awards, http://industry.shortyawards.com/nominee/7th_annual/opL/horse-with-harden (accessed August 19, 2015).
7. Ann-Christine Diaz, "Reebok Makes You Run to Watch This Movie." August 19, 2015, http://creativity-online.com/work/reebok-run-the-movie/43046 (accessed August 22, 2015).
8. Eugenia Nazarova, "Get Moving, Get Pumped in the Subway with Reebok in Korea," April 17, 2015, http://eugenianazarova.com/?p=472 (accessed August 22, 2015).
9. Alexandra Jardine, "Google Turns Your Words into Poetry with an Interactive Billboard," August 27, 2015, http://creativity-online.com/work/google-poetrics/43099 (accessed August 29, 2015).
10. www.creativeguerrillamarketing.com/guerrilla-marketing/seeds-change-invites-eat-endangered-species/ (accessed August 29, 2015).
11. www.dandad.org/awards/new-blood/2014/unilever-solve-megacity-problems/2595/saving-the-planet-so-easy-a-human-can-do-it/ (accessed August 29, 2015).
12. http://media.subaru.com/pressrelease/704/1/subaru-launches-share-love-campaign (accessed August 27, 2015).
13. www.nonprofithub.org/social-media/the-top-4-nonprofit-social-media-campaigns-of-2013-and-what-you-can-learn/ (accessed August 27, 2015).
14. www.creativeguerrillamarketing.com/guerrilla-marketing/netflix-transforms-building-facade-prison-promoting-orange-new-black/ (accessed August 27m 2015).
15. Michael Barris, "Top 10 mobile advertising campaigns of Q2," July 1, 2015, www.mobilemarketer.com/cms/news/advertising/20785.html (accessed August 21, 2015).
16. Chantal Tode, "Mondelez's Triscuit Tries to Close Gap between Inspiration, Trial on Social," June 23, 2015, www.mobilemarketer.com/cms/news/advertising/20720.html (accessed September 27, 2015).
17. Alex Samuely, "Schick Sharpens Mobile-Optimized Interactive Video to Promote Razors," April 16, 2015, www.mobilemarketer.com/cms/news/advertising/20236.html (accessed September 29, 2015).
18. Ann-Christine Diaz, "Your Stupid Big Hands Get in the Way in B-Reel's Virtual Reality Game," August 19, 2015, http://creativity-online.com/work/breel-stupid-big-hands/43045 (accessed August 22, 2015).
19. Kitty Dann and Matthew Jenkin, "Back from the Brink: Five Successful Eebrands and Why They Worked," July 23, 2015, www.theguardian.com/small-business-network/2015/jul/23/five-successful-rebrands-why-worked?utm_content (accessed July 29, 2015).
20. Judith Aquino, "10 Most Successful Rebranding Campaigns Ever," February 10, 2011, www.businessinsider.com/10-most-successful-rebranding-campaigns-2011-2?op=1&IR=T&IR=T (accessed August 27, 2015).

10

GLOBAL STRATEGY
Architectural Blueprint

As we've seen in earlier chapters, strategic thinking guides the overall campaign direction. Each component needs to be included in the creative process. As advertising teams develop the campaign, they move through each step, checking that each is on-strategy. These steps include the:

1. Conceptual idea
2. Audience insights
3. Verbal message
4. Visual communication
5. Multimedia choices
6. Multiplatform integration

Box 10.1 Strategies for Global Campaigns

1. *Universal Truths (as described in Chapters 1, 3, 5 and 7*

2. *One Unified Message*

3. *One Modified Message*
   a. One core message that is slightly modified
   b. Several messages for myriad markets

4. *Audience- and Culture-Specific Campaign*

5. *Media-Specific Campaign*

6. *Interactive Campaign*

7. *Educational Campaign*

8. *Cause-Related Campaign*

They become the actual blueprint from which to build the message. Without a clear plan, the advertising would not reach the target market(s) with a relevant, clear and authentic brand position.

The entire structural foundation lies in the development of ideas that address, resonate with and respond to audiences' needs and desires, as well as their core values. What's important to the target should be clear in the ads.

Before we continue, let's take a quick look at a few possible global strategies you may want to incorporate when creating an international campaign (Box 10.1).

Universal Truths

One way to begin thinking about a core message is through the use of universal truths. To review, these are common sayings that most people can agree on and accept. People of all ages, cultures and nationalities understand the basic meaning. Although it might be stated differently in other languages, the intent behind it is the same.
Here are few examples.

> *The best things in life are free.*
> *Use moderation in all things.*
> *Patience is a virtue.*
> *Waste not, want not.*
> *Look for the silver lining.*
> *Practice makes perfect.*
> *Don't cry over spilled milk.*

There are, of course, many more. The challenge is to use one that tells the brand's story and is relatable to the audience. Often, these globally adopted phrases are implied and not actually stated. They communicate on a deeper level, which is why they can manage to bypass consumers' ad-aversion blockers.

Here is one example of a TV spot that speaks to the heart of parents with teenagers. The spot shows a teen dressed in Goth clothes and makeup as she enters school. Kids stare at her, toss a frog on her desk and avoid her. It's obvious. She doesn't fit in, especially in gym class when the others girls are in white uniforms and she sits on the sidelines in her self-imposed, all-black attire. Nothing changes as she walks home after school. People gawk in

Figure 10.1 Universal Truths

horror when she passes by. No wonder. Her black hair, dark nails, brooding eyeliner and morbid outfit disrupt the commonly adopted *mode actuelle* or current fashion.

Then, as she opens the gate to her home, she notices wet, black paint on her hands. She looks down and sees a black pathway up to her home, where her dad is on a ladder painting the entire house black. She smiles for the first time. So, what could be the universal truth?

> *I'd do anything for my daughter.*
> *There's nothing like a parent's love.*
> *See the world through someone's eyes.*
> *If you can't beat them, join them.*

It doesn't matter which one of these or others is relevant to you. What matters is that the bond between parent and child is universal. Regardless of country or culture, it touches the deepest part of each of us. It's penetratingly profound.

The dad created a bridge to connect with his withdrawn, solitary daughter. He joined her in her Goth style and made her feel welcome in a disapproving world. Not a word was spoken. The only thing that was felt was love.[1] (See the commercial at www.youtube.com/watch?v=Cmg8ghXhAt8.)

One Unified Message

Even when you're using one specific message, there are many ways to present it. Just deciding on one core idea is only the beginning. Next, you need to consider how to execute. Which strategies will you use? Which creative direction? What kind of copy (verbal communication)? What type of visuals? Which media? Which platforms? What kind of consumer engagement? In short, what tactics or execution, such as consumer touchpoints, will you incorporate?

Before selecting one strategy for developing a single idea, let's review a list of possible options (Box 10.2). Look these over as you start your conceptual process. Don't forget to find other approaches as you continue to review effective campaigns.

These strategies can be used one at a time or in combination. Let's look at a few examples. First, we'll see how a campaign used these strategies together to: 1) spark an emotion (#3), 2) reflect the audience (#5) and 3) portray brand value (#8). In China, Listerine wanted to encourage people to use mouthwash twice a day. It created the "Kabe-don" campaign featuring film-star heartthrob, Gregory Wong. It showed one important, social benefit of using a mouthwash: getting close to someone attractive whom you want to meet. To do this, Wong demonstrated a common, passion-filled move called "Kabe-don" as shown in manga comics. The words translate into "wall" (kabe) and "hit" (strike). Kabe-don describes the action done when a character slams his open hand(s) against a wall, close to the girl he wants to impress. It's a masculine move of passion, not violence.

In the video, Wong used his Kabe-don move and discovered, as he got closer to the girl, that her breath wasn't fresh. He backed off. Viewers were left thinking about themselves in a similar scenario (audience reflection), wondering if they'd pass or fail an unexpected, up-close encounter. As they became concerned about their breath (emotional response), they were reminded of the value of oral care. Although, using Listerine twice a day also fights dental-disease-causing plaque, the focus was on the instant, not long-term, benefits of the brand.[2]

Box 10.2 Strategies for One Message

1. *Engage the audience*

2. *Share humor*

3. *Spark an emotion*

4. *Reward the consumer*

5. *Reflect the audience*

6. *Epitomize consumer opinions*

7. *Show compassion*

8. *Portray brand value*

9. *Reinforce brand positioning*

10. *Change audience perception or behavior*

11. *Support a cause*

12. *Play with the audience (Figure 10.2)*

Now, let's look at a second campaign that combined two strategies: 1) engage the audience (#1) and 2) change audience perception or behavior (#10). A particularly clear example is the Volkswagen "Think Blue" campaign, which ran in various areas of Russia.[3] Volkswagen customized vending machines, changing the coin slot for one that would allow consumers to "deposit" old batteries as credit to get free items from various local stores. They could choose from T-shirts, stress balls, bottles of water and so on. In just one month, one machine collected more than 8,000 batteries compared to 1,000 deposits in the preceding year at an ordinary, designated collection place. (See the video at www.youtube.com/watch?v=4Cm3kDmgSqc.)

Here's a third campaign that integrated several strategies: Heineken "Dream Island." It engaged the audience (#1), sparked emotion (#3), rewarded the consumer (#4), changed audience's perception (#10) and played with the audience (#12).

It invited people at bars around the world to confide their dreams over a beer. Then, they were entered into a contest to win a dream vacation: an all-expense-paid week in Thailand. The six winners were flown to a deserted island. When they arrived, they found the dream they expressed was actually fulfilled. One guy, who wanted to sail around the world, found an abandoned sailboat on the beach. Another young guy found the beachfront

Figure 10.2 Play with the Audience

bar he dreamed of owning, with his name on it. A third winner, who wanted to be a rock star with a red guitar, found a band set up with a red guitar at the front. Each was amazed to discover their dreams waiting for them, as they read Heineken signs stating, "Don't let your dreams die." Instantly, they got the message: Don't abandon your dreams. They just might come true. Heineken can keep them alive just as one passion can fuel another. (See the campaign at www.youtube.com/watch?t=4&v=wLSJzmMCcIs.)

Let's move to the next strategy: relevant global messaging. Here, we'll see two ways to accomplish this, in addition to using one core message.

Relevant Global Messaging

With many ways to develop on-target, on-strategy campaigns, let's simplify them down to two. These would be 1) modified messages for different cultures and 2) several messages for myriad markets. This will help you focus your creative energy on two specific strategies.

Often campaign concepts need to be "transcreated" (or recreated in another language) for various cultures. Just translating might not work because the meaning is lost or the literal translation means something entirely different in a different language. For example, "Got Milk?" when translated means, "Are you lactating?" in Mexico.[4]

So, the question becomes how do you decide whether to just translate, transcreate or create a similar, but localized message?

1. *You must look at the question strategically.* Start by carefully responding to this list of questions:

    • Which key campaign points are relevant in that area of the world?
    • Should you focus on other messages instead?
    • Are the core brand values, promises and features relatable?
    • Do the benefits solve local needs or desires?
    • Would one main message work or do you need to create several campaigns?

2. *Next, evaluate the creative content and execution.* Think about answering these questions:

    • Do the campaign headlines have the same meaning when translated?

- Would the headlines work better if transcreated (slightly modified to clarify the meaning) or completely rewritten for each audience?
- Do the visuals fit the audience and culture? Are they appropriate or offensive?
- Are the core brand values, promises and features relatable?

3. *Lastly, review the local culture and attitudes.* Consider the following:

- Does the core idea need to be completely changed for this region?
- Do the messages in the headlines need to be rewritten and/or completely changed to mean more to the local audience? Do you need to add more cultural references, such as idiomatic phrases or colloquialisms? Do you need to reflect popular beliefs? Finally, does the message sound authentic and relevant?
- Do the visual references need to be further refined to feel authentic to people of that region?
- Do the media and platform choices need to be revised to hit more consumer touchpoints?

You also might want to study the original six cultural-differentiation categories established by Dutch professor Geert Hofstede. These are commonly referred to in many articles and books on global marketing. They are frequently listed as follows.

1. *Power distance*—How do people of different ranks interact? Do lower-station workers challenge or instantly accept or bow to authority? Or do the powerful believe only a few should have it? In short, is it equally or unequally distributed?
2. *Individualism*—Does this society revere individuals' accomplishments or does it honor collective achievements more? (Figure 10.3)

Figure 10.3 Individualism

3. *Masculinity*—Does the region support the male role model in the workplace? Does the society praise men for their accomplishments authority and power? Or are women considered equally capable of recognition for their abilities? Is it centered on competitiveness (masculine-oriented leadership) or encouragement and acknowledgment of others' efforts (feminine-type leadership)?

4. *Uncertainty avoidance*—How well or poorly do people tolerate a lack of structure, uncertainty or unexpected events?

5. *Long-term orientation*—Does this society work toward long-term goals by saving, building with perseverance for future rewards and preserving nature? Or does it have a short-term point of view, blending yesterday and today, respecting tradition, slowly building relations, believing in national pride and committing to its social obligations? Societies with short-term orientation enjoy finding happiness right now, rather than carefully protecting tomorrow's peace of mind.

6. *Indulgence*—Are people in this culture allowed to have more freedom to have fun? Or are they more restricted in the way they view gratification, preferring more stringent standards of behavior? It boils down to this: indulgence or restraint?

As you look at global campaigns, consider how the message is crafted to speak to the audience. Think about how these categories influence the design of a brand's communication, as discussed below.

Why These Different Approaches Matter

Before developing a global strategy, you must first understand cultural differences and beliefs. That means you wouldn't talk about how much fun social media is if they have a more rigid society or are long-term oriented. Those consumers might think fun activities are a waste of time (#6 Indulgence reluctance). Instead, they would praise you for developing skills needed for future success (#5 Long-term orientation).

Campaigns that challenge superiors or are irreverent to elders would be offensive to cultures that believe in respecting authority (#1 Power distance). This means that each campaign needs to be strategically and methodically examined and prepared for each region. What are the language's nuances? What are the audience's core values? How do they relate to ambiguous or unfamiliar situations (#4 Uncertainty avoidance)? What is their business climate? Is it masculine-oriented with a male-dominated hierarchy or more of a nurturing type of environment?

Understanding the audience on many levels is crucial in crafting an effective campaign. It must be sensitive to the common *mores* (customs) of the culture. Then, you need to look at how the visual and verb communication matches that specific society. Words, such as "glocal" and "cultural adaptation," explain how global brands make their message relevant and authentic (Figure 10.4). Still, questions must be asked to accomplish this. Which media

Figure 10.4 Glocal

would be most effective? What do you need to tweak, revise or redo for that campaign to resonate with that audience?

Just for simplification, here are three methods: 1) one message for multiple markets, 2) one core message that is slightly modified or "transcreated" and 3) several messages for myriad markets for a multi-themed communication.

Global companies strive to design relatable messages. They create advertising that is relevant and authentic to global and local markets. These are called "glocal" and "cultural adaptation" campaigns.

1. One Message for Multiple Markets

Realizing how instantly people respond to their names, Coca-Cola presented an unforgettably innovative idea: Put the most popular names on its cans and bottles. Who wouldn't be thrilled to see their own name on Coke? As we discussed in Chapter 4, it was an instant hit! Not just in the USA, but also across the world.

Originating in Australia in 2014, it swept the globe being noticed, loved and shared. A simple, direct message, it didn't need any translation. Just invite people to "Share a Coke with ____(name)." Then, show people's names and everyone immediately "gets it." Starting with 250 million cans and bottles targeting Australia's population of 23 million, it continued to excite people in 70 countries, including Turkey, Great Britain, Spain, China and finally the USA.

The unexpected response was that people lined up to customize a Coke at kiosks. But, they didn't use their own names, they created surprise bottles and cans for loved ones serving overseas, recovering at hospitals and visiting over holidays. They also created virtual bottles to share on social media. People saw their names in lights on giant digital signs. People in Sydney, Australia could submit names and hope to see them light up. In preparation for the probability of profanity, the campaign included the preparation of a list of more than 5,000 blocked words.[5]

In short, this singular idea resonated with people from all background, cultures and nationalities. It broke through with the power of one singular, enticing, play-along message.

In 2014, Pepsi-Cola launched its "Now is What You Make It" soccer-focused campaign to appeal to current global fans and attract more U.S. fans. This campaign, which launched in Brazil, moved around the world, inviting soccer and sports fans to interact with a video. Participants could change the story in the video by clicking on different pop-up icons. Once they did, the video would freeze and give a shutter click as if they took a picture. Or the frame would stop and a soccer player would reach his hand out inviting you to write your name in the blank box that pops up. Then, he'd sign the ball, inserting your name into this phrase, "_____(name). You are my hero." He'd hold the ball up for you to see.

Pepsi, as it has done in many campaigns, included celebrities, choosing the most popular ones from a particular region. In Brazil, it featured these soccer stars: Leo Messi, Sergio Ramos and Jack Wilshere. In the U.S., it highlighted Seattle Sounders star Clint Dempsey.

The music behind the 30- and 60-second TV spots and two-minute interactive video was an updated version of the David Bowie hit, "Heroes," sung by Janelle Monae. The chorus of "We can be heroes for just one day" drives home the point that people everywhere can achieve their goals. In the background, Stony, a digital-beat, YouTube sudden celebrity, provided the percussion accompaniment, with one sound that resembled a spray-paint can being shaken.

A true competitor, the Pepsi campaign launched the same day as its rival Coca-Cola, the soccer-sponsor for the World Cup, released its campaign.

What's interesting to note is how both brands used interactivity in different ways. Coke had people order customized bottles and cans both online at kiosks. Consumers could also send in name suggestions. The word spread quickly and personalized Coke became the coolest Christmas gift.

On the other hand, Pepsi invited consumers to interact with a video that allowed them to enhance, change and score points by clicking on suddenly appearing icons. Although the Pepsi "Now is What You Make It" campaign went global, it didn't reach the enthusiastic response of the "Share a Coke" campaign.

2. One Modified ("Transcreated") Message

To promote *FIFA 16*, a soccer ("football") simulation video game, EA Sport, the design team, worked with global communication firm, Freedman International, to develop a campaign that created buzz. Here are a few reasons why. It was the first in the series to feature female players. It released a seamless transcreation and localization of the message.

This $40 million global campaign, which ran throughout Europe, America and Asia, included digital media and television spots across the world. It customized ads for different formats on YouTube, Instagram and Facebook. An online promotional video used a famous Neapolitan song "Funiculì, Funiculà", animation and world-class sports celebrities who displayed great moves from Sergio Agüero, Pele Alex Morgan to Kobe Bryant. The spots and videos were tweaked to work in different languages. For example, the voiceover would be in English along with French subtitles. The slogan "Play beautiful" became *Faites du beau-jeu* in French.

Just watching the promotional two-minute videos and commercials made the game seem breathtakingly exciting. Mixing live action with animation, in addition to high action, fast plays and authentic characters made the game seem live. If you weren't a gamer before, this is the kind of enticement that might convert you.

3. Several Messages for Myriad Markets

IKEA advertised in several countries. Although the messages are similar, they are specific to each country. This is often called "cultural adaptation," as mentioned earlier.[6] Both the visuals and the concepts changed for each market. Here's a list of the messages and visuals in several of the countries, which included Sweden, Norway, Italy, USA, United Kingdom, Turkey, Russia, Portugal and China (Box 10.3).

Once you look at the campaigns, you can easily see how people would see the connection to their region and IKEA. Playful and fun, the images and language tell the brand's story and how its products can benefit consumers. This wonderfully clever campaign works so well because of the marriage of the visual and the copy and the perfect pairing of the "bride" (brand) and "groom" (audience) (Figure 10.5).

Audience- and Culture-Specific Campaign

In 2015, McDonald's created 24-hour, around-the-world events. As part of the "imlovinit24" campaign, the "Gifts of 'Joy'" event started in Sydney, Australia and traveled the globe,

Box 10.3 Messages for Myriad Markets

Country	Message	Visual
1. China	*"Create More Space"*	a) Furniture out of blocks like a video game b) People and furniture spelling out words c) Various size cabinets show more storage
2. Portugal	*"Live Your Home"*	Whimsical, tropical images, such as: a) A bikini stretched around a dresser b) Flip-flops under each table leg c) A Hawaiian shirt draped around a lamp base
3. Italy	*"You Get More"*	Furniture made out of IKEA cartons: a) Beds b) Desks c) Lamps
4. Germany	*"Play"*	Floor plans that spell out words: a) Play b) Create
5. USA	*"NY Gets Flat-packed"*	Iconic New York cityscape miniatures are made out of IKEA boxes, depicting: a) Area around the Empire State Building b) One of Manhattan's many bridges

Figure 10.5 Marriage of Brand and Audience

Box 10.4 List of McDonald's "24-Hour Gifts of 'Joy'" Events[7]

1. *Have A Ball Café*—Sydney

2. *Motorbike Drive-Thru*—Ho Chi Minh City

3. *Sound Bites*—Auckland

4. *McTollBooth*—Manila

5. *McD Photo Booth*—Tokyo

6. *Fry Luggage Tag*—Guangzhou

7. *Pajama Party*—Milan

8. *Pajama Party*—Catania, Italy

9. *Big Mac Song*—Seoul

10. *Jingle Bench*—Warsaw

11. *BigMacSelfie*—Dubai

12. *Giant Jigsaw*—Madrid

13. *Welcome to McDonald's*—Toronto

14. *Party Up*—Hong Kong

15. *McOrchestra*—Vienna

16. *McBike Thru*—Copenhagen

17. *Romania's Joy Maze*—Bucharest

18. *Big Mac Fashion Show*—Stockholm

19. *Ice Coupon Machine*—Rio de Janeiro

20. *Pop Up Library*—Paris

21. *Jessie J Boom Bus Tour*—London

22. *Crazy Straws*—Mar del Plata

23. *People in Concert*—Lisbon

24. *Ne-Yo's Lovin Anthem*—Los Angeles

ending up in Los Angeles, USA. Its interactive, fun experiences rewarded participants with free food, free books and more. For example, in Sydney, commuters could interrupt their normal morning routine by jumping into an outdoor, giant inflatable cup of lightweight, colorful balls. As they exited, they received a free McCafé coffee as a reward.

That moment of 'joy' continued with a tollbooth, which was converted into a McDonald's pick-up window. Unsuspecting travelers didn't pay tolls. Instead, they received a free McDonald's breakfast. Other events included a Paris pajama party. People who showed up in PJs, got a complimentary breakfast up until 10 a.m.

Other events included a free concert in the USA of international R&B hit maker Ne-Yo, who performed the original "Lovin'" theme song: "Every Day with Love." People who couldn't attend, could see it unfold at the http://imlovinit.com. (See the campaign at www.youtube.com/watch?v=As-p6OxGTIQ.)

The campaign included social media, which invited Big Mac fans in New Zealand on Facebook to jump in. Londoners enjoyed a free concert by pop musician Jessie J, who performed on an open, double-decker bus. It also incorporated various sound effects at the events to enhance the experiences. Videos were posted online to heighten event awareness. Millions of people around the world were involved in a 24-hour period (Box 10.4).

Media-Specific Campaign

Using primarily social media, focusing on Twitter, Facebook and Instagram, Vogue Eyewear featured female celebrities from three areas of the world: Brazilian top model Adriana Lima, Indian actress Deepika Padukone and Chinese star Liu Shishi. Famous, glamorous stars instantly speak to fashion-focused women, who are following trends through social media.

Vogue Eyewear wanted to project its brand's message in a "glocal" way: showing international flair and local appeal. The "Meet the Muses" campaign made its luxurious frames relevant to fashionable women everywhere (Figure 10.6). The campaign shared Instagram shots, tweets and Facebook posts of the celebrities during their everyday life. In addition, the brand invited Vogue eyeglass wearers to upload images of themselves to be recognized on "FanFriday." Then, brand bloggers added casual comments about how terrific the frames looked.

Figure 10.6 Fashion

A few of the countries were Afghanistan, Albania, Ethiopia, Thailand, Vietnam, Slovakia and Switzerland.

Built on polar opposites and close likenesses, the campaign showed that one commonality was the necessity of food to live. It didn't matter where you lived—north, south, east or west—or whether you were a member of the haves or have-nots, everyone must eat. Food for life impacts everyone.

Havas Worldwide Milan created the thirty- and sixty-second broadcast messages. Accompanied by original music by Ferdinand Arno, the campaign aired on radio and TV, including both digital and satellite stations.[11] (See the video at www.youtube.com/watch?v=QnfUFaIlZVM.)

Unexpected and Exciting Concepts

Keep an eye on innovative campaigns all over the world. For example, in Barcelona, Pepsi Max connected with soccer fans with its "Genius" video campaign. It redesigned an everyday court into one with amazing visual effects. A drone dropped a soccer ball into the lit-up, fenced-in neighborhood field to start the game. LED lights celebrated goals with spectacular starbursts and illuminated countdowns. Goal boxes were even more challenging because they were demarcated by rectangles of moving lights. The drone captured the action and showed it from all angles, adding an exhilarating experience projected on surrounding apartment housings, the "Football Drone" visuals appeared as exciting, action-filled holograms. Viewers watched as the drone continued the action by grabbing the ball. A yellow placard appeared to "flag" a foul. Initiated in a digital platform, the game extended beyond the stadium and moved into social media with the hashtag #LiveForNow.

The video of the event made the campaign instantly praised for its ingenious element of surprise.[12] (See the video at www.youtube.com/watch?v=lX_DLdpygzw.)

To introduce its new clothing collection, Rag & Bone demolished a prized, 1979 Porsche 911 SC with a giant block of falling concrete. Trendy fashion fans gasped in disbelief as they watched this barely one-minute video. Actress Gabriella Wilde blithely walks toward the camera in a casually chic outfit of cool clothes and a shiny, sleek black coat. She flinches as the car is crushed behind her. The irreverent act of demolishing a revered car demonstrated the brand's gutsy, who-cares attitude.

For car lovers everywhere, relax. It wasn't a real Porsche 911 SC, just the shell, which was found in a junkyard. But, the truth is, anyone watching it shuddered in horror thinking it was mercilessly squashed to death.

Car or fashion aficionado or not, the impact was unforgettable and the new line of 2015 Rag & Bone designs was brought to life with a bang.[13] (See the shocking video at www.youtube.com/watch?t=1&v=pvJLAq8vGGc.)

Great Copy

Sometimes the simplest ads get the most attention. Normally, when people are thinking of holiday shopping, they're trying to find the best gifts they can. Well, in 2013, Harvey Nichols created a line of obviously cheap gifts and sold them online and on-site in no-frills packaging. The surprise came when people read the honest and unabashedly selfish, gift-collection message: "Sorry, I Spent it on Myself." Under that was the product's measly price and description, which included silly items, such as "Authentic Lincolnshire Gravel," "Multi-

Figure 10.8 I Come First

Bristled Toothbrush," "100% Real Wood Toothpicks" and "Christmas Lunch with Most of the Trimmings."

The copy in this award-winning campaign delivered its tongue-in-cheek message in these and other media: ads, packages, TV, in-store window flyers and displays, social media via the "#SpentItOnMyself" hashtag and a printable holiday e-card. The agency, adam&eve DDB in London, created this award-winning campaign. The simple message, which told shoppers to splurge on themselves, made it difficult to overlook. Perhaps, some even took the advice at the detriment of their gift recipients (Figure 10.8).[14]

Compelling Visuals

One print campaign, "Skyline," for the United Nations Environment Programme (UNEP), stood up to the overwhelming influence of digital and interactive messages with its stunningly powerful visual. Cause-related and provocative, it featured stalactites, which are hanging ice formations created by dripping water from the ceilings of caves, to create a *tromp d'oeil* (optical illusion). Set against a blue sky over a body of cool blue water, the ice crystals also looked like a big-city skyline. The striking two-in-one image told the story of global warming.[15] "A single line of copy sat at an angle over the water: "Melting Icebergs Lead to Sinking Skylines." Nothing else needed to be said. The image delivered an impossible statement. It could be restated as different universal truths, any of which could serve as "global warnings":

You're at the point of no return.
There's no turning back now.
It's later than you think.
You'll be sorry.

Other more motivating, take-action-now universal truths could also be considered:

It's not too late.
Time is of the essence.

Don't sit idly by.
There's no time to lose.

Another visually invigorating campaign for Hyundai showed an astronaut who got a loving message from Stephanie, his daughter. He was away from home for long periods of time. Missing him, she wanted to send him a message that expressed her love and would be visible to him from his post on the International Space Station. Imagine his surprise, when he was engaged in precision-demanding tasks and looked down to find a note to him. To accomplish this, eleven precision drivers in Hyundai cars moved across an open desert area and, in perfectly synchronized movement, carved out a message in the sand. Amazingly, it resembled Stephanie's handwriting. What did it spell out? "Steph loves you." Instead of the word "love" a heart was drawn followed by an apostrophe and an "s."

As she predicted earlier, her dad, who was a photography buff, grabbed his camera and took a picture. Instantly, he called her and told her he loved it. She was sitting in the control tower and could hear his voice. The entire team involved cheered from the control center on earth.

The visual set a Guinness World Record in 2015 for the largest tire track image. (See the unforgettable video at www.youtube.com/watch?v=3EOAXrTrsOE.)

As you can see in these and other campaign examples, compelling graphics can often express a thought faster than words (Figure 10.9). When combined with excellent copy, campaigns can deliver a hard-to-duck, one–two punch.[16]

Figure 10.9 Compelling Visual

Innovative Use of Media

Audi used a typical out-of-home promotional medium, billboards, in a novel way. To illustrate its water-only emission system in its electric cars, it presented a disappearing billboard. Just as water evaporates in a harmless, fume-free way, the Audi image of its eco-respectful A7 Sportback H-TronQuattro vanished. To replicate normally invisible evaporation, the billboard lit up at night creating a ghost-like image. What an innovative way to promote Audi's h-tron engine technology in major cities through an inventive, hi-tech approach to a traditional medium.[17]

Box 10.5 Short List of Creative References

1. *AdExchanger*—www.adexchanger.com
2. *Advertising Age*—www.adage.com
3. *AdWeek*—www.adweek.com
4. *Ads of the World*—www.adsoftheworld.com
5. *Artefact*—www.artefactgroup.com
6. *Big Ideas Machine*—www.bigideasmachine.com
7. *Business Insider*—www.businessinsider.com
8. *BuzzFeed*—www.buzzfeed.com
9. *Cannes Lions Award winners*—www.canneslions.com (current) www.canneslions archive.com/winners/categories/cannes-lions/ (past)
10. *CMYK Magazine*—https://cmykmag.com
11. *Communication Arts Magazine*—www.commarts.com
12. *Content Marketing Institute*—www.contentinstitute.com
13. *Convince & Convert Digital Marketing*—www.convinceandconvert.com
14. *Copyranter*—www.copyranter.blogspot.com
15. *Creative Bloq*—www.creativebloq.com
16. *Creative Review*—www.creativereview.co.uk
17. *Creativity Online*—www.creativity-online.com
18. *Digital Buzz blog*—www.digitalbuzzblog.com
19. *Fast Company*—**www.fastcompany.com**
20. *Graphic Design Magazine*—www.gdusa.com
21. *How*—www.howdesign.com
22. *HubSpot*—www.hubspot.com
23. *International Advertising Community*—www.adcglobal.org (referred by www.ihavean idea.org)
24. *Marketo*—www.marketco.com
25. *Media Daily News*—www.mediapost.com
26. *Millward Brown*—www.millwardbrown.com
27. *One Club*—www.oneclub.org
28. *Print Magazine*—printmag.com
29. *ROI Online*—www.getroionline.com
30. *Webby Awards*—www.webbyawards.com

One other visually stimulating ad is the campaign by Penguin Books. Looking to promote its line of audiobooks, it presented headsets that resembled famous authors. For example, two Shakespeare bodies were curved together. Their feet met at the top to form the crown of the headset. At the bottom, the two faces confronted each other. The separation between them allowed wearers' heads to fit between them. The soft-sculpted characters created the ear covers. The immediately recognizable writers made the headsets both amusing and informative. Audiobook fans would enjoy the pun, and non-listeners would find the unique headsets intriguing.[18]

Make it a habit to regularly visit blogs, agency websites, industry-related publications, advertising organizations and Award Show sites that share creative ideas and inspiring campaigns. Check the quick list below and constantly compile new sites (Box 10.5).

Global Campaign Strategy Summary

Now, let's review this chapter. This summary will help remind you of what to consider when developing global campaigns. There are many different strategies to consider. These include the following.

1. *Universal Truths (as described in Chapters 1, 3, 5 and 7)*
2. *One Unified Message*

    a. Engage the audience
    b. Share humor
    c. Spark an emotion
    d. Reward the consumer
    e. Reflect the audience
    f. Epitomize consumer opinions
    g. Show compassion
    h. Portray brand value
    i. Reinforce brand positioning
    j. Change audience perception or behavior
    k. Support a cause
    l. Play with the audience

3. *One Modified Message*

    a. One core message that is slightly modified or "transcreated"
    b. Several messages for myriad markets for a multi-themed communication

4. *Audience- and Culture-Specific Campaign*
5. *Media-Specific Campaign*
6. *Interactive Campaign*
7. *Educational Campaign*
8. *Cause-Related Campaign*

In addition to the above list, there are also global campaigns with 1) unexpected and exciting concepts, 2) great copy, 3) compelling visuals and 4) innovative uses of media.

When designing an international campaign, it's crucial to create a relevant message for each culture and region. Next, you need to decide whether to translate, transcreate or write another related, but locally targeted message. Start with these three steps.

Figure 10.10 Observe

1. *Strategically re-examine the brand, message and market.*
2. *Critically analyze the creative content and proposed execution.*
3. *Carefully study the specific culture and attitudes in that region.*

Remind yourself to reacquaint yourself with the six cultural categories determined by professor Geert Hofstede. These are:

1. *Power distance*
2. *Individualism*
3. *Masculinity*
4. *Uncertainty avoidance*
5. *Long-term orientation*
6. *Indulgence*

Take your time to design a methodically detailed architectural blueprint (Figure 10.10). This will help you construct a campaign that has a stable foundation. Then, each brick will align with the next, creating a communication structure that will withstand challenges and be modularly designed. That way, you can strategically modify certain components and keep others, while the campaign holds fast until it is time to rebuild, reconfigure or redesign the next one.

Global Campaign Strategy Exercises

Exercise 1: Identify one global campaign that uses one unified message and a universal truth. Answer the following:

a. State the universal truth.
b. Which type of message did it use? For example: engage the audience, share humor, spark an emotion, reward the consumer, reflect the audience, etc.
c. What media were chosen?

Exercise 2: Find and name one global campaign that modified or "transcreated" the original message. Answer the following:

a.   Name the product, company or brand.
b.   Where did it run (which countries)?

Exercise 3: What global campaign used interactivity?

How was it used? For example: social media shares, games, apps, etc.?

Exercise 4: Name one global campaign that addressed a cause or worldwide problem?

a.   In what countries did the message appear?
b.   How was the message delivered? For example: word of mouth, flyers, solution-driven inventions, etc.?

Exercise 5: What type of companies or campaigns would focus on an "uncertainty avoidance" audience? For example: healthcare, pharmaceuticals, etc.

Exercise 6: Name two characteristics of a country that has a masculinity orientation.

Exercise 7: Cite one global campaign that presented compelling visuals.

Exercise 8: Identify one global campaign that created exciting copy.

Exercise 9: Find one global campaign that used innovative use of media.

Notes

1. Caroline Bologna, "German Ad Doesn't Need Words to Speak Volumes about Supporting your Kids," September 9, 2014, www.huffingtonpost.com/2014/09/04/german-ad-celebrates-supportive-dad_n_5766182.html (accessed September 7, 2014).
2. Staff writer, "Case Study: Listerine Breaks Records with Social Engagement," June 30, 2015, www.marketing-interactive.com/case-study-listerine-breaks-records-with-social-engagement/ (accessed July 4, 2015).
3. Craig Knowles, "Volkswagen Created Vending Machine that Uses Old Batteries as Payment," April 14, 2015, http://prexamples.com/2015/04/volkswagen-create-vending-machine-that-uses-old-batteries-as-payment/ (accessed September 26, 2015).
4. Margo Berman, *The Brains behind Great Ad Campaigns: Creative Collaboration between Copywriters and Art Directors* (Lanham, Maryland: Rowman & Littlefield, 2009), 149.
5. Jay Moye, "Share a Coke: How the Groundbreaking Campaign Got its Start 'Down Under'," September 25, 2014, www.coca-colacompany.com/stories/share-a-coke-how-the-groundbreaking-campaign-got-its-start-down-under (accessed September 22, 2015).
6. Adhibition, "IKEA's Internationalization: Advertising in Different Countries," July, 27, 2012, http://adhibition.tumblr.com/post/17950628838/ikeas-internationalization-advertising-in-different-coun (accessed September 30, 2015).
7. McDonald's, "24 Gifts of Joy. In 24 Cities. Over 24 Hours. #imlovinit" http://imlovinit24.com (accessed October 4, 2015).

8. Vogue Eyewear Luxottica, www.luxottica.com/en/one-brand-many-faces-one-voice-speaks-many-languages-global-heart-different-beats (accessed September 30, 2015).

9. Artefact, "How Can Design Help Improve a Global Health Issue," www.artefactgroup.com/content/work/path/ (accessed June 20, 2015).

10. Eugene Kim, "Samsung is Testing a New 'Safety Truck' to Change the Way People Drive," June 21, 2015, www.businessinsider.com/samsung-safety-truck-makes-driving-safe-2015-6 (accessed September 26, 2015).

11. Expo Milano 2015, "The Expo Milano 2015 Communication Campaign: Food is Life," October 30, 2015, www.expo2015.org/en/the-expo-milano-2015-communication-campaign—food-is-life- (accessed September 29, 2015).

12. DAN, "Pepsi Global Ad Campaign: Drone Football," October 5, 2015, http://digitalagencynetwork.com/pepsi-global-ad-campaign-drone-football/ (accessed September 28, 2015).

13. Alexandra Ilyashov, "Rag & Bone Pulverized a Porsche in its New Campaign Film," July 28, 2015, www.refinery29.com/2015/07/91441/rag-and-bone-porsche-film-fall-2015 (accessed September 27, 2015).

14. Bibbi Sowray, "'Sorry, I Spent it on Myself': Harvey Nichols' Self-Indulgent Christmas Campaign," November 27, 2013, http://fashion.telegraph.co.uk/columns/bibby-sowray/TMG10477935/Sorry-I-spent-it-on-myself-Harvey-Nichols-self-indulgent-Christmas-campaign.html (accessed October 5, 2015).

15. Creative Bloq, "100 Brilliant Print Adverts," July 14, 2014, www.creativebloq.com/inspiration/print-ads-1233780 (accessed October 5, 2015).

16. Hyundai, "Hyundai's New Thinking Campaign: A Message to Space," http://worldwide.hyundai.com/WW/Experience/Campaign/AMessagetoSpace/index.html (accessed October 5, 2015).

17. Creativity Online, "These Audi 'Billboards' are Nothing but Hot Air," March 23, 2015, http://creativity-online.com/work/audi-the-disappearing-billboard/40094 (accessed October 5, 2015).

18. Creative Bloq, "100 Brilliant Print Adverts," July 13, 2014, www.creativebloq.com/inspiration/print-ads-1233780 (accessed October 5, 2015).

INDEX